"Rich Georgian
Strangely Shot"

T0040476

"Rich Georgian Strangely Shot"

Eugene Grace, "Daisy of the Leopard Spots" and the Great Atlanta Shooting of 1912

TOM HUGHES

McFarland & Company, Inc., Publishers
Jefferson, North Carolina, and London

LIBRARY OF CONGRESS CATALOGUING-IN-PUBLICATION DATA

Hughes, Tom, 1948–
    "Rich Georgian strangely shot" : Eugene Grace,
"Daisy of the Leopard Spots" and the Great
Atlanta Shooting of 1912 / Tom Hughes.
        p.   cm.
    Includes bibliographical references and index.

    ISBN 978-0-7864-7078-5
    softcover : acid free paper ∞

    1. Grace, Daisy.   2. Murder — Georgia —
Atlanta — Case studies.   3. Atlanta (Ga.) —
History — 20th century.   I. Title.
HV6534.A7H84 2012
364.152'3092 — dc23   2012040184

BRITISH LIBRARY CATALOGUING DATA ARE AVAILABLE

On the cover: Mrs. Daisy Grace on way to court,
Bain News Service, 1912 (Library of Congress);
background image © 2012 Shutterstock

Manufactured in the United States of America

McFarland & Company, Inc., Publishers
    Box 611, Jefferson, North Carolina 28640
    www.mcfarlandpub.com

Even the most lurid melodrama is tame when contrasted with the Grace case.... Balzac and other realists have never discovered anything more remarkable than the mysterious shooting of Eugene Grace and the history of his marriage with his suspected wife.

—*Spartanburg Herald-Journal,* August 3, 1912

Table of Contents

Table of Contents

Preface

Atlanta has always been a city that craves recognition, a city hoping to force itself into the conversation when people discuss the great cities of America. In the late twentieth century the boosters demanded attention by self-anointing Atlanta "the world's next great international city" or boasting of "the world's busiest airport." Superlatives were always readily employed.

None of this was new. Atlanta was always proclaiming its exceptionalism. By 1912, Atlanta was selling itself as "the Energetic City of the South."[1] When Hartsfield Airport was still just a field, folks in the region were already moaning that to get to heaven you had to go through Atlanta. "All roads lead to Atlanta." The railroad had built the city, and the iron road established Atlanta and not Birmingham as the hub of the Deep South. The new Terminal Station, erected in 1905, was the symbol of Atlanta's pull on the entire region:

> You first feel that you are in this heart of the New South when you alight from your train within the Atlanta Terminal, whose trainshed is so vast and so resounding, so awe-inspiring by its very size, if you please, as to be at once remindful of the great stations in Boston and in St. Louis. And you feel it again when you go driving from the station up to your hotel through streets so brisk, so canyoned with modern skyscrapers, so filled with the toil and the turmoil of a real city that your old-time impression of Southern towns — dignified and delicate and a bit moldering, perhaps — is at once swept away.[2]

Atlanta was certainly a crowded place. A curiously angled downtown street plan, with a railroad gulch to be crossed, and a generational hodgepodge of vehicles meant daily congestion. "The sidewalks and stores were generally crowded daytimes with walkers — businessmen, countrymen with 'fascinators' around their necks, women shoppers, colored people — and the streets were filled with streetcars, carriages, country carts, drays."[3] Since the census of 1890 the population had more than doubled in two decades; the 1912 city directory put the number at 157,835 people. South of Washington, D.C., only New Orleans had more residents. But New Orleans was a somewhat

1

decadent (moldering perhaps) port city with its almost foreign rhythms governed by the languid pace of the river and the cotton trade. Atlanta, meantime, was "chock full of life."[4] Banking, shipping, merchandising, even the infant "convention" trade all kept Atlanta growing and profitable. Walter Cooper, one of the first leaders of the Atlanta Chamber of Commerce, came up with a neat description: "Atlanta is the busiest town in the world for its size."[5] Fifty years later, Atlantans still prided themselves on staying busy. In the Civil Rights era, of course, it was — at least by slogan — "the city too busy to hate."

There was a lot going on in the early months of 1912. A great automobile show was held in February. The motorcar was remaking Atlanta. The shoe industry chose Atlanta for a major meeting in March. The Metropolitan Opera, headlined by the great Caruso, was making a return visit in April. In the background was a constant political buzz. There was political ferment. Hoke Smith had stepped down as governor to enter the U.S. Senate. There was a scramble to find his successor. Nationally, it was a presidential year, and while Georgia was a yellow dog Democrat state, the party was split amongst three solid choices — Senator Champ Clark of Missouri, Senator Oscar Underwood of Alabama, who had the bulk of the Georgia support as a fellow southerner, and a third candidate, Governor Woodrow Wilson of New Jersey, who had practiced law on Atlanta's Marietta Street and had "wooed his bride on the banks of the Etowah." (Wilson, however, despaired of ever finding intellectual satisfaction in the city and, after a year or so, opted to leave "slow, ignorant, uninteresting Georgia."[6])

There was a construction boom. The Peachtree-Whitehall commercial district (of course it would be called "the Broadway of the South") spanned one of the new viaducts over the railroad gulch. The roadway had just been ripped up and repaved, and new street car tracks put down. The new "million-dollar hotel," the Georgian Terrace, was said to be the finest and most well-appointed anywhere. An art museum was announced for Piedmont Park, and inevitably the backers immediately proclaimed this proof of Atlanta's new status as the "art center of the South." (With the opera now coming to town annually, Atlanta had already announced its status as the undisputed "music center of the south.") Piedmont Park itself had been vastly improved by the Olmsted brothers, who ripped down the last dilapidated remnants of the old Cotton States Exposition of 1895. The Exposition was Atlanta's first "Big Show" on the national scene. Lastly, the old Fulton County Courthouse on Forsyth Street had been knocked down, and the site had been cleared for the erection of a new "Temple of Justice" befitting its setting. In the meantime, the courts were lodged in rented space all about the downtown area, including the soon-to-be-infamous M. L. Thrower Building at Mitchell and Pryor streets.

But perhaps the most significant change in Atlanta for the purposes of this story was the sale of the *Georgian*, a fading afternoon paper with an anemic circulation, to the controversial publishing giant William Randolph Hearst.[7] He had failed in his bids to purchase either the morning *Constitution* or the afternoon *Journal*. The *Georgian* would be Hearst's first masthead in the South. His reputation preceded him, of course, and while he received a friendly welcome from his rival editors, there was concern that Atlanta journalism was about to change. F.L. Seely, who sold the *Georgian* and then took his money off to build the Grove Park Inn in Asheville, NC, reassured his readers on the day the sale became official (February 5, 1912): "I believe that nothing has happened to Atlanta in a long time that will so advertize it to the world and place it so large on the map as Mr. Hearst's advent [here]."

If Hearst's new team at the *Georgian* was looking for something to ignite new interest in the paper, they had only to wait four weeks. The story of "Daisy of the Leopard Spots," the well-dressed, alluring and wealthy suspect in the shooting of her debonair husband, "scion of one of Georgia's aristocratic families," was heaven-sent for newspaper sales. Not that the *Georgian* would have the field to itself by any means. The *Constitution* and *Journal* were quick to mobilize their forces, and day by day for weeks the three papers went through tons of newsprint covering this mystery in the minutest detail. As the *Macon Telegraph* put it, the Atlanta papers "have gone dippy." The story of the "Rich Georgian Strangely Shot" was soon read in papers across the country. But, truly, in Atlanta, the busiest city had all but dropped everything to follow "the great shooting story." Within a week, James R. Gray, the editor of the *Journal*, admitted, "It would be unreasonable to expect a very decided revival of business until a certain shooting mystery is cleared up."

In this book, this singular mystery is recreated, relying heavily on the voluminous contemporary press accounts. In addition, the book is informed by drawing upon the people and places, mores and prejudices of the pre–World War I South and Atlanta. The names and faces of Daisy and Eugene Grace may have been known to millions of Americans in 1912 but they are largely unknown today. This is the story of the tragic romance between "the Adonis from a country town" and the woman known to all as "Daisy of the Leopard Spots."

The research for this book has been conducted in the libraries of Emory University in Atlanta, the University of Georgia in Athens, the Library of Congress in Washington, the Free Library of Philadelphia and the Atlanta History Center. The author is grateful for the assistance of the staff at each of these research facilities. Modern researchers have also been greatly assisted by the increasing digitization of newspaper archives. The Library of Congress's

Chronicling America project was quite helpful. I also wish to especially recognize the outstanding Digital Library of Georgia and its collection of newspapers from Atlanta and throughout the state.

I also personally extend my thanks to Paul Milich, professor of law and director of the Litigation Program at Georgia State University, College of Law. Professor Milich is the leading scholar on Georgia's Rules of Evidence, which played a defining role in the fate of Daisy Grace. The interpretations of the law and any faults herein are mine. I also enjoyed meeting and talking with Tom Redwine of the Newnan-Coweta Historical Society. Lastly, of course, I thank my wife, Kathleen McGraw, for her support, encouragement and her nonpareil proofreading skills.

CHAPTER 1

"Rich Georgian Strangely Shot"[1]

It was a bit odd for Mrs. Grace to actually come down into the kitchen in the morning.[2] But on Tuesday, March 5, 1912, at about eight o'clock, wearing her blue silk kimono, Daisy Grace came in to ask Martha, her colored servant, to "be a dear" and fix her a couple of soft-boiled eggs and a cup of coffee. She sat and ate the light breakfast there in the kitchen and told Martha that she would also be needing a tray for "Mister Gene." She requested two eggs, some toast, coffee and a large glass of cold water. She commented to Martha that she didn't know whether Gene would even want any of it because he was feeling no better that morning. But she ordered that the breakfast be made ready anyway, so that Martha could get started on cleaning up the kitchen and then be off. Daisy carried the tray upstairs herself. Martha Ruffin and her husband, J.C., who was rather grandly titled "the butler," were the only two servants for Mr. and Mrs. Eugene H. Grace. The Ruffins lived out in the back in a one-room "servants' quarters" behind the Graces' elegant home at 29 West Eleventh Street, just off Peachtree.

There was a good deal of activity in the house that Tuesday morning. Mr. Grace was going to be leaving on an early afternoon train for Philadelphia. It was a business trip. Mrs. Grace was also going away; she had plans to spend the next three days in Newnan, south of Atlanta, where she would be staying at the home of her husband's mother and stepfather. Before she carried the tray up to Gene, Daisy reminded the Ruffins that the sooner they got everything straightened up downstairs, the quicker they'd be free to spend the rest of the day and the next two as a holiday. Daisy was planning to return to Atlanta on Friday.

The Ruffins were well aware of all these plans: the night before, Martha had heard the Graces discussing the Philadelphia trip during dinner.[3] Although

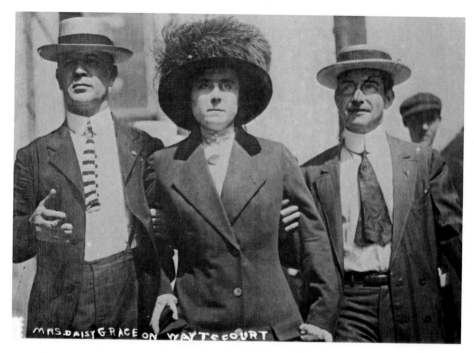

Mrs. Daisy Grace being escorted to court at the Thrower Building by her private detective, C.W. Burke (left), and Bradford Byrd, a reporter for the *Atlanta Journal* (Bain Collection, Library of Congress).

Mr. Grace was obviously not feeling all that well on Monday night, Martha thought he was still in good spirits. He talked about his plans to buy a motorcar, and he joked that he might even train J.C. to be the chauffeur. Martha had thought the Graces were a "mighty loving" couple, and they did a lot of "kissing and hugging." After dinner, the Graces had gone out; as usual on Monday nights, they went to the theater. While they were out, a seamstress came to the house, and she was shown up to Daisy's dressing area for some final work on the outfits that Daisy wanted to take with her to Newnan for the entertainments planned for her visit. The Graces were a very fashionable couple; they always made it a point to be well-dressed. In her short time in Atlanta, Daisy had already drawn notice for her stylish clothes, "handsomely set off by her leopard skin furs."

The Graces came home from the show at about eleven and retired for the night. Tuesday morning came and, as mentioned, Gene was no better. When the Ruffins came in the house that morning they found a note from Daisy asking that they be very quiet and not come upstairs until called. Thus it was a surprise when Daisy had shown up in the kitchen. It wasn't until about nine that Martha went upstairs; Daisy called her up to light the fire in the master bedroom. Martha heard Mr. Grace groaning from the bed. But Daisy told him that he was going to be fine. Martha returned to the bedroom a short time later to fasten up Daisy's traveling dress. Daisy then asked Martha to send J.C. up to get her luggage for her trip to Newnan. When J.C. climbed the stairs, he found the bag set outside the closed door of the bedroom. He brought it down to the lower hall. It was then about time for the Ruffins to be off. Daisy urged them again to enjoy themselves and gave them each a dollar. Actually, the next day, Wednesday, was to be their usual payday, and they were owed seven dollars. The time off would surely have been more enjoyable with a bit more cash in hand. But Daisy sent them on their way. Before they left she told them, "Gene's been asking about a doctor, but I don't think he needs one." The Ruffins set off to go downtown. The only two people remaining in the house were Daisy and Gene.

A cab arrived for Daisy at a little after eleven o'clock to take her to the Terminal Station for the train to Newnan. Gene's train north would also leave from the Terminal but not until 2:30. He was not due back in Atlanta until Sunday.

It wasn't the best weather for the Ruffins' holiday in Atlanta as it rained most of the day. After a particularly wet winter, Atlanta was quite eager for spring and some sunshine. The Southern Shoe Retailers Association was holding its meeting at the Piedmont Hotel. But it was definitely not a day for stepping out wearing the new vogue in footwear — the "low cut shoe." Over at Poncey Park, a few miles northeast of downtown, the spring-training New York Yankees were unable to hold their workouts. The field was the summer home to the Crackers of the Southern League. But the diamond was now a "sea of mud." That Tuesday the *New York Times* correspondent wearily filed his copy: "The Yankees are having their troubles with the weather, and today, by way of variety, a downpour visited them. It rained hard in the morning and rained still harder in the afternoon."[4]

More importantly for our story, the rain spoiled the half-day off for J.C. and Martha Ruffin. The Ruffins had decided to take in the "negro moving pictures" at the Arcade, one of the "colored" theaters on Decatur Street. Leaving the show and caught in another cloudburst, they decided to go back home. They caught a Georgia Railway and Electric trolley up Peachtree Street for the nickel fare. The cars required that "colored passengers occupy the rear seats" and exit only through the rear doors. Whites were seated from the front back.[5]

It was mid-afternoon when the Ruffins approached 29 West Eleventh Street. J.C. noticed that two blue-uniformed policemen were standing on the front porch. The cops were white, but, of course, the entire force in Atlanta was white, then and for many decades longer (until 1948).[6] Ruffin approached the officers warily. He explained who he was and asked the policemen their business. Officer Wood said they had received a phone call from a man giving this address who claimed he had been shot. They had just arrived but had not been able to rouse anyone in the house, and everything seemed to be locked up. J.C. said he was surprised to hear all this because both the master and mistress were gone, and the house should have been empty.

The Ruffins, as was typical in the day, were only allowed the key to the rear servants' door of the house. J.C. led the officers around to the back. Once inside the home the police found nothing amiss on the ground floor. Ruffin said if there had been a phone call, there was only one telephone in the house and that was up in the master's bedroom, directly at the top of the stairs. The bedroom door was found to be locked. The smaller of the two policemen, Dorsett, boosted up by Ruffin and Wood, managed to peer through the transom window. He saw the body of a man, his head hanging off a large four-poster bed. He could not tell from that view whether the man was alive or dead.

The thick wooden door would not yield to boots or shoulders; Ruffin said they had an axe in the backyard. With the tool soon in hand, the police were finally able to smash their way into the bedroom. The man found sprawled across the mahogany bed was alive but delirious. Ruffin confirmed that the victim was "Mr. Gene." Eugene Grace moaned in pain and seemed unable to move. He begged for water. When it was brought to him, he drank it down in great gulps. His blue silk nightshirt was marked with a large blood stain, as was the top pillow. All the pillows had been piled up on the right side of the bed.

Two plainclothes detectives had now arrived at the scene; one of them, George Bullard, crouched down beside Grace and asked him what had happened. The man replied feebly that he didn't really remember having been shot. Maybe he had been drugged, he mumbled. He said he did not even know he had been shot until he put his hand under his nightshirt and felt the blood. The police later described Grace as incoherent; his sentences were "disjointed." He was finally asked bluntly, "Who shot you?" Grace's reply was curious: "The person that shot me I thought was my friend. I will tell you about it later." The policeman asked if it was his wife who shot him. "I don't know, I think she did." But then, in an agonized whisper, Grace pleaded, "Don't arrest anybody, for God's sake."

According to Grace, his wife had left in a cab sometime after 11:00 to catch a train for Newnan, but she had promised to get him a doctor. Yet no help ever came. He had been hollering and whistling, but no one had heard him. He told the police that he could not move his legs.

A police ambulance then arrived, and with it came Dr. W.S. Goldsmith of St. Joseph's Infirmary. It was one of the new ambulances with pneumatic tires. Much of Atlanta, including this portion of West Eleventh Street, was still "paved" with crushed rubble. Goldsmith said Grace would have to be moved to the infirmary on Courtland Street. The detectives would follow.

By now, 29 West Eleventh Street had become the center of intense excitement. Neighbors had been attracted, as they ever will be, and a crowd had formed in the street. Some were even able to get inside and gawp about. Reporters from the three Atlanta newspapers had also arrived. A crime of violence in this highly desirable neighborhood, with so many homes of "socially prominent families," was quite rare, and a story must lie behind it. In fact, it was the *Constitution's* scribe on the scene who scored the first great "beat" of the ensuing newspaper "war" when he found the gun. Reporters were apparently allowed to simply roam about the house, and while poking around on the first floor, Oze van Wyck espied a pistol only half-hidden on a ledge behind some drapes. He proudly handed the gun to Officer Dorsett, who "broke it," examined the chamber, raised the gun to his nose for a good sniff, and declared that one round had been recently fired. The gun was a .32 caliber Smith and Wesson blue-steel, hammerless revolver. There were four more bullets chambered; only one spent shell had been found in the bedroom.

The police were finally able to clear out the curious and sundry onlookers. The reporters had gone off to chase the prone victim to the infirmary, and things were quiet again on West Eleventh Street. The police simply locked the place up and went away. They left entirely to their memory what the room had been like when they first arrived. They took no photographs. They left the bloody bed clothing right where it was.

Circa 1912, the Atlanta police force was not generally held in high esteem.[7] The police had been greatly disgraced in the events leading to and during the Great Race Riot of 1906.[8] Beyond issues of black and white, there were also charges of corruption. The word from Atlanta's pulpits was that the police had been bought off by the purveyors of sex and liquor. The new chief's much touted "flying squads" had done nothing, and the city was still plagued by whore-houses and gin mills, near-beer peddlers and "blind tigers."[9] Amid such charges of racism and corruption, the competence of the force, under Chief James Beavers as an investigative agency rarely entered the discussion, and, frankly, for good reason. Most of the "call officers" were recruited from country towns and chosen more for their toughness and willingness to go into Darktown and other places decent white folk did not care to tread. A week or two of training and they were outfitted in a blue tunic, handed a billy club and sent out on the street for a salary of $75 a month. There were no classes in evidence collection or crime scene preservation. In July of the previous year the *Constitution* had expressed some exasperation: "What is the matter with the Atlanta police?"[10] A grand jury had more recently condemned the force for its "inefficiency."[11] The police had responded as they always did — with an appeal for more men, rather than for better training or equipment.

One more note: the police took J.C. and Martha Ruffin away with them to the police station on Decatur Street. Not simply because they could but because the detectives thought the servants would serve as important material witnesses. They were to remain in custody for six weeks.

CHAPTER 2

"What have you told these people, Gene?"

That Tuesday morning, Daisy Grace had left 29 West Eleventh Street by horse-drawn cab in plenty of time to make her 2:00 train for Newnan. It was Allan Hardaway's cab that answered her call. Being a "cripple," the driver well remembered how he had to lug the big suitcase out of the front hall and down those stone porch steps to his cab. He was happy then to hand it over to the porter at the station. But the nice lady had tipped him well and said if he was free Friday morning she would be returning from Newnan. Daisy traveled via the Atlanta and West Point Railroad southwest from the Terminal Station to the Newnan depot, a journey that took just over an hour and, at the fare of two cents a mile, was an affordable 78 cents.

Daisy would have had no idea at the time, but she was actually under observation while aboard that train. Trox Bankston was the editor and proprietor of the *West Point News*, and he was heading back to that riverside Georgia town after handling some business in Atlanta. He took immediate notice of this stylishly dressed woman as she came on board. It was a somewhat unusual sight on that particular line, which was often derided as "the goober train"[1] because it carried so many peanut farmers and their rustic kinfolk back and forth to the capital city for business and shopping. Bankston admitted that he never spoke with the woman, but he did see her exchange a smile and a pleasant word or two with other passengers. She spent most of the time simply staring out at the mist-shrouded fields along the way. Bankston recalled being shocked when he subsequently saw this woman's picture in the papers and read about the shooting in Atlanta. While he had been watching her that afternoon she had betrayed no concern of any kind. "She seemed merely a handsome woman whose thoughts were pleasant." If she had only just shot her husband and left him to die at

11

home, then, Bankston declared, "She is a greater actress than I have ever seen in the theatres."[2]

This most interesting woman got off the train at Newnan. In the years before the First World War, "Newnan must have seemed to have been in the center of the South."[3] A prosperous agricultural town with an "intelligent and progressive population" of about 6,000 residents, Newnan claimed to have "all the conveniences of a modern city." Cotton was king in Newnan, with several mills, ginneries, and cotton oil manufacturing plants. The town and county's employment was dominated by the industry. Served by both the A&WP and the Central of Georgia rail lines, Newnan was at the crossing of a north-south, east-west axis ideal for the moving of peaches and other food crops. Georgia's first winery had been established in the eastern part of the county. There were more "millionaires" per capita in Newnan than in Atlanta, the locals boasted. Newnan was then, as it is now, the seat of Coweta County.[4]

But if Newnan was known at all outside the borders of the state, it was for the lynching of Sam Hose, a black farmhand charged with murder and rape.[5] Hose was dragged off a train in Newnan, and despite the appeals of the Governor, W.Y. Atkinson, who was a resident of Newnan, Hose was strung up before a crowd of 2,000 people on April 23, 1899. His body was then mutilated. It wasn't Georgia's first lynching, nor was it the last, but the brutality of the crime and savagery of the participants led to denunciations from Atlanta to New York to London. Bill Arp, writing in the Georgia weekly *The Sunny South*, yawned, "The fulminations of the northern press nor the apprehensions of editors nearer home amount to nothing. History is just repeating itself."[6] "Bill Arp" was a pseudonym for Major Charles H. Smith, a one-time Confederate officer and lawyer whose "homely philosophies and dry witticisms" were carried in newspapers across the South.

Daisy Grace's train slowed as it passed the two block long red-brick face of the sprawling Newnan Cotton Mill before halting at the new A&WP depot. Sam Hill, her husband's stepfather, was waiting for her; he had come down with the farm wagon for her luggage. Sam turned his horses out of the depot and up East Broad Street towards the courthouse, built only a few years before in the classic "Villa Rotondo" style. From the square it was then only six-tenths of a mile to the southeast, down past the post office, and on to Greenville Street and the Hill farmhouse. On the short journey Sam and Daisy were talking only of Eugene's upcoming trip to Philadelphia and the entertainments that were planned for Daisy's stay in Newnan.

Daisy had arrived on the 3:14. Word of the shooting had already reached the farmhouse. A little after three in the afternoon, Mrs. Ida Hill, Eugene Grace's mother, received a wire from Atlanta stating only that Gene had been shot and that he had been taken for treatment to the St. Joseph's Infirmary. The sender was one of those "nosy neighbors," John Owens, a banker who lived next door to the Graces. Mrs. Hill sent her youngest son, Hamilton, Eugene's stepbrother, scampering off by foot to meet the carriage with this dreadful news. When the lad in his knickerbockers met the wagon he breathlessly spilled the limited details he had. Mrs. Grace was shocked. "I don't believe it," she cried. Once at the farm, and upon receiving more information, Daisy and the Hills quickly agreed that they must take the 5:00 train that afternoon to Atlanta. "Mother Hill" and Sam would be joining Daisy for support. What terrible news indeed. Mrs. Lewis Hill (Ruth) who was married to one of Sam's brothers, and who lived in Atlanta, also called the farm that afternoon with a few more details of what she knew about the shooting. Daisy spoke with Ruth for some time on the phone.

The somber party now reversed the wagon journey back to the Newnan depot and boarded the 5:00 train to Atlanta. Sitting with the Hills on the train, Daisy seemed at a loss to explain what possibly could have happened. Eugene, she said, had no enemies. Gene had always had guns, and Mother Hill thought it might just have been a clumsy accident. Daisy did not think so. Instead, she wondered if perhaps the "negro butler" might have been involved. Gene had recently been cross with J.C. for roughing up Martha. Or it might have been a burglar. There had been money left lying around the bedroom, and if it was missing, Daisy was certain that theft was the cause of the shooting.

The train clattered into Atlanta's massive Terminal Station at about six. On the platform the Newnan party was met by detectives Bullard and Doyal. Pressed with questions for more information on the shooting, the police said little. Eugene was still alive, but any details on his condition would have to come from the doctors. Stairs led up from the platform shed into the great vaulted waiting room, always one of the busiest places in Atlanta. Daisy and the others, with their lawmen escort, walked amidst the home-going crowds and shoppers, past the restaurants (separate eateries for white and colored diners), stores, laundries and shoeshine men. They would have also passed several newsstands. The *Georgian's* "Extra" edition was already on the street with the front page news: "Man, Badly Shot, Phones to Police, Then Faints Away." The *Journal's* "Last Edition" alerted readers that "Mysterious Call Takes Police to Grace Home." Did Daisy see either of those papers? Did a newsboy offer her one? Some travelers thought the Terminal's persistent newsboys were becoming a nuisance.

Out through the arched doorways, framed by the Terminal's famous twin "Spanish Renaissance" terra cotta towers, Daisy Grace, the Hills and the plainclothesmen silently crossed the grassy plaza to the cab stand in front of the Jacobs Drug store. They were now joined by Morris Prioleau, whom Daisy knew as one of Eugene's closest Atlanta friends. He climbed in the cab with her. Mrs. Hill, understandably quite overcome, went with her husband in another cab.

Daisy Grace arrived at St. Joseph's Infirmary at about 6:30 in the evening. The cab had pulled up at Courtland and Baker streets at the entrance to the infirmary's brand new main building. Daisy climbed the semicircle of concrete steps under a marquee of iron and glass to enter the reception room. She was met by one of the nurses from the Sisters of Mercy who led her down a corridor to her husband's room on the first floor. There were glum-faced policemen everywhere. Though Daisy surely did not know him, the man who seemed to be in charge of things was Newton Lanford, the Atlanta chief of detectives. The Hills' cab had arrived at the infirmary shortly before Daisy's. When Daisy neared the room, she saw that Sam Hill was off to one side having a quiet palaver with his two brothers, Lewis and Preston, the latter of whom was an Atlanta attorney. Only Prioleau stayed with Daisy.

Reaching Gene's room, Daisy showed no nervousness and entered. Her husband lay flat on his back, able only to raise his head to look at her. She did not kiss him. Dr. Goldsmith was there along with a colleague. The police, the doctors, Prioleau and others were all lurking nearby for this sensational reunion. The *Journal* described it as "one of the more dramatic scenes ever witnessed" in the city. The ensuing conversation between Daisy Grace and her wounded husband Eugene — in any of the innumerable print versions, all only slightly different — would soon be as familiar to Atlantans as the lines to a popular song. This is the *Journal's* version:

> DAISY: What have you told these people, Gene, to make them act in this strange manner?
> EUGENE: I don't know, it seems like you must have shot me.
> DAISY: The idea!
> EUGENE: Why did you leave me alone when you knew I was hurt?
> DAISY: You were alright when I left and you know it.
> EUGENE: Why didn't you get a doctor?
> DAISY: You didn't need one. What you say makes me out a murderess, Gene.
> EUGENE: Well, who shot me?
> DAISY: If you keep talking like this, I will take away your Power of Attorney.
> EUGENE (beginning to weaken): Ohhh, I don't know who did it.
> DAISY: They are going to take me to jail.
> EUGENE: No, not that![7]

At that point, Eugene Grace became greatly excited. He began spasms of coughing and spitting up some blood. Dr. Goldsmith chased everyone out of the room; the conversation would have to end.

Leaving Gene's bedside, Daisy was met in the hall by a policeman who asked her to step down to another room where she found Mr. Lanford waiting with a stenographer. He questioned her closely on the subject of her movements that day. From his questions, it was clear that the detective had been able to make some good use of the information already extracted from the Ruffins, who had been interrogated separately.

J.C. had told the police about that morning note from Mrs. Grace asking them to be extra quiet. She had specifically requested that they not be disturbed until at least nine o'clock, as Mr. Grace was unwell. Thus, J.C. said he was a bit puzzled when Mrs. Grace came down at about eight. She had a small meal herself and then took Mr. Gene's tray up herself, which was his job. He always took up Mr. Grace's meals; she had never done it before.

Martha Ruffin said the mistress called her up to the bedroom about nine to make a fire. While in the room she heard Mr. Gene groan from the bed. She heard him say he was sick and in pain, but Mrs. Grace told him, "You ain't sick, Gene, you're just sleepy." Martha said she left the room but returned around ten to help "hook up" Mrs. Grace's dress. The mistress then urged her to be on her way with J.C. and to enjoy the free days before her return on Friday. Mr. Grace was still in bed; he had not touched his breakfast. The last thing that morning, before she and J.C. left to go uptown, Mrs. Grace came into the kitchen and said to them that if "Dr. Cromer comes, send him away. My husband says he doesn't need him." Dr. James Dawkins Cromer lived around the corner at 568 West Peachtree Street.

The statements from the Ruffins convinced the police that they had enough to hold Mrs. Grace for questioning. A magistrate's warrant soon arrived at the infirmary, and Lanford told Mrs. Grace that, unfortunately, she would have to come with him to Decatur Street. She was to be placed under arrest on the charge of assault with intent to murder. Daisy was quite distressed and spoke briefly with the Hills, protesting her complete innocence. The Hills had, at first, given Daisy their complete support. Mother Hill thought Gene must be out of his mind with pain to even make such a claim. Preston Hill urged Daisy to get an attorney, and he agreed to help find one for her as soon as possible.

John Wesley Moore, of the firm of Moore and Branch in the Peters Building, came to police headquarters late that night. The city court was in the same building, and Moore arranged with magistrate Judge J.B. Ridley that Daisy would be freed on a bond of $7500. That was a high number, but Ridley reminded Moore that this was a serious charge. Mr. Grace was said to be very near death. Additionally, Mrs. Grace was relatively new to the city and might be a flight risk. The bond money was put up by Isaac Clark, a dodgy character who ran a lucrative side business as a bondsman out of his near-beer saloon quite near the police court.

Daisy was now quite free to leave, but the police told her she would not be allowed to return to 29 West Eleventh Street. Attorney Moore took her to the famous Kimball House hotel at Five Points, adjacent to the building housing his office. Daisy Grace was given room 613.

On the morning of Wednesday, March 6, 1912, the morning paper, *The Constitution* featured the first of what would be hundreds of photographs of the principals that appeared in the city's three papers over the next several months. It was a sizeable front page photograph of "Mr. and Mrs. Grace," but otherwise the *Constitution* offered only the most limited details of the shooting. According to this first report, Eugene H. Grace had suffered for hours in "one of the most luxurious residences in the city." It seemed almost certain that young Grace would not long survive his wound. "Developments are watched for with eagerness."

But it was the afternoon papers that really spring-boarded this domestic mystery into the national headlines. With the additional hours allowed to meet their afternoon deadline, the *Journal* writers had industriously delved into what was obviously going to be a sensational story. The paper's Wednesday afternoon banner headline shouted: "'DAISY OF THE LEOPARD SPOTS' WAS A WIDOW ONLY SIXTEEN DAYS." The Atlanta reports were avidly picked up by the Associated Press for papers nationally; the *Georgian's* coverage was exclusively shared with the rest of the Hearst papers. Soon all the nation was learning about the strange shooting in an Atlanta bedroom involving the "widow of a Philadelphia millionaire" and the "scion of an aristocratic Georgian family."[8]

Who were these people?

CHAPTER 3

"Adonis from a Country Town"

At the time of the shooting, Eugene Hamilton Grace was 28. He was born in Macon on August 6, 1883.[1] His claim to any personal "aristocratic" lineage seems altogether dubious. His father was William Florence Grace, who ran a tobacco store on Cherry Street in downtown Macon. William was a popular fellow in Macon, a "prominent merchant," and a bachelor until he was forty. On October 25, 1882, William was married to Ida Hamilton of "the beautiful little city of Cuthbert" in southwest Georgia. She was the daughter of the late Dr. Alexander Hamilton, who had been president of the Andrew Female College in Cuthbert, a 2-year Methodist institution that "bears favorable comparison with similar establishments in any part of the country." Ida was an excellent catch; she was well-educated and "highly accomplished."[2] Mr. Grace was to be congratulated "upon securing such a lively companion to gladden his pathway through life."

Alas, the remaining path was to be a short one. William died when his only son Gene was two. On January 21, 1890, Ida Grace took a second husband—Samuel Lane Hill of Newnan. They were married in Camilla in Mitchell County, Georgia. Sam's first wife had also died. It should not be misunderstood—the Hills were certainly a prominent family in Newnan. Gene's stepfather, Sam, was the oldest of his generation, and managed the cotton and orchards. In that future summer of 1912 he would send 13 carloads of peaches to market, something over 100 tons of fruit. He also managed a quarry in the southeastern corner of Coweta County, breaking up granite for the track beds of the Central of Georgia railway. Sam's brother, Lewis Hill, was on the board and treasurer of the Newnan Cotton Mills. The Hill sisters had all married well—Fannie, Hettie and Callie, aligning themselves, respectively, with the Cole, Herring and Freeman families, all of them leaders in both business and the entertainments of Newnan.[3]

Eugene and his mother had come to Newnan when he was six. Sam

Hill's farmhouse was on Greenville Street, a pretty street running south out of Newnan and (still) lined with some of the town's finest antebellum homes. The Hill house was one of the more modest in the area; it was a small, Victorian-style home with a touch of gingerbread detailing and a nice summer porch running half the front of the structure. It was wooded out back, screening the house from the A&WP tracks about a half-mile away.

Gene attended the new Newnan High School and was a good Methodist church-going lad, such that his mother had thought he would make a fine preacher someday. When he was ten his half-sister Nannie Sue Hill was born, and three years later Hamilton Hill arrived, the already introduced tale-bearing lad.[4]

Eugene grew to a height of 6-foot-3 and was a handsome young man with a fine athletic physique. In 1899 he went up to Atlanta to enter the rolls of the Georgia School of Technology as one of the first students in the new Textile Engineering program.[5] The student directories at Georgia Tech are a bit conflicting, but they indicate that Eugene attended classes on "the Hill" — the old campus — for about three years. He was listed as a sub-apprentice, then apprentice, and eventually he took courses described as "Special Textile 1" and "Special Textile 2." The academic regimen, including courses in Carding and Spinning, Warp Preparation, Weaving and Finishing, and Bleaching and Dyeing, was certainly one well mapped out for the stepson of a cotton planter.[6] But Gene left Tech in 1902, not officially taking a degree. While at the school he had joined the *Alpha Tau Omega* fraternity. The ATO stickpin can be seen fixed in Grace's tie in the so-called "last photo."

At the age of 20, having left Tech, Gene went to work for Southern Bell at their Atlanta offices, staying with the firm for three years. From there he put those textile courses to some use by taking a sales position in North Carolina with the German dye-making firm Farbenfabriken. He spent three years with them, picking up at least a smattering of German phrases. But after that, Eugene's resume becomes a bit spottier. He spent only a short time on the road selling paint for the Detroit Graphite Company. In 1910 he moved again, this time to Philadelphia. He had taken a sales position with the American Pulley Company, working from their offices in Philadelphia at 29th and Bristol streets. Again Grace's stay was brief, as he left to try his hand at the more lucrative profession of a bond salesman in the Philadelphia offices of Fitkin and Co. of Wall Street. He was living at Green's Hotel at South 8th and Chestnut. Green's was one of Center City's most popular gathering places, especially for the "showy bar" fitted out in an Arctic theme.[7] It was while in Philadelphia that Gene would meet his future wife.

Gene and Daisy made quite the striking couple and won speedy notice among those who enjoyed what was called the "gilded café life" of Philadelphia. They "flittered about in a high-powered automobile." Few people were perhaps aware that the motorcar actually belonged to Daisy Opie's first husband, who was, at the time, lying near death in a hospital.

CHAPTER 4

The Philadelphia Belle

Daisy Ulrich was born in Lebanon, Pennsylvania, some 90 miles northwest of Philadelphia. Most of the local folks were farmers of German descent. At the time of the shooting, reports of Daisy's age varied wildly. Her enemies said she was a dozen years older than Gene, but it was probably closer to six, and that puts her birth at 1877. That matched the census data, which, admittedly, was not always faultless.[1] Her father, Stanley Ulrich, was a Yale-educated lawyer,[2] and her mother, Mattie, was from the Susquehanna River village of Selinsgrove, Pennsylvania. The Ulrichs lived on North Fourth Street in Lebanon. They were a well-connected family, and Daisy, their eldest daughter, was a popular girl who sang in the Lutheran church choir, showing off what her mother later said was a "sweet, strong soprano voice."

Ideas of feminine beauty will vary from generation; some characteristics are prized in one era more than another. Daisy was an attractive girl, but more to be admired for her full figure and carriage than her beauty. Her hair was thick and dark. She was also rather tall for a woman at the time, standing about 5-foot-7.

The Ulrich home was just steps from Cumberland Street, the main thoroughfare in Lebanon. There was a commercial hotel called *The Eagle* on Cumberland Street (on the Ben Franklin Highway) where the men of the town, and visiting salesmen, would gather on the porch to smoke and spit and swap their stories. They could also watch the local women pass by as they made their various calls or visits to the shops. When Daisy strolled past, she attracted more than a few admiring glances. One of the interested gentlemen was a young salesman, Webster Opie, who came to Lebanon regularly, peddling "paper bags, wrapping paper and kindred supplies." Daisy returned the young drummer's compliments with a smile, and Opie contrived to be introduced. A suitable courtship led to their marriage. The Lebanon County Historical Society records show that Daisy Elizabeth Ulrich and Webster Hughes Opie were wed on January 21, 1897.[3]

Opie was something of a success, if not the "millionaire" the press made him out to be. He was soon a partner managing the Philadelphia end of the business for the statewide Pennsylvania paper supply firm Huff, Barnes and Opie, Inc. He bought a large new home at 4246 Spruce Street in West Philadelphia. The newlyweds' efforts to start a family yielded only tragic results. The first two babies, both girls, died at or soon after birth. In 1903 a son was born. The infant, named Webster after his father, soon developed vision problems, and an operation did nothing but blind him for life.

These successive heartbreaks — said those who claimed to know — changed Daisy. Abandoning the hopes of further children, she remade herself from the choir girl of Lebanon into a regular on the Philadelphia social scene. The Opie home was in Spruce Hill, a "streetcar suburb" just west of the University of Pennsylvania, developed in the late nineteenth century. It was a street of "semi-detached villas" with what the preservationists today call "exuberant Queen Anne detailing."[4] It was a sought after residential area, with no commercial aspect to it at all and boasting several large, well-endowed churches. The West Philadelphia historian R.M. Skaler says the neighborhood was a "testament to the affluence and piety of the residents."[5]

If that was the case, Webster and Daisy may not have fit the neighborhood profile. They entertained lavishly at 4246 Spruce Street, which grew notorious with the neighbors for the "bohemian parties." When not hosting various gaieties, they were off to Center City. The nexus of all that was exciting in Philadelphia was the magnificent Bellevue Stratford Hotel, scene of many gala events. Anyone in attendance would never forget the night the Wideners provided "a troupe of Hindus and writhing reptiles" to entertain their guests. Mrs. Craig Biddle, the queen of Philadelphia's "400," had shocked the world by lighting up her own cigarette in one of the public rooms of the hotel. Mrs. Biddle had also smiled favorably on the latest ragtime dances, such as the "turkey trot."[6] The trot had been banned in many other hotels, condemned as being no more than "indecent antics to the accompaniment of music." The Bellevue Stratford's ballroom and roof garden were packed nightly with young Philadelphians daring to engage in a "swinging motion of the body with shoulder movements up and down" to tunes such as George Botsford's "Grizzly Bear Rag." The Boston Dropstep had become "so last year."[7]

Opie drank more than was good for him, and this led to arguments. By 1910 the Opies were living apart. Daisy went to live with her mother, who was now widowed and also living in West Philly (on South 60th Street). Though a separation agreement had been drawn up, Daisy and Opie agreed to try to salvage their marriage and were in the process of working things out when the accident happened. While driving back from Atlantic City, Opie's "high-powered" car sputtered to a halt. Prior to 1912, most every American motor car had to be hand-cranked to start the engine. The chore was not anything like winding a watch. There were very strict instructions to be followed or risk a backfire which would set the crank spinning dangerously. The resulting injury had even created a new medical term: a "chauffeur's fracture."[8] Something of the sort happened to Webster Opie. He thought nothing of the slight scrape he had received, but in a few days his arm had swollen and he was down with a serious fever. He entered Philadelphia's Garretson Hospital, but he never came out.

Eugene Grace, at this time, was beginning to attract some notice as a dashing new figure on the city's café scene. He was, as noted, a tall man and quite good looking. His black hair was brilliantined, his "imperial moustache" perfectly curled at each end and meticulously clipped. He spoke in the slow, drooping tones of the rural South, in what one writer of the period called "that homely Georgia drawl, so charming to Northern ears and so impossible to reproduce in type."[9] He dressed very well. It was said that a local men's shop had provided him with the latest suits to wear out in Philadelphia society. Gene would serve as their walking advertisement. The admiring ladies would send their gentlemen in pursuit of suits of a similar "elegant fit."

One of those admiring ladies was most certainly Daisy Opie. While her husband fought for his life in the hospital, Daisy gave some encouragement, quite clearly, to this new young man. Daisy (helpfully) saved many of her letters from Gene, and they would (selectively) later become public. Gene either did not save her letters to him or did not think that releasing them would be helpful. On February 7 Gene wrote to Daisy from his room at Green's Hotel:

> You must pardon my frank admission, but it seems rather difficult to believe that you would desire me for a friend, even an acquaintance. And I can hardly grasp the matter as I have been going with silly young girls, who continually try to have you think that they are wild about you and such nonsensical stuff, that when one, who I believe to be sincere, makes a little flattering remark it seems like a flash of lightning out of a clear sky. But when I am conclusively known, as I trust I will be, believe me, I am true blue to the core. And now that I know you, I will truthfully say that I wish I could find someone who I call "my friend." I would be so happy just to know that should I get sick or some adversity should befall me, I would know that I had one friend who would grasp my hand and say, "I am with you." But, my dear, these kinds of friends are so scarce that only a microscopic examination of the heart or some severe and crucial test will discover them. I have been misled once or twice in my short career, and I am only trying to forcibly emphasize the fact that in the future, to use slang, "I have got to be shown," a la Missouri. I do not wish to give vent to my feelings, but will add that it is now up to you entirely, and I think you will be a true friend, and that which goes with it. For I do think an awful lot of you, but a woman is

sometimes cruel and I do not wish to venture too far into the game unless I am sure to win. Do you think I will win? It seems so strange that you should be impressed with me, for I know you are a woman with experience and who has had admiration, while I am nothing but a mere man, and while a trifle weak, not too susceptible to flattery, and it comes so sudden from sincere lips that when I do hear it honestly spoken I am forced to "sit up and take notice." Anyway, we will let my almost previous and unwarranted remarks go for the night, as in a few hours, the lips may impart that which a pen dare not attempt to write. Take good care of yourself and do not worry, for remember someone cares for your welfare a whole lot.

Yours till Niagara Falls (10)derly X[10]

This is quite a letter, it must be said. Poor Webster Opie isn't even dead yet, and Gene Grace is assaying his chances as his successor with "Do you think I will win?" He is bold enough to explicitly ask this woman "with experience" for her friendship "and that which goes with it." From the concluding words, we can surmise that he had already made some "unwarranted" approaches in that direction. Jauntily, he signs off with a winking mention of that favorite elopement destination, Niagara Falls.

Two weeks later, Webster Opie died at Garretson Hospital; the date was February 20, 1911. The cause of death was officially reported as blood poisoning. He was 37. Apparently there were no questions raised about the death at the time. It does truly seem to have been an accident. Opie left a will that had been drawn up only twelve days before he died. He left everything to "my darling wife Daisy." But just how much was "everything?" The press would have a field day in wild speculation on the young widow's fortune. Estimates ranged from the preposterous but headline-worthy figure of a million dollars to the more likely sum of about $75,000. The estimation of the purchasing power of a dollar in 1912, as opposed to a dollar a century later, is an inexact science at the minimum. According to modern estimates $75,000 in 1912 would have had the purchasing power of more than $1.5 million today.[11] In addition, Opie's will left to Daisy the lifetime use of the home at 4246 Spruce Street, but the value of the property was to be held in trust for his sightless namesake son. Webster was now eight years old.

Three days after Opie's funeral, which Gene attended, the infatuated swain wrote again to the young widow. He made his love for her quite plain, while admitting his manifold faults:

My Dear Girl, I know that you now feel more at ease since your mind has been relieved of the severe ordeal you have had to undergo these last few weeks and the only sensible thing for you now to do is to look only to the future, forget your troubles and endeavor to be happy and — although certain reverses prevent me from doing what I should be happy to do, if I can in any way make your future a happy one, believe me, I stand in readiness to respond to your call.

Of course, dear, I have absolutely nothing but a heart and my true friendship to offer anyone for I have been a rank failure in a business way during the last six months and can truthfully say it was caused by fast women. But I am now through with such women and shall from henceforth make every effort to make a man out of myself. What I have witnessed, and I say this absolutely free of sentimental feeling, has been a revelation to me, in that is shows that the finis to such fast living to be death. I shall never again be misled by the sweet silver tongue of an accomplished morally perverse woman into the depths of depravity. Neither shall I again drink whisky. I do not make these statements for your benefit or through any affection but solely for my welfare and for this reason I shall make every effort to adhere to them. For my only curse has been women. I know that this is not the kind of letter that you desired or expected, but I wish you to know my inner feelings. You need not have any future fear of my vacillating from the resolution which I have faithfully pledged myself to. You can rely on me to be true blue to the core. I just want to be the kind of a friend that you can know, down in the depths of your heart, if you have one true friend in the world, it is I. Not the kind that sticks only as long as good fellowship lasts but the kind that grasps you by the hand and says, "No matter what your trouble is or what is wrong, I am with you to the finish." I am willing to be such a friend and in return for such a friend who I could thus rely on I'd gladly give my life. In the time of trouble or adversity you can pick the ones that are friends. You will find both the true friend and the false friend near you in the time of trouble, but it does not require acute discernment to pick the weeds from the flowers, for that false friend has not the clear conscientious look of the loyal one. For today at a glance I could pick those whom you could rely on from the Judas type, and you can see similar types during the next few weeks. Pay strict attention to all that you shall hear in the way of advice and suggestions regarding your affairs but do not reply to any or commit yourself in any manner, neither should you be influenced by all you hear. Just listen, say nothing, and use your own judgment.

I want to have a good talk with you prior to your taking any steps other than consulting with your lawyer and the physician in regard to the insurance. In the latter do not pledge too much to the doctor. Upon reading this letter carefully give close thought to that which I have said, and if you think me worthy of such a friendship as that I mention, phone me today and just say, "I agree with what you say." Good night, dear, think of me a little tiny bit now and then. As ever, G[12]

Daisy must have made that phone call, for in the days following Opie's death the turkey trotting went on; Gene and Daisy were seen together in the Philadelphia clubs "night after night." Given the circumstances, this caused some comment. And then they were gone. The couple who had inspired so much interest and gossip disappeared, but not for long. In March, Daisy and Gene returned to Philadelphia as man and wife. Daisy had been a widow just 16 days.

CHAPTER 5

"A heart broken man"

In 1911, if you stopped someone on the streets of Manhattan and leaned close to inquire where you might find a church for a wedding on a wink and a nod, canny New Yorkers would confidentially whisper, "There's a little church around the corner." Officially known as the Church of the Transfiguration on 29th Street between Madison and Fifth in the Chelsea district, the church was, according to legend, a place to get married where the clergy wouldn't ask too many questions. As to how that legend got started, stories vary, but the church became a magnet for "runaway couples" — to the point that the harried rector had to put an announcement in the *Times* that it wasn't true.[1] Yet Daisy appeared at her mother's home on South 60th Street in Philadelphia to announce that she and Gene had been married at "the Little Church Around the Corner."

Regardless of this charming story, Daisy's mother was not entirely pleased to receive the news of her daughter's hasty second nuptials. What did anyone know about this Gene Grace from Georgia? Daisy assured her mother that Gene was from a good family that owned a prosperous plantation. He had a college education and was working as a bond salesman for a Wall Street firm. Martha Ulrich thought the Gene Grace she knew never seemed to be about any business at all, and she surmised that he was simply after her daughter's money — that, and he smoked altogether too much. Gene was not exactly made to feel welcome in the bosom of his new mother-in-law. Feeling this chill, Gene reasoned with Daisy that, given time, her mother would accept this marriage. But in the meantime, he wanted to take a honeymoon.

It is at this point, in late March 1911, one year before the shooting in Atlanta, that we begin to get into matters that would eventually come into dispute. However, there is a certain framework of data that is reliable and can be provided here. Gene quit his job with Fitkin and Co. He and Daisy left Philadelphia. Traveling indirectly, but via Niagara Falls, they eventually arrived in the spa community of Hot Springs, Arkansas. There they remained several weeks at the Park Hotel, "the most elegant bathhouse in the country, catering to a select patronage." They would, of course, take the regimen of famous baths. The curative waters in Hot Springs were recommended for many things, including "rheumatism, venereal diseases, asthma, catarrh, sexual disorders, and general debility."

Refreshed, and with any of their debilities vanquished, Gene and Daisy moved south to New Orleans where they took a room at the Grunewald Hotel off Canal Street. The travelers no doubt selected the Grunewald for its celebrated night life; the "subterranean supper club" The Cave featured waterfalls and faux concrete stalagmites and stalactites.[2] Even Philadelphia could not match that. But while in the Crescent City, Gene and Daisy took time to transact some important business, as will be discussed later. The Graces then moved on to Mobile, but the Alabama port city on the Gulf of Mexico failed to charm either of them. It was time for Gene to bring the bride home to meet his family.

According to Daisy, and this is solely her version of events, they had been spending anywhere from $500 to $800 a week, all of it hers. It was while they were on the train coming north from Montgomery to Newnan that Gene first admitted that his family was not quite as wealthy as he had been telling her. His stepfather was a farmer; Sam Hill made a good living, but the family home was nothing like a plantation. There was no great antebellum mansion waiting for her in Newnan, peopled with servants. Daisy seemed to take this news without great disappointment. It was made easier by the much warmer welcome extended on her arrival in Newnan than Gene had received in West Philadelphia. Still, Newnan was a different place; the evenings were of a much more sedate nature. For instance, when Gene's mother hosted the "Mesdames" of the local Salmagundi Club, the highlight was "a salad course with coffee followed by a game of dominoes."[3] So much for night life. Daisy remained several weeks on Greenville Street, getting to know Mother Hill and Gene's siblings.

It eventually came time for Daisy to return to Philadelphia; she professed to care very deeply for her son, little Webster, and she missed him. She had now been away for some time. The boy was being schooled at the Overbrook Institute for Blind Children during the week and stayed with his grandmother on weekends and holidays. Daisy and Gene went back to Atlanta and took the train to Savannah where they could catch a steamer to Philadelphia. While in Savannah, Gene decided that his wife should have a proper ring when she re-entered society. At Van Keuren's jewelry store on Bull Street, Daisy selected a diamond ring worth $1,475, which she, as a matter of course, paid for herself.

Gene and Daisy took up where they left off in Philadelphia. The home on Spruce Street having been let, the Graces took rooms at the Bellevue Stratford and delighted in the ragtime gaieties of the day. They also made a foray into New York society, lodging for a week or so at the Plaza Hotel on Central Park. They were seen at the finest "lobster palaces," the Edwardian term for today's high-end steakhouses and clubs.

Gene and Daisy took a delayed honeymoon cruise out of New York to the Canadian Maritimes. They sailed aboard the Red Cross Line's new SS *Florizel*,[4] a powerful vessel with an ice ram for the winter crossings but otherwise outfitted with every luxury for the 145 first class tourist cabins. It was a twelve-day cruise, seven at sea and five in port in Halifax, Nova Scotia, and St. John's, Newfoundland. The ship was their floating hotel. The cuisine aboard came highly recommended, and an orchestra played the latest dance numbers. The passage in and out of St. John's Harbor is a beautiful one. As they steamed home, Gene and Daisy could see above them, off the port side, the looming Signal Hill and the Battery. That summit had earlier been the scene of a memorable walk. But now the *Florizel* was bound for Gotham. The honeymooners had settled in their cabin with their new pet, a large black Newfoundland dog. They named him "Nig," and he'd become their inseparable companion.

Back in Philadelphia, Gene's relations with his mother-in-law improved somewhat. He thoughtfully invited Mother Hill and her sisters-in-law to come up to Philadelphia for their first ever visit to one of the great cities of the North. The visit went very well, and Gene and Daisy treated the Georgians to a drive across New Jersey to Atlantic City. Daisy took rooms for them all at Haddon Hall, the best hotel on the Boardwalk. The glimpse of the ocean even led Gene to suggest that they all might book a passage to Europe. Mother Hill said there was no chance of that ever happening, as she had a great fear of the wide and dark Atlantic. Mother Ulrich, meantime, was continuing to wonder when Gene would ever get back to work. And so was Daisy.

There was trouble in paradise. The rollicking and expensive travels *a deux* and entertainments of the in-laws had run through a goodly portion of the money that had been left to Daisy by her late and oh so briefly lamented husband. There were quarrels, and they became increasingly heated ones. Following the worst of these blow-ups, there were the inevitable apologies and pledges that they would work to ensure that such would not happen again. On August 11, 1911, the two of them signed a bizarre "contract":

> To whom it may concern: This is to certify that I, Daisy O. Grace, being of sound mind and fully knowing what I am doing, do hereby solemnly swear and promise, that after this date, August 11, 1911, should I speak unkindly, harsh or

fuss in any manner with my lawfully wedded husband, E.H. Grace, I shall forfeit to my husband the sum of $25,000 cash, and my home, located at 4246 Spruce Street, this city. In consideration of the foregoing promise and pledge, my husband, E.H. Grace, also promises to not fuss unless given proper reasons for so doing.

Once again, Daisy was the only half of the partnership putting up the money.

Gene did finally bestir himself to make a bid to get his old job back at Fitkin and Co., but he was told that the only work was in the New York office, and he wasn't keen about that. He reluctantly went up to Manhattan and wrote to Daisy from there on October 26. He had been told that the sole position open at Fitkin would require that he stay at the office until as late as 9 P.M., putting a crimp, of course, in their nightlife. "It certainly does not look very encouraging," he complained. New York wasn't for Gene Grace: "I do not like this town. It's too big a place. No country air or nothing. Nothing but abominable strange faces all the time. I am sick of it already." On the back of the envelope of this saved letter, Daisy wrote, "I have made Gene look for work and refused to support him any longer. This is the letter he writes about it."

There was more than just finding a steady paycheck for Gene that was making the Graces miserable. In that same letter from New York, Gene accused Daisy of paying too much attention to "evil minds and wicked tongues." Was he slipping back into old habits? Was he flirting again? "No matter what anyone says or what you have done or what I have said or done, I swear before God I love you. How happy we would have been had other people left their vile and slanderous tongues between their teeth or had we turned a deaf ear on their remarks or called them down for their insults." In his hotel room alone, Gene wrote, "I am a heart broken man."[5]

While in New York, Grace ran into J.S. Slicer, an Atlanta attorney and bank executive. They got to chatting about the Atlanta residential real estate market, a subject on which Slicer was quite bullish. There was money to be made in the construction of new homes, as the former fields between downtown and remote Buckhead were now being laid out in tracts. With Eugene's good looks and his salesmanship skills, plus that "Georgia Tech" background, he would make an ideal addition to any firm. In fact, Slicer knew a man looking for an investor. Ellis Lawrence was the fellow's name; he was a good, solid, sensible draughtsman who had an office in Slicer's building, and he was in need of a partner willing to put some capital into the business.

This was an ideal opportunity and the answer to everything, at least as Gene saw it. It was time to leave "rotten Philadelphia." He agreed that he would go south to investigate.

Gene arrived in Newnan on the first of November, broke.

I had to borrow $20 from [Uncle] Preston as you know I was broke when I landed, so if you want me to come send me about $50 to pay him and my car fare to Philadelphia. I am too ashamed to ask Papa or anyone here to loan me $50 as it looks bad. I don't want my folks or anyone to know of my shape. I would even pawn the clothes off my back if I had not faithfully promised you that I would never pawn anything again.

Something had to break right for Gene.

I do not know what to do. I hate to say it but I must tell you and be honest — if something does not happen within a few days so I can see or be with you, I shall not be responsible for what happens. I am getting afraid of myself and can't hold out much longer.[6]

But within a day or so, Gene was feeling more optimistic about the opportunity in Atlanta. But it would be Daisy, of course, who would have to come up with the money:

I am positively not going to live in Philadelphia. I was in Atlanta yesterday and also today. I had picked out a dandy furnished place and almost arranged to go into a beautiful business that I could make 200 percent on the money — the building business. It would only require about $6,000.[7]

To get that money he begged Daisy to once again tap into her inheritance. Some of Opie's money had been put in the stock market; she owned several thousand dollars worth of shares in Baldwin Locomotive. The company, at their plant in the Spring Garden section of Philadelphia, was the largest manufacturer of steam locomotives in the world. It was a good stock, selling at a little over $100 a share, and would remain a good stock until diesel engines came along and derailed Baldwin after the First World War. Gene gave Daisy instructions on how to turn those shares into cash. Then she could join him in Atlanta for their new life. Otherwise, he would have to return to Philadelphia, pending her sending him the $50, of course, and go back to Fitkin and Co. on Wall Street. It was obvious what he wanted:

I can make $1,000 to $2,000 a month on this as a building proposition is the thing. I am so anxious to go to work and show you that you have a husband who is a good businessman. Now if you want to sell your stock and can raise $6000, do so and come down at once.... I know that we shall be the two happiest people in the world in the future. We are not going to fuss or even disagree again. We had to do those things until we knew and understood each other. Now we can stop it, forget it, forgive and be happy. The folks were awful anxious to see you and ask every time I get a letter when you are coming. With all my love and devotion and kisses, your devoted husband, Gene.[8]

As previously noted, we do not have any of Daisy's letters to Gene. But one of Daisy's must have arrived soon after Gene had sent off the previous letter. He hastily wrote another one and took the wagon to the Newnan depot to make sure the letter made the last night train to Atlanta and then north. Daisy appears to have suggested that Gene ask his father for the money. "Papa is holding his cotton, and he could not possibly sell any of his farming lands at anything near their true value until next spring. He is worth $75,000 but it's tied up. You know nearly everyone may be worth lots of money but often say they cannot raise actual cash at once." Here, Gene criticized Daisy for not taking his advice following Opie's death and getting more of her late husband's money in cash:

I am sorry that you foolishly tied your money up and only wish you had taken my advice. You know this world is full of crooked people who are tickled to death to get on to some woman ignorant of business who has a little money. Of course, it has placed me in a very awkward position, as I came down here and practically closed up all arrangements. I don't know what they will think of me but I can't help it. I know I could have made good for I was going to work hard as a man could. I was so ambitious to make good so that you and everyone else could have been proud of me. I can match my brains with any man and be there at the finish.

I love you better than life Daisy and this I swear as God is my judge, and I know that you love me, so it nearly kills me to be away from you. Of course, I love my folks but home is not now what it was before I married you. I have you who God has made nearer and dearer to me than even my blood kin and you cannot ever know how my heart bleeds and yearns to have you again pillow your head on my bosom and go to sleep. How I miss those "Hello, Dearie" and "Good-bye, Dearie" kisses that I have gotten from you every day for over eight months. You have been my sole partner and companion both night and day for months and to now be separated for so long is like having a keen edged dagger continually thrust in my heart.

I am willing to abide by your decision. You can sell your stock and come to me, or I will come to you. I wanted to come south for I knew this to be the most promising country for business in the whole United States, and I knew that in a few years we could be wealthy, and I am so anxious to make something and make you happy. If ever a woman should be happy and forget her past unhappiness it is my dear wife, and I knew that by coming to Atlanta, where we could make money and new and good honorable friends, we could be so happy. I am sorry that things are like they are but maybe things will adjust themselves after all. I am going to try and make myself a good true and devoted and loyal husband no matter what position in life our station will be. I am going to be good and also win your confidence. There is never again to be any ill-temper or other things which tend to make life unhappy. I shall live only for you and you shall live only for me. I am grieved beyond expression when I think of my financial condition. God knows that if I were able, I would never taunt you on money matters. I never saved any money because I never knew that I could ever love any woman enough to get married, therefore, I only lived for the present, not caring what the future might bring, but there has entered my life a new hope, a new light and awakening to the realization that life is worth living after all and there is more to life than merely playing "the Great White Way," café's and parasitic women. Oh! If I only had you in my arms to tell you how much I love you, and how I long to be with you. Write me, dear partner, at once so I am to know if I am to come to you or you to me. With all my devotion and loving kisses, your loving husband, Gene.[9]

Gene had been up to Atlanta and met with young Lawrence, and between them they had arrived at the necessary figure of $6,000 to get their partnership established. In the end, Daisy did not disappoint. The money was provided, and in December 1911 the nameplate for the Grace-Lawrence Building Company was added to the directory in the lobby of the Empire Building at Broad and Marietta. The new firm could be found on the seventh floor, room 718. Now this was an excellent address. The Empire Building opened in 1901 and was one of the first of the Chicago-style steel skyscrapers on the Atlanta skyline. In 1911 the *Constitution* enthused that the Empire "throbs with the commercial life of the South."[10]

At this moment of great opportunity, at last, Daisy rejoined her husband in Atlanta late in 1911.

CHAPTER 6

Between the Peachtrees

When Daisy first arrived in Atlanta, she and Gene stayed at the "splendidly appointed" Piedmont Hotel, at the pie-shaped corner of Peachtree and Luckie streets. The Piedmont must have reminded the Graces of Philadelphia. Opened in 1903, the Piedmont was "Atlanta's first gesture in imitation of the hotel civilization of the effete east," wrote the legendary Atlanta historian Franklin Garrett.[1] This faux–Yankee establishment, then, met with some local resistance. The hotel was soon notorious for the "Gal in the Fountain." The grand lobby saloon bar featured a fountain in which stood a bronzed maiden, and "upon her form [was] a tunic admirably adapted to a tropic clime." Governor Hoke Smith, who was part owner of the Piedmont, was taunted by political hecklers for allowing this shocking display in his "palatial hell-gate."[2] Alas, by the time Daisy and Gene had come to Atlanta, you could not get a legal drink anywhere in the city except at private clubs. The sad bronzed maiden was still in the fountain, but now she presided over a coffee and tea room "instead of the rattle of the bartender's spoon as he mixed a festive cocktail."[3] However interesting the lore of the Piedmont might have been, a hotel could never be home. After stopping at the Piedmont for a week or so, Gene rented some rooms at 471 North Boulevard, near Rankin Street in the Bedford-Pine section. Gene soon decreed that the place wasn't grand enough.

On January 15, 1912, Eugene and Daisy Grace, with faithful Nig, signed a lease to rent the "Kiser home" at 29 West Eleventh Street. This was the perfect setting for their planned splash in Atlanta society. John Kiser, heir to a dry good fortune, and his wife spent a good deal of their time in the North Carolina mountains or in Florida. Their luxurious home was only two years old. Standing on the north side of the street, it was a green shingled, two-story house. Handsome stone steps led to a stone porch that ran across the entire front of the home. Four large stone pillars supported the roof. Above right, a small sitting porch opened off the second floor room where the Graces

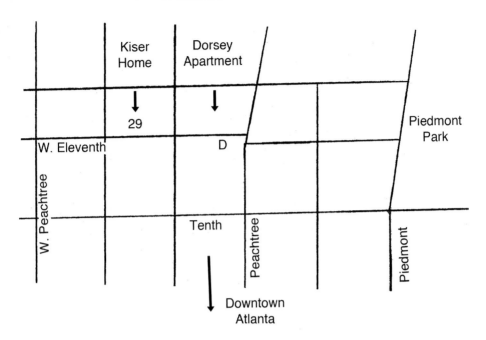

A map of West Eleventh Street, 1912. D marks the site of Solicitor Dorsey's apartment, approximately 300 feet to the east of the Kiser home (29 West Eleventh Street) where Grace was shot.

slept. They had leased the property fully furnished. The reception room, or drawing room, was all done in a rich red décor and had been the scene of many fashionable events. The carpets throughout were of the highest quality. Paintings, tapestries and prints adorned many of the walls. The divan and chairs were upholstered in the finest fabrics. When Gene let Nig have the run of the house, Daisy was quick to put a halt to that. Think of the damage the dog will do. "It's all in the lease, Gene," she fretted. In truth, however, the Kisers had also kept a pet, "a very smart and cute little monkey." Upstairs at the front of the Kiser house were two large bedrooms. They were connected by an interior door, and each room had a door opening off the hall as well.

The Graces began to socialize, as they must. They dined with Gene's partner, Ellis Lawrence, and his wife. Colquitt Carter, a man of good family with Newnan ties, also lived on Eleventh Street. Morris Prioleau, a fellow Tech man who had worked with Gene at Southern Bell, came around frequently. He actually was a clubman; his sister was a prominent socialite, and the Prioleau family was active at the Driving Club. They were good people to know. Gene and Daisy were being seen out publicly; it was said that the couple had been "prominent in the fashion parades on Peachtree and White-hall."

The Graces' new neighborhood was now one of Atlanta's finest. It had not always been so. The Kiser residence was in an area of new homes and streets laid out in the wake of the 1895 Cotton States Exposition in Piedmont Park. In preparation for the fair, the city fathers had finally done something about a long-standing plague spot known as "Tight Squeeze."[4]

The route of Peachtree Street began at Five Points and ran to the north, following an old Indian trail. Six miles to the north, Peachtree reached the settlement at Buckhead. There the road divided three ways. To the northwest, via Paces Ferry, the road led to Marietta. To the north, the next major town was Roswell. To the northeast, the road led toward Athens. By the 1880s, residential Atlanta had only reached what is now Tenth Street (then called Bleckley Avenue). Peachtree was a well-paved and lit boulevard as far as Tenth. Immediately beyond Tenth, there was a ravine or gully, some thirty feet deep, running downhill to the east toward Piedmont Avenue. Peachtree Street was forced to take a jog to the west to avoid this ravine and here the road narrowed. Though some of the better local residents "affected" to call the area "Blooming Hill," most folks knew the bottleneck and crime-ridden stretch as "Tight Squeeze." The gully was a refuge for the homeless and for men on the run. Anyone trying to move goods through the area by wagon was susceptible to having the contents pilfered by bold thieves. All around were taverns and low lodging places. There was a chain gang convict camp nearby. All said, it was an insalubrious part of town, and no one wished to be in the area after dark. The locals would warn you, "It's a tight squeeze you'll make it out in one piece."

For the Cotton States Exposition this area had to be tamed. For a cosmetic start, in 1883, Tight Squeeze, Georgia, was officially re-named "North Atlanta." The gully was filled in. Peachtree was finally straightened, and, continuing beyond Tenth Street, the road would carry a new street car line to bring visitors from the downtown hotels out to the Exposition. The chain gangs and the homeless were moved out.

After the Exposition, west of the park, from Tenth Street north to the new Ansley Park, "magnificent wide streets" and sidewalks were laid out in what had once been a wasteland of tangled underbrush.[5] New lots were platted in a grid: numerical streets running east-west crossed the vertical arteries of Piedmont, Peachtree and the newly laid out West Peachtree Street. At first the developers were fearful that West Eleventh Street had been tainted by its past propinquity to the "Tight Squeeze," and so they renamed it "Peachtree View." Even then, Atlanta developers took great delight and refuge in the proliferation of *Peachtrees*. But when a new Buckhead development co-opted the name, the street went back once again to the ever serviceable West Eleventh Street.

There was a demand for these new homes of quality in "north Atlanta." The formerly white residential enclave in the Fourth Ward, east of downtown, was being pressed by the growing black population. Whites were complaining that they could not find seats on the Irwin Street trolley line anymore. A resolution had been passed to "stop the encroachment of the Negro."[6] Similar demographic changes were happening west and south of the business district. Thus, there occurred the rapid growth of the old Tight Squeeze to the north, now home to bankers, lawyers, and other white professionals proud to boast of an address "between the Peachtrees."

The Grace-Lawrence Building Company quickly began making its mark. The *Constitution* had a daily real estate page, "Atlanta's Strides, Day by Day." The paper would note the latest sales, proposed new developments, etc., all written in the classic boosterish style. On January 24, 1912, the Grace-Lawrence Building Company made its first appearance in the column with an announcement that they were planning to build five houses on land located on Lake Avenue at Krog Street. The lots were convenient to the streetcar — the Fair-Irwin line terminated not far away. In February, more notices appeared in the *Constitution* that the company had plans to build on lots on Douglas Street and Vedado Way. They had hit the market at exactly the right time; the *Constitution* reported that "agents say that they have more prospects and deals on hand now than they had this time last year, which was considered a good real estate year."

All seemed to bid fair for the young partnership. Lawrence would remain at his drafting table, designing his soffits and fascia, while the aptly named Grace would once again serve as that walking sandwich board. With his good looks and the resources of his vivacious wife, he would push forward, striving to cross the needed social thresholds of Atlanta — such as the Piedmont Driving Club, the Capitol City Club, and the Atlanta Athletic Club. He would be the firm's "rain-maker." Messrs. Grace and Lawrence envisioned new clients who would demand homes far afield of Lake Avenue, which was, after all, in the shadow of the rail line and the Stove Works. These sought-after clients, high-end gentlemen, would pay very dearly for the Grace-Lawrence Building Co. to design their homes in the more desirable purlieus, such as Ansley Park or even beyond towards Buckhead.

The sign was up in the throbbing lobby of the Empire Building. The glass had been etched in the doorway to room 718. But in the contracting business there is quite a lag between laying out money for buildable lots and getting the check from the happy new homeowner. The Grace-Lawrence Building Company had only just acquired its first lots. They would build to suit. But now was no time for a spending spree. Yet Gene, as ever, was impatient. He and Daisy would stay only at the Piedmont Hotel upon their arrival in Atlanta. They had a weekly box at the theater. Then the rooms they rented on North Boulevard were not upmarket enough; they had to lease the Kiser house at twice the monthly payments. Gene had already asked Lawrence to put down a few ideas for a new home in Druid Hills. He was also eager to join the right social and business organizations. He had Daisy pay the $100 for his new advanced degree in the Masons. "That's money well spent," he assured her. And didn't he need a motorcar? On March 4, the day before the shooting, he had bumped into Olen Teate, an old friend, at the Jacobs Drugs on Whitehall Street where he had gone in to buy some of Dr. King's Special Mixture for his cold. Teate said Gene was feeling very poorly, so Teate bought him some hot lemonade. Teate was in the insurance business, and Gene asked if he handled automobile insurance. He said he did not but he knew people who did. Gene told him he was in the market for a motorcar, maybe two (one for Daisy). He thought the new American Traveler models were the thing, but he had not yet decided on the coupe or the semi-torpedo. Gene knew a chap who would make him a deal for something around $2,000 apiece.[7]

It should be made clear that the Grace-Lawrence Building Company had not taken in a penny just yet. But Gene had something else in hand — he now had Daisy's power of attorney. On Saturday, March 2, in the presence of a witness (the realtor J.P. Sturgeon), Daisy had signed the document authorizing Gene to go to Philadelphia and cash out her remaining investments, and also look into the sale or mortgaging of the home at 4246 Spruce Street. This was the home, it will be recalled, that the late Opie had intended would be held in trust for his son. Gene Grace would be leaving on the Tuesday afternoon train.

After leaving the drug store and Mr. Teate, Gene came home to West Eleventh Street for dinner. The Ruffins were there, and, as noted, they heard Gene and Daisy discussing their separate travels for the following day. Monday night was the Graces' theatre night. Atlanta had five theatres offering live shows every night but Sunday. Eugene and Daisy had standing tickets for the Monday night performances at the Forsyth Theatre, across the street from the Piedmont Hotel. On the night of March 4, 1912, after dining at home and discussing their mutual travel for the following day, they took the streetcar downtown to the Forsyth (now the Rialto).

The Forsyth was touted as "Atlanta's busiest theatre." Seating a thousand under a domed roof, and decorated in the rather florid "French Renaissance" style, it was perhaps the grandest theatre in the city.[8] Alas, the bill did not necessarily rise to the setting. That Monday night featured a troupe of performers from the famous "Keith's Vaudeville" stable. The evening shows began at 8:30, but the audience came and went according to their tastes and schedule. Mr. Keith, the impresario, had certainly put together a varied bill for Atlanta: he offered "Cheyenne Days," a brief extravaganza starring seven cowboys and five bucking broncos, said to have been "a remarkable and most sensational feature"; a well-known actress in the form of Hermine Shone, a "charming and clever entertainer," was featured in a playlet called *The Little Goddess*; a few laughs from Lou Anger, the German soldier (a monologist); Forsini, an accordionist; Marseilles, a novelty gymnast; and Cook and Lorenze, two "grotesque comedians" who did piano stunts.

After however much of that gallimaufry of entertainment options they chose to enjoy, the Graces wearily made their journey back to West Eleventh Street. They retired shortly after midnight. The next day was to be busy for both of them. It was the last night that either Eugene or Daisy would ever spend in the "Kiser house."

CHAPTER 7

Burglar or Butler?

A very interesting hypothetical question can be raised: if this shooting had taken place while the Graces were living in rented rooms at 471 North Boulevard in Atlanta, would it have generated anywhere near as much attention? Sometimes in journalism it is not so much the who or the what but the where that really matters. The scene of the shooting of Eugene Grace was identified in the papers as, simply, "the Kiser house," as if all Atlantans should know it well. And they *would* know it had they been reading their daily society pages attentively. Every party, dance or dinner was chronicled. "A fairly continuous spate of parties shuffled the elect from house to house with the same names generally on the roster."[1] The Kisers were among the elect.

John Franklin Kiser was heir to a dry goods fortune. The legendary "Major" M.C. Kiser came to Atlanta after the war.[2] Marion Columbus Kiser was a farm boy who, along with his brother, made a great family fortune in dry goods with a store at Pryor and Wall Streets. He also expanded into real estate, and, at the end of his life, he launched a popular line of shoes under the Shield brand. When the major died in 1893, he was carried off to a massive new mausoleum in Oakland Cemetery but left a million dollar fortune mainly to his two young sons. John was just ten years old. John seems to have left the job of continuing the Kiser family businesses to his older brother, William.

In June of 1906, John married Mary Washington Read at All Saints Episcopal Church on West Peachtree. It was Atlanta's wedding of the year, "one of the most popular young women in the city and a prominent young businessman well known in the social world."[3] Mary Kiser was soon established as one of the most admired society leaders in Atlanta. "Her superb jewels and exquisite gowns are chosen with so much taste and worn so beautifully that she is always surrounded by so many admirers." The Kisers were regulars in the fashionable columns. Their movements were followed with curious interest; John was among the first to have a motorcar in Atlanta and also one of the first to have his license pulled for speeding. The Kisers wintered in Palm Beach; they sailed to Europe for the summer of 1910; whenever they visited New York they stayed only at the Waldorf. While in Atlanta, their "charming new home" between the Peachtrees was the scene of Mrs. Kiser's "lovely little luncheons" and "gay receptions," and, to the great joy of all, a "very pretty birthday party" in 1911 for Master John F. Kiser, Jr. To think that such an awful thing as this shooting could have occurred in the very same house where the Kisers only months before had entertained the Baron and Baroness Rosenkrantz from London was simply too horrid to contemplate. The *New York Age* reported that "Atlanta high society had cold shivers up and down its spinal column while it held down its proud head with sorrow and shame."[4] The *Macon Telegraph* informed their readers in mid–Georgia: "Not in years has Atlanta been stirred as it has today when details of the mystery became generally known."[5]

On Wednesday, the day after the shooting, the police gave reporters the first update on their investigation. Desk sergeant Guy Lindsay had been on duty at police headquarters on Decatur Street. He had taken the call when it came in at about 2:15 on what had been a rather quiet Tuesday afternoon. The number for the police was Bell Main 21. A man was on the line and spoke quite feebly, "I'm E.H. Grace of 29 West Eleventh Street. I am shot. I am all alone. Send help." Then there was the sound perhaps of the phone dropping to the floor and silence. Two "call officers," Wood and Dorsett, were dispatched, and it took them ten minutes to reach the address. We cannot say how the police got there; at the time, Atlanta police moved on horseback, bicycles, by the streetcar or the new "auto patrol." However they reached West Eleventh Street, the patrolmen arrived to find the Graces' home "securely locked as if a fortress ... care was taken that no one reach the interior." On the arrival of the Ruffins, the police were taken inside. Once they had chopped their way into the bedroom, they found Mr. Eugene Grace lying on the bed, gasping for water. The room itself was in disarray. Chief of Detectives Lanford told the *Journal* that his men described it as though "a cyclone" had blown through the room. There was an empty suitcase on a chair, the bureau drawers were left open, and papers were found scattered and rumpled on the floor.

Mr. Grace had told the police that, at first, he thought he only had a bit of indigestion and a pain in his side. But when he reached to rub it, he discovered he had been bleeding. The blood on his nightshirt was dried, according to Lanford, and that, the detective asserted, was the most important fact that had yet come to his attention. The blood on the nightshirt had dried into a brown crusty stain, and the blood on the pillows had dried in the same way. Lanford shared with the reporters the knowledge that it takes three hours for blood to dry. (The detective may have been a little too certain in that finding. In the C.S.I. world of a century later, "new and innovative techniques" are employed to establish the age of bloodstains. The science was unknown in 1912. The German researcher Dr. Schwarzacher, as late as 1930, wrote, "All investigations in the direction of development of a practical method for determination of the age of bloodstains [blutspuren] have proven abortive."[6] Still, three hours was the bloody round number.) The bloodstains proved to Lanford that if the victim made his phone call for help soon after 2:00 on Tuesday afternoon, that put the shooting at no later than 11:00 that morning. Mrs. Grace had told police that she left West Eleventh Street for Newnan a little after eleven. It certainly put her "in the frame."

There was also the puzzling question of the keys. The house at 29 West Eleventh Street had been locked up tight, "with care," the police had said. At police headquarters, where she was brought following her arrest, Daisy had allowed the detectives to look inside her "stylish" alligator bag. Inside were two "large and heavy bunches of keys." These key rings, she promptly explained, included the keys to all the doors at West Eleventh Street, including the interior bedroom doors, various keys for bureaus and suitcases, the keys to their house in Philadelphia, the keys to Eugene's office at the Empire Building, his desk, etc. Daisy had complained that the police had actually busted through the bedroom door because there was always a key to the bedroom left in a small vase on a hall table upstairs. The police, in fact, later found the key right where she said it was. But why did Daisy have Gene's keys with her?

The papers reported that Mrs. Grace had been "put through a grilling" by Detective Lanford. Yet even the police had been impressed by her poise and resolution in denying any role in the attack on her husband. The idea was simply preposterous to her. She loved her husband very much; they were living together quite happily. She had recently given him a large sum of money to join a business that was showing great prospects. They had spent a pleasant evening the night before at the theatre. Eugene had not been feeling well, but she thought it was no more than a winter cold. Before bed on Monday evening he took some quinine and a dose of Dr. King's Special Mixture, a cough medicine. The combination of these patent medicines had left Eugene rather drowsy when he awoke, but otherwise she thought he was in good health. She last saw him sitting on the side of the bed, planning to dress for his business trip to Philadelphia. She left the house sometime after eleven, having called a cab to take her to the station to board the 2:00 train to Newnan. She was going to spend three nights there at the home of Gene's mother on Greenville Street. Only on her arrival in Newnan, through the words of 13-year-old Hamilton Hill, was she told that her husband had been found shot.

Pressed by police for any alternative theories to help them find the gunman, Mrs. Grace went back to the burglar idea. It was a suggestion not without merit. The *Constitution* only a few months earlier had reported that a "Burglary Wave" had swept Atlanta. "A dozen or more burglaries daily are being reported at the police station and a veritable epidemic seems to have struck the city."[7] The paper blasted police for tolerating an "aura of lawlessness." In mid–February, only two weeks before the shooting, police rounded up a ring of "negro men and women" in connection with a string of residential break-ins.[8] Certainly a burglar could not be ruled out. Daisy said that she had left a purse and some money on a mantel in the bedroom; if it was gone, then that would prove that a burglar had been involved. Police conceded that there was no money found in the room.

Mrs. Grace was also willing to throw some shadow of suspicion on the Ruffins; after all, she must have known that the servants had been freely talking to the detectives. Daisy said that her husband had quarreled quite recently with J.C. Ruffin. She said J.C. had twisted Martha's arm badly during an argument. Eugene had warned J.C. that if he hurt his wife again he would "take a cane to him." J.C. had not taken the lecture gracefully.

Late that Wednesday afternoon Mrs. Grace left her room at the Kimball House and went back to 29 West Eleventh Street. She was heavily veiled. "Do you think I enjoy being stared at," she barked at one reporter. When she arrived at the house, at least Nig was glad to see her. The poor dog had been locked out on the back porch when Daisy and Gene had gone to bed on Monday night, and the animal was still there, unfed. The police were also there to greet Daisy, and she was instructed that the second floor crime scene was off limits to her. She insisted that she had only come to get some of her things and perhaps "straighten up" the room. She had earlier told Mother Hill that she did not want the police poking around in her "soiled things." The police would not permit it. She sulked and complained to the trailing reporters that the police had made a mess of the place. The first floor looked like "vandals" had taken roost. Daisy fixed herself a light supper from the kitchen; the Ruffins, of course, had gone over to the police. It didn't even feel like her home anymore. Daisy went back to the Kimball House.

Mrs. Grace may have been kept out of the locked bedroom, but newspaper readers were taken there vicariously. Both the *Journal* and the *Georgian* helpfully provided their readers with photographs of the "magnificently furnished" house, which was said to be located in "probably the most fashionable section of the city." The *Journal* published a diagram of the bedroom where Mr. Grace was found. The *Georgian* went a little farther, offering a small artist's sketch of the wounded man abed.

Wednesday also marked the arrival of the first of many, and not all necessarily accurate, reports from Philadelphia. The early claims that Daisy Opie had inherited as much as a million dollars from her first husband were denied. The *New York Times* reported that the late Webster Opie had left her a "handful of unset diamonds and some real estate."[9] No one could put a dollar figure on her fortune, but the seven figure surmises were being discredited. Daisy Grace was clearly making fascinating news-copy nonetheless. A Philadelphia correspondent told Atlanta readers that "she is a striking brunette, 5 feet 7 inches tall, with a splendid figure and clothes that drew envious glances. She wore furs that won her the sobriquet of 'Daisy of the Leopard Skins.'"[10] Over the several months that this case would garner headlines, the sobriquet varied from "Leopard Skin" to "Leopard Spots."

Eugene Grace was also well-remembered from his meteoric transit across the Philadelphia society landscape. "He is eight years younger [than Mrs. Grace] and a boy in disposition and appearance despite his height of 6 feet 3 inches. [He] is popular everywhere."[11] The *Constitution* echoed the positive thoughts on the young man's reputation: since arriving in Atlanta, Mr. Grace had become "one of the most popular of the younger married set" and was "well known in the business way." Though new in town, Grace had already made himself "popular with his associates" and was described as "optimistic, energetic, buoyant and enthusiastic."

Late on Wednesday afternoon, however, the doctors at St. Joseph's Infirmary reported that the very popular and estimable Eugene H. Grace was in grave condition, and his death could be expected at any time. According to Dr. Goldsmith, Grace was "all right about the chest" and able to move his arms, but he was "totally incapable of movement below the wound." It seemed most likely that the bullet had severed the man's spinal cord. Such a wound would certainly be mortal — Grace was going to die and likely very soon.

CHAPTER 8

To the Tower

The Kimball House at Five Points was the best known hotel in Atlanta. Opened in 1870 as the largest hotel south of Washington, DC, the first Kimball House burned down in 1883.[1] It was rebuilt with remarkable speed, and the new structure covered most of the block made up by Peachtree, Pryor, Wall and Decatur Streets. It offered over 400 rooms, arrayed along open hallways, overlooking the naturally lit seven-story atrium lobby — or "the rotunda," as it was known. The Kimball House was rebuilt of brick, iron and stone, with a terra cotta finish. It was "Atlanta's pride," and it was now fireproof.[2]

Thursday morning, in room 613 of the Kimball House, Daisy (I will henceforth drop the more formal Mrs. Grace except where appropriate) entertained the press. She no doubt admired the front page photo in the morning editions of the *Constitution*. According to the caption, she is "noted for her stunning figure which shows off well her exquisite clothes." Her face was now appearing on newspaper front pages throughout the country. For editors and headline writers, "Daisy of the Leopard Spots" was simply too good to pass up. Yet Daisy was indignant. She went right after the man from the *Georgian*, where the sobriquet had first appeared: "I had a leopard skin coat but I never knew anyone who called me Daisy of the Leopard Spots." She doth protest too late. The *Georgian's* sketch artist had already put out a drawing of Daisy in a leopard coat and hat. This was based on a Philadelphia news item that reported she had been seen frequently wearing a coat made of five leopard skins, plus a "saucy little hat" of the same material and matching shoes. The *Constitution* also remarked on Daisy's "affectation of leopard skin furs." Their report also expressed something like disappointment that "the costume has been worn in Atlanta but seldom." Certainly the climate did not provide a lady of fashion with as many opportunities to wear a leopard skin coat in Atlanta as in Philadelphia. You could not even buy such a coat in Atlanta.

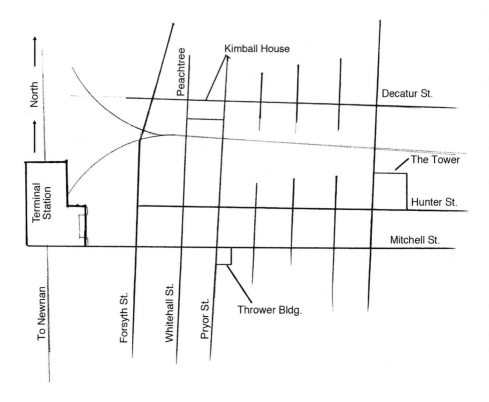

A map of downtown Atlanta 1912.

The Whitehall Street shops did offer their high end clientele various fur coats of mink and lynx, but they sold a good deal more of the more affordable Russian Pony Coats. A leopard skin coat in New York at the time was selling on the rack for $295. But the *San Francisco Call* joked that an actress had one made especially for her and paid $1200, spot cash![3] The leopard skin's rarity and its association with demi-monde characters like actresses and courtesans led to the air of sensuality that surrounded those who wore it.

As for Eugene, the increasingly gloomy reports from St. Joseph's Infirmary on her husband's condition brought a frown to Daisy's face and prompted her to extend to him her very best wishes for a recovery. "When he gets better and his wind clears up, he will straighten all this out. I am innocent of this charge, God knows."

While Daisy was exchanging quips and quibbles with the delighted members of the press, the police were busy telling other scribes that her alternative theory suggestions held no water. Chief of Detectives Lanford declared the idea that either of the Ruffins had been involved "cannot be held for a moment." The police had examined Martha's body and found no signs of any recent violence. If either of the Ruffins had shot their master, Daisy would have been in the house and certainly heard the shot. As for a burglar, it was certainly possible, but police had found no evidence of a break-in. Nothing was taken. A purse belonging to Mrs. Grace with a check for $2,000 was left untouched on the mantel. Why would any burglar, having created such a disturbance, including the loud crack of a gunshot in a quiet residential neighborhood, then leave the gun downstairs and take the additional time to lock all the doors behind him. No, Lanford concluded, "Mrs. Daisy Grace is our only suspect."

At 2:30 Thursday afternoon, almost exactly 48 hours after Eugene's desperate phone call, Chief of Detectives Lanford and detectives Bullard and Doyal went to the Kimball House hotel and instructed the elevator boy to take them to the sixth floor. Daisy answered their knock at room 613. With her were her two attorneys, John W. Moore and his partner James A. Branch. Apparently they had been tipped off as to what was about to happen. Lanford announced that upon instructions from the offices of the Fulton County Solicitor General, Daisy Grace was being re-arrested. Solicitor Hugh Dorsey had issued a statement that he was acting in the belief that Mr. Grace's condition had become so dire that it was no longer proper or wise for Mrs. Grace to remain at large.

The Hill family had been reading the papers too. To them, as they sat expecting "dear Gene's" death at any moment, it seemed too much to bear that the woman the police were saying had shot him was free, posing for pictures and being extolled for her "exquisite clothes." What if Gene were to die suddenly? There were 125 trains a day through Atlanta, going in all directions, including toward the port of Savannah. A woman of Daisy's undetermined fortune might easily slip away and book passage to foreign climes. Italy, for some reason, was the rumored bolt-hole for Daisy. The Hills now had their own lawyer, Lamar Hill. My apologies for introducing another Hill, but Lamar was not apparently related to the Newnan family. Lamar Hill insisted that the family was making no formal accusation. However, he asserted that the "members of Mr. Grace's family are not of the firm opinion that Mrs. Grace is innocent. They simply desire to see justice done."

At the Kimball House, Lanford told Daisy that there was a cab downstairs to take her the few blocks to the Fulton County Jail, known ominously as "the Tower." Daisy eschewed the cab — "I have no money to hire a cab," she huffed — and opted instead to walk. Emerging from the elevator, she crossed the glass-walled rotunda as hotel guests and employees stared down at her from the parlor level. She left via the main hotel doors onto Pryor Street. It was a cool, cloudy afternoon (the Yankees actually got in their workout). Daisy's route to the Tower was down Decatur Street, four blocks to the east, then right on Butler Street. The cab had been offered for a reason. It was not the most pleasant of walks; just a block or two off Peachtree brings the walker to the stretch of Decatur Street known as the "plague spot" where the race riots had begun. It was lined with fish stalls, "negro beer saloons" and (according to *Harper's Weekly*) "other establishments catering to Negro trade and Negro vice."[4] The Associated Press correspondent said Daisy seemed troubled not at all, and "she marched" her way along Decatur Street, accompanied by the detectives, her two attorneys, several reporters, and a small crowd of "the curious." Apropos of nothing, perhaps, Daisy declared to the pressmen that she should never have accepted room 613 at the hotel because it was a "hoodoo" number. The marching party reached the jail in about ten minutes.

Franklin Garrett, in his 1960s classic *Atlanta and Environs*, referred to this jail as "the grim old Fulton County tower."[5] The blacks called it "the big rock."[6] The facing of the five-story jail was done entirely in Stone Mountain granite. Opened in 1898, at the corner of Butler and Hunter streets, the jail was proclaimed to be "as fine a building as there is in the city." The landmark granite tower rose an additional sixty feet above the cell blocks (110 feet in all). The four wings behind were built of brick. The floors were concrete. The cells of "chilled steel" were secured with the very latest locks. As with everything in Atlanta, the jail inmates were separated by race. Whites were housed from the top down, blacks from the basement up — and the conditions varied accordingly.

Daisy was to be housed in the women's ward, known as "Third West" or "Third floor front." The 12-bed ward, with cold cement floors, was entered through a locked and forbidding iron door. The ward was well lit by numerous, if barred, windows. She had the place to herself; those of her sex who were being held for common crimes (such as prostitution or drunkenness) were kept at the police station on Decatur Street. Not many women came to the Tower. In early 1911 a young woman — "prominently connected" — charged with passing bad checks at the Daniels Brothers store on Peachtree Street drank poison five minutes after she arrived at the Tower.[7] The most recent woman in "Third West" had been moved out to an insane asylum.

In such surroundings, coffee and toast were sent up for Daisy's refreshment. Regardless of the amenities, the Kimball House it was not. Attorney Moore told the trailing pressmen that Daisy's re-arrest was totally without precedent. Still, they intended to fully cooperate with Mr. Dorsey until this regrettable matter could be resolved. His client was entirely innocent. Lanford, his duties done, left the Tower with the parting remark, "I hate to say it, boys, but she's the only suspect."

Daisy proceeded to give the first of her series of jailhouse interviews. "I am as innocent as a new born babe," she protested. She would never have done anything to injure Gene: "He is dearer to me than life. It's all a dreadful mystery. How can I explain it? I know no more about it than you do." Daisy wondered why the police had so quickly dismissed her theory that it had been an intruder. It happened every day in the better sections of Atlanta. She understood the feelings of the Hill family but expressed confidence that it would all be straightened out. She is a patient woman and will let her attorneys resolve this mystery. Her only regret at being incarcerated was that it would keep her from seeing Gene: "My regret at being here is great, but from only one cause — that I cannot be with the man whom I love better than anyone else I ever met.... Should he recover and be paralyzed, I will wheel him around in a chair until death takes him from me.... Will you give him my love?" It should be noted that in the 24-plus hours of freedom she enjoyed from being bonded out to her re-arrest, she had not made any effort to visit the infirmary to see her apparently dying husband. To be fair, after the dramatics of Tuesday evening her attorneys may have advised her to keep her distance.

If the afternoon papers were brought to her ward, and they no doubt were, Daisy would have perused a statement given to reporters in Philadelphia by her mother. Daisy had earlier alerted her mother by wire to the developments in Atlanta: "Accused of shooting Gene. I am innocent. He is improving." Reporters had found Mother Ulrich at 900 South 60th Street, where she lived with her married daughter Martha and her husband Henry Kreider, an accountant. Henry confided that, at first, he thought Grace was a jewel, but now the whole family thought him to be a complete wretch. Mrs. Ulrich declared, "If she did shoot him, it was in self-defense. They always argued about money." We already know that Gene's relationship with his distant mother-in-law was just that. Mother Ulrich would consistently denounce him. "They quarreled frequently, I understand, because of Gene's hatred of work. He always posed as one of those Southern gentlemen and took great delight in boasting of Southern chivalry. But he seldom gave an exhibition of it personally." A note of interest: Gene's father fought for the Confederacy while Daisy's father wore the blue of the Union army. Forget? Hell, no.[8]

CHAPTER 9

"A diabolical plot"

Daisy Grace awoke alone on Friday morning in Third West complaining of a sore throat. As the "star guest" in residence at the Tower, Daisy received unusually prompt medical attention. Dr. S. H. Green, the jail medico on call, visited her cell and diagnosed the problem as a mild case of tonsillitis. Her throat was swollen, and she could only talk in a hoarse whisper. It seemed plain that the fetid jail air, even in her select quarter of the facility, was doing her no good. A jail official assured Daisy's friends that she would continue to receive every "legitimate courtesy" under her present status.

Had she slept well? Had she had any strange dreams? According to the *Constitution*, Eugene Grace had been telling visitors that his wife suffered from nightmares. For several weeks prior to the shooting she would wake up in the night in a great fret and cry out things about her first husband. One night she pleaded, "Take him away! That's Opie, he's trying to get in, oh, take him away." She seemed quite afraid of Opie and had begged Gene to protect her from his ghost. After one such fitful night, she warned her husband, "I might kill you at anytime, Gene." The *Constitution* headlined this new development: "Was Eugene Grace shot while asleep?"

The new theory had come from Gene Grace himself. He had been feeling somewhat better at the infirmary and was now wondering whether Daisy might have shot him while she was in a somnambulant state. Perhaps, he suggested, she did not realize that she had shot him, or even remember now what she had done. Grace admitted that both he and his wife had guns, and his was kept under his pillow. The *Constitution* suggested that this "might explain many things." The police quickly cast the "dream" scenario aside — Chief of Detectives Lanford said flatly, "The gunshot would surely have woken her up."

The more important developments at the end of the first week were two: the presence of significant life insurance policies which might have been a motive for the shooting and a mysterious letter "which fell into the hands of Eugene H. Grace's relatives instead of reaching Mrs. Daisy Grace."

Gene Grace was well enough on Friday morning to stand a visit from Judge J. B. Ridley, the same magistrate who had bonded Daisy from jail several nights before. On this occasion Ridley came with a possessory warrant for Grace to sign. Such warrants in Georgia are issued when a person — in this case Gene Grace — claims that some personal property "has been taken, enticed, or carried away, either by fraud, violence, seduction, or other means," or may have "disappeared without his consent."[1] This property, he now believed, is in the possession of the party complained against (i.e., Daisy Grace). The Hill clan was going after the three life insurance policies taken out on Gene's life the previous December. Daisy had been named the sole beneficiary. Those policies were nowhere to be found at 29 West Eleventh Street, and the Hills believed Daisy had placed them beyond anyone's reach. It was now Eugene's wish — according to Lamar Hill — that the policies be changed, with the money going instead to his mother and the Hill family. Gene signed. When the paper was brought to Daisy's cell in the Tower, she claimed not to recognize Gene's signature. She huffed that Eugene would never have signed the warrant if he had been in control of the situation. She realized the Hills had now all turned on her. As for the policies, she could not get them while she was locked up in jail, and she would not reveal their current whereabouts.

There would be no more doubts where the Hills of Newnan stood on the matter after reporters were called to the office of attorney Reuben Rose Arnold in the Gould Building on Decatur Street.[2] Regarded as one of the leading criminal lawyers in the South, Arnold said he had been employed by the Hill family to ensure that the person who shot Eugene H. Grace will not escape punishment. That person was his wife Daisy. "Mrs. Grace," he began, "drugged her husband and then shot him. Mr. Grace has reiterated that he was drugged before he was shot. That explains why he did not hear the shot or know just when it was fired." Arnold said that prior to the shooting Grace had been given so many opiates "she could have amputated his leg." On the day of the shooting, Mrs. Grace put into motion "the execution of a diabolical plot to murder Eugene H. Grace for his insurance money." There was "not a shadow of a doubt" that she had fired that gun.

> She had even stuffed the telephone transmitter with cotton so he could not talk over it. She had stuffed the bell with the same material in order that the ringing of the telephone, should it ring, would not be heard by the neighbors. Then she secretly left for Newnan, to visit his parents, to establish a perfect alibi. She had

made every arrangement to prevent his body being found for four or five days and she was ready to declare that for almost a week she had been with his mother.

Arnold said that they were now in possession of an envelope that had fallen into their hands. It actually contained two letters — one written in pencil, the other typed. These were forgeries done by Mrs. Grace to establish, if necessary, an alibi for the day of her husband's death.

The motive for this murderous plot was perfectly clear. Arnold said the newspapers had misled everyone with this talk of Daisy being the widow of a millionaire. In truth, she was in straitened circumstances. "We can prove she was hard pressed for money. She tried to murder him to collect the $27,000 on his insurance policies. Why, the very fact that even now she is clinging to those policies like grim death is enough to show why she shot him." Not willing to reveal his entire docket of information against Mrs. Grace, Arnold teased the reporters with the idea that he held back "one crowning bit of evidence" which would not be divulged until the trial but would demonstrate very clearly "the brutal nature of this woman's plan."

When Arnold had concluded his statement, Lamar Hill added — if only for emphasis — that Mr. Grace's family is now "fully convinced" that Gene was shot by his wife and no one else. As for the efforts to retrieve the life insurance policies, Hill said that the family had no interest in "blood money," but they were stirred to take the steps they had "to keep the woman we believe was willing to kill a man for money from sharing in the profits of her crime."

The close-knit world of the Atlanta bar in 1912 put most of the offices of the leading lawyers and law firms all within a short walk of the courthouse. It was not but a block or two for reporters to scurry from the scene of Reuben Arnold's ringing indictment of Daisy Grace to get the response from her lawyers, Moore and Branch in the Peters Building on Pryor Street. J.W. Moore placidly listened as breathless scribes relayed Arnold's charges. He assured them all that Mrs. Grace was innocent, and such talk of a "diabolical plot" was nonsense. He scoffed at how, seemingly overnight, Daisy had somehow gone from a great heiress to a woman driven by financial straits to shoot her husband. This newly crafted theory that she was in great debt would be "fully exploded," he promised. In fact, Moore declared that Mrs. Grace had never been in a better financial position than she was at present. He allowed that Mrs. Grace's home on Spruce Street in Philadelphia had been mortgaged for something near $4,000, but the property was easily worth $25,000. The insurance policies, so much now under discussion, had actually been taken out directly at the wishes of Mr. Grace. They were none of her doing.

Moore wondered why the police had so blithely dropped the idea that

Grace had been shot during a bungled burglary. Still fresh in everyone's mind in Atlanta was the tragic death of businessman and civic leader Daniel Dougherty the previous fall. He had accidentally shot himself while investigating a prowler at his splendid residence at 459 Peachtree, only a short distance from the Kiser house.[3] Had the police not been freely criticized only a few weeks before the Grace case for being incapable of dealing with break-ins? Why, even Reuben Arnold had been a victim — a "professional negro burglar" had broken into the attorney's home on Ponce de Leon Boulevard in 1911 and made off with several thousand dollars worth of Mrs. Arnold's jewelry.[4] Moore insisted that that was what had also happened in the home of Eugene and Daisy Grace. It was a Negro burglar, and "we will prove it." Moore denied trying to single out the Ruffins as suspects, but, nevertheless, he asked, "Does it not look like a Negro's hand played a part in this?" The police had said it could not have been a burglar because nothing was taken. There was a check for $2,000 left on the mantel. Moore was incredulous; a Negro takes what he can easily sell. Mrs. Arnold's jewelry comes to mind. What would a Negro thief do with a check for $2,000? The same could be said for the tapestries and artwork on the walls of the Kiser home. The Negro thief came for money. "Negroes often steal money and small articles and pass the more valuable ones over." If they were caught in the act, they fought. "Anyone who is familiar with the habits of Negroes knows that a darky will do most anything to cover up a theft, no matter if it is a small amount of money." Mr. Moore was apparently more than willing to share his knowledge of the Negro criminal classes.

Another expert on the criminal mind was former Atlanta Police Chief John W. Ball, whose stormy tenure as "top cop" had ended in 1905.[5] He was still around town, and he was put to work by the *Atlanta Georgian* as their crime-solving consultant. Ball called it "the queerest case I've ever studied and the queerest part of it is Mrs. Daisy Grace herself." Though it was early in the investigation, the ex-chief thought the net was tightening. "It would have been a beautiful plot if that bullet had killed Grace but it didn't." He was also sold on the blood evidence. If it was dried, as the police insisted, then Mrs. Grace had to have been in the house when the shot was fired. If someone else had fired the shot, she would have heard it. Ball believed the Ruffins were telling the truth about being hurried off by Daisy, who had also told them to send away any doctor who might come by. Ball did not necessarily credit the Ruffins as trustworthy, mind you, but rather, "It's not the kind of story a Negro could invent." The gun that was left downstairs behind the drapes was a curious thing. But Ball reminded his readers that if Mrs. Grace had left the gun in the bedroom, it might have begun to look like a suicide.

Most life insurance contracts stipulate that they will not pay out for a suicide within a year of the policy's start date. To collect the insurance, best leave the gun somewhere else. Finally, it was certainly a mistake that the shooter had not just cut the phone line. Ball concluded that Daisy must have been sure that her husband could not get to the phone for help. "A man would have pulled the wires out of the wall but women are afraid of electricity," said the old copper. The new claim that some cotton had been stuffed in the telephone was telling. Ball said that was almost surely "women's work."

Amid all the theories and speculation, the week ended on a somewhat lighter note. Had police received a tip that would break the case so quickly? Judge Nash Broyles had since 1898 presided over the Atlanta Recorder's court. It was there, hard by the police station on Decatur Street, that the routine fistfights, cuttings, disorderly conducts, and general affrays of urban life in Atlanta were brought before the bar of justice. "Jedge Briles," as the blacks knew him, was feared for his swift and severe sentences. The stockade on Glenwood Avenue was being expanded to make room. The grateful white voters re-elected him time and time again.[6] Broyles showed the press a letter he had received from a "negress" named Mattie Gibbs. She had written:

> I seen what ther was in the paper abaout Mrs. Grase and I don't want her to go to no stokade. My husban got a lot of munny a few days ago and I beleave he stole it from Mr. Grase and shot him. I don't want her to suffer for what he done.

Broyles said he did not know anyone by the name of Mattie Gibbs but the letter was obviously written by a colored woman and probably one who had had a fight with her man and thought she would get him in some trouble with the police. The reporters shared a laugh with Broyles, and their editors happily printed the letter orthographically intact.

CHAPTER 10

"Hell, no, I'm not going to die"

As the week ended, 72 hours having passed since the shooting, the *Philadelphia Evening Item* concluded, "The Atlanta police are completely at a loss how to proceed." It was not until Saturday that two Atlanta detectives went back to 29 West Eleventh Street and removed the blood-stained bedding. They were seen leaving the house carrying a bundle of items.

The arrival of the weekend would also allow time for everyone to take a pause. Atlantans (or, as the *Journal* then preferred to describe the city's residents, "Atlantians") were obsessed with the case. "The sensational shooting affair has become the one topic upon Atlanta's streets and in Atlanta society circles."

The sun had finally come out. The weekend gave the "morbidly curious" the free time to have a look for themselves at the scene of this most mysterious shooting. They came on foot and by streetcar. A steady parade trooped along West Eleventh Street. In front of number 29, they would halt and point up at the window, second floor right, that looked in upon the now infamous four-poster mahogany bed. They exchanged theories on the dark deed that had taken place therein. Then, perhaps with a shake of the head and some censorious reflection on the lifestyles of such fast-living folks, they shuffled off. It was a short stroll to enjoy the newly redesigned Piedmont Park. The Olmsted brothers had laid out a golf course and a five-mile "driveway" meandering through the park, the high point (literally) being the site of the Exposition midway.[1] All the old buildings, including the massive feudal castle at 14th Street that had served as entrance and administration headquarters, had been torn down in 1909. They had become white elephants and "were for so long a time such an eyesore."[2]

While others could enjoy some reminiscing on a rare fair day, the two principals remained in their respective places. Daisy was in her cell, Gene was at the infirmary. Daisy had been given no roommates; Moore had requested that the jailers "ameliorate" her stay in the Tower as much as possible. She wanted her privacy. The lawyer also requested that no more reporters be allowed to see her without his permission. The papers, he said, were just looking for "skyrocket" comments, and Daisy need not give them any. It was not necessarily helpful, as things she said to the papers now might later be used against her.

Even though slightly muzzled, Daisy was the dominant subject for the weekend editions of the Atlanta papers — although the *Georgian* did not publish on Sunday. Each day since the shooting, the papers had vied to put a new photograph or sketch of Mrs. Grace on their front pages. Her clothing style was parsed in knowing terms. The great interest shown in Daisy Grace's wardrobe, and the minuteness of the detail, were only unique in that the woman under observation was being charged with trying to murder her husband. The Sunday fashion sections were regularly filled with photographs and elaborate detail on who wore what where at the latest society gala. Atlanta was a very fashion-conscious metropolis. The merchants on Whitehall Street, "the Broadway of the South," raced against each other to bring the newest styles to their display windows to meet this demand. "It is little wonder that Atlanta's fame as a shopping center is widespread or that many thousands of women, as well as men, residing in the surrounding territory flock to this City to gratify their desire for smart apparel."[3] The new "French" styles were not universally greeted with approval: Dr. Len G. Broughton of the Baptist Tabernacle on Luckie Street equated the new fashions with licentiousness. "The styles you women in Atlanta wear come from New York, the New York styles come from Paris and the Paris styles come from hell."[4]

The good cleric's concerns notwithstanding, new photographs of the accused gun-woman appeared daily. The *Georgian's* reporter studied her intently:

> In appearance, Mrs. Grace is anything but criminal. She is large for a woman, almost robust, but it is a graceful magnitude. Her figure is striking. She wears excellent clothes and knows how to wear them. Her eyes are luminous and far apart. Her smile is infectious and her manner good natured, though there is a tilt to her head that would suggest hauteur.

The *Journal* on their Sunday front page opted to print a curious photograph of Daisy — from happier days in Atlanta — "feeding the chickens in the backyard on 11th Street." Even in the finest residential neighborhoods, fresh eggs were prized. But the *Journal's* biggest coup was a curious exclusive — if reporters were being kept out, why could a fellow inmate not fill the bill as a cub reporter? Bert Walmsley happened to be serving six months in the Tower for forgery, a crime he blamed on "the cigarette and its attendant evils."[5] He had formerly been a press agent of some sort, and by way of picking up a little freelance work, he penned his observations of his fellow inmate. In the florid style of his ilk, Walmsley began:

"I am so terribly lonely," she exclaimed appealingly to one of the deputy sheriffs this morning and her dark eyes were misty as she turned yearningly towards the barred windows.

Perhaps auditioning to someday be Daisy's press agent, Walmsley described her as a compelling woman:

> [She] has brilliant provocative eyes under high arched brows [and] a figure of opulent curves.... She is Niobe now but the presence of a storm is in her tearful quietude and when it breaks all the subtle pacification for which John Moore, her lawyer, is noted will be swept aside and she will denounce her enemies, cost her what it may.

Walmsley concluded, "If she is guilty, then her poise is marvelous."

As for the wounded Gene, there was better news from the infirmary by the weekend. He was slightly improved and able to see his first visitors. St. Joseph's Infirmary was about eight blocks north of the Tower and was located on the block where now stands the Marriott Marquis hotel. The hospital had been established by the Sisters of Mercy, and in the 30 plus years since it had opened, the infirmary had become "a veritable synonym of all that is kindliest, most comfortable and best among Atlantans, Georgians, and Southerners generally."[6] The main building fronting Courtland Street was topped by a cupola and boasted elaborately detailed wooden porches that ran the length of the structure, allowing the patients to take the morning sun. As recently as 1909, a four-storey surgical annex was added, elevating the infirmary "to the front rank among the hospitals of the South." They had also opened the first nursing school in Georgia.

Gene was being cared for primarily by two nurses, Miss Gibossi and Miss Ballinger, who did their best to make him comfortable and keep him clean. Beyond that, however, there was little that could be done for Eugene Grace. He remained under the care of Dr. Goldsmith, who was now consulting with Dr. Thomas S. Bailey, a respected surgeon and Greenville Street neighbor of the Hills from Newnan. The bullet was still in Grace's body. Goldsmith had determined that the shot had been fired from a fairly close range; the bullet pierced the left lung, missing the heart, and then — he believed but did not know for certain — the projectile severed the spinal cord but was blocked from passing out of the body by the spinal vertebrae where it was now lodged.

The early twentieth century had produced a good deal of new research on gunshot wounds to the spine, using the wounds suffered by U.S. soldiers in the Spanish-American War. None of it, unfortunately, would have brought much cheer to Grace's medical team. Dr. N.B. Carson of St. Louis had advised:

> When a radiograph shows that the bullet or a splinter of bone is causing compression of the cord, then operation for the relief of such pressure is indicated. The question of waiting until the wound caused by the projectile or weapon has healed is one that must be settled in each individual case. If fitting treatment can be employed, it is perhaps better to wait, as thus the danger of infection is made less. However, it must be remembered that pressure upon the spinal cord or its membranes, when continued for long, is apt to result in local destruction of the cord.[7]

From Texas, Dr. J.E. Thompson was even gloomier:

> The spinal cord is incapable of regeneration ... the indications for operation can thus be reduced to absolute simplicity. Any injury attended by the immediate onset of paralysis and anesthesia has probably destroyed the conductivity of the cord. An operation can hold out no hope of improving the condition of the portion of cord actually injured. What possible good can we expect from mere exposure of the cord? Are we not more likely to do harm by the extra risk of sepsis? [He added] I have removed bullets but I never expected to cure the patients by the operation, because I knew that the mere removal of the bullet could not arrest the degeneration or favor regeneration.[8]

Goldsmith and Bailey never gave Grace, his family, or the public any false hope. The wound suffered by Eugene Grace, they insisted, would — at the least — leave him permanently paralyzed. "Wounds of the spinal cord below the cervical region virtually never cause immediate death, though the termination is frequently fatal from the complications arising from paralysis. The principal of these are cystitis with ascending infection of the kidneys, infections and exhaustion from extensive bedsores, etc."[9] Eventually, an infection would be fatal. There was no hope for recovery.

All this medical crepe-hanging notwithstanding, Eugene Grace was perversely upbeat and was not about to have his obituary published prematurely. "Hell, no, I'm not going to die," he chirped. He joked to a reporter that he was more likely to starve to death on the regimen of gruel and broth that the doctors had put him on. If not so pleased with his doctors, Grace was happy with his lawyers. He was encouraged by the aggressive approach taken by Reuben Arnold. Grace made a strange admission from his hospital room: he had actually written one of those mysterious notes that Arnold now had in his possession. It was the one scratched in pencil. Gene said, "I wrote it in a spirit of fun, just to please Daisy who was in one of her teasing moods." But he had never seen the typewritten note nor had he signed it; that was Daisy's forgery. He also wanted to clear up any misconceptions about his being confused about the shooting. He had been drugged all right, but "I know very well who shot me, Daisy shot me." His wife's daily press briefings (in today's parlance) had sucked the air out of the room all week. By Saturday, however, Gene was feeling a little stronger, and some news began to come out of the infirmary. The most startling development was Gene's vow that "once I am well enough, I'm going to sue her for divorce."

Her jailers reported that when Daisy read that on Sunday morning she threw herself across her jail bed in tears. Daisy had remained in her cell for the Sabbath, choosing not to attend services. The *Constitution* thought that she (quite reasonably) feared "the curious glances which would inevitably be leveled at the only woman prisoner in the gathering, a beautiful woman at that." We know she read the papers, but she was also said to have read a Bible that was brought to her floor. The Reverend J.W. Ham, the assistant to the pastor of the Baptist Tabernacle on Luckie Street, made the rounds of the jail that Sunday. He found her to be low in spirits. She talked freely with him, insisting that she would return to her husband once this was cleared up, should he live. Ham believed that she was truly suffering, but it was a "tearless suffering." There were no public visitors allowed on Sunday. Many women — the "tender-hearted sex" — were turned away when they asked at the gates to be allowed to visit her. A prominent businessman arrived with a bouquet of violets for her, but his name was "withheld at his request." When asked why not one of her many "society friends" in Atlanta had come to call upon her, Daisy philosophically shrugged and replied, "It is the way of the world." She was very much alone: "Practically every human soul she had become acquainted with in this city openly express the belief that she is guilty, and have extended her no word of sympathy or consolation in her prison cell."[10]

The first published female perspective on Daisy's incarceration appeared in the *Georgian*.[11] Their writer, Martha Randolph, had been able to closely observe Daisy's demeanor in the Tower. She seemed to pace her cell as a tigress caged. She stared blankly through the bars at the railroad yards three stories below. Any moment she expected to receive word of her husband's death. For such a woman as Daisy Grace to be imprisoned and unable to control events must have been a torture. Randolph left the Tower thinking Daisy was "the most pathetic figure in God's bright world today."

CHAPTER 11

The House of Mystery

The first court appearance for Daisy Grace had been set for Tuesday, March 12, one week after the shooting. The excitement in the city was high. That morning the *Constitution* published separate photographs of the two lead figures taken by William Lenney, a well-known society photographer of Whitehall Street. The paper dared to caption one of the photos as "the last picture of Eugene Grace." Daisy was shown wearing another of what must have been a rather large collection of plumed hats. For a week, Atlantans had been trying to figure this woman out. What kind of woman was she?

"Daisy of the Leopard Spots" whose opulent charms decked out in expensive baubles and gewgaws have been displayed on the front pages of Atlanta newspapers oftener than that of any other woman! Is it possible that this woman can be a cold-blooded murderer? Do you believe she would drug a man, shoot him while he slept the heavy sleep that only comes of narcotics, call to the room a servant that she might see the man while he slept; that she then locked the stricken man — the husband of her breast — in the house and departed on a visit to his mother in a distant town, leaving him to welter in his blood, helpless and dying?

If the police were sure of their findings, the press was not quite as ready to accept the case as closed. "The chronology of the shooting has never been established ... it is baffling in its mystery," declared the *Constitution*. The shooting could only be compared to *The Mystery of the Yellow Room*, the 1907 best-selling novel about a murder victim found in a locked room in Paris.

Modern readers might be wondering how much of a mystery this all could be. Once Mr. Grace was strong enough to be called to testify, certainly he would tell a jury in his own words exactly what happened in that locked bedroom on West Eleventh Street. Alas for his sake, he most certainly could not take the stand, and that was the looming problem for the prosecution. Under Georgia law of that day, Penal Code 1910, § 1037, par. 4, a husband could not testify, or in the legal phrase, was not competent to testify, against his wife in any criminal proceeding.[1] The prosecution would have to rely on other lines of inquiry to lead a jury to believe that Mrs. Grace had done the shooting. This would involve the far murkier circumstantial questions of motive, intent, opportunity and malice aforethought. Or they could simply wait, a stenographer at the ready, for Gene Grace to show signs that he was imminently prepared to cross the bar.

The prosecution was quite prepared to take that latter course. Solicitor Dorsey asked Judge Ridley for a postponement. They needed more time to better understand Mr. Grace's condition and prospects. Grace had been taken by ambulance to the West Peachtree offices of Dr. Michael Hoke, one of the city's leading orthopedic surgeons. There he would be x-rayed for the first time. If the bullet could be located, the options for its removal would be better understood. To put it bluntly, the state needed to get some certainty as to whether Gene Grace was really at death's door. Obviously, if he died the assault case became a homicide. There was an ironic but very important legal twist at play as well. If the doctors were willing to state under oath that Grace was, as the lawyers called it, "in the articles of death," the police would be allowed to take his ante-mortem statement (also called a dying declaration).

As stated, Gene Grace would never be allowed to get into a witness box and accuse his wife of shooting him. However, he *would* be allowed to make a dying declaration.[2] A person "at the point of death and when *every hope* of this world is gone" is allowed to make such a statement, and it would be admissible in court as an exception to the rules of hearsay evidence. This exception was based upon the religious belief that no one expecting to imminently face his Creator would wish to leave this world with a lie on his lips.[3] Gene Grace would be able to swear to what happened to him, and how and by whom he had been mortally wounded. That statement would be taken down by the police. There are two key points to be kept in mind with dying declarations. First, the witness must be facing a certain death: he cannot simply understand that his prognosis is grim and that he will die eventually. If any hope remains, the human will to live persists. Such a person then "may be actuated by motives of revenge and an irritated mind to declare what possibly may not be true." Thus, in the words of Justice Cardozo in a later 1933 Supreme Court opinion, "the patient must have spoken with the consciousness of *a swift and certain doom*."[4] The second point, and one brutally simple, is that Gene Grace's dying declaration would be totally worthless unless he then very promptly shuffled off his mortal coil and joined the choir invisible. He had to go ahead and die.

In the event, Monday's first x-ray at Dr. Hoke's was inconclusive. More plates were taken Tuesday at the offices of Dr. John Derr. The second set revealed the location of the elusive bullet. It had been found lodged in the spinal column, against the cord, in the area of the ninth dorsal vertebra at the lower end of the rib cage. The picture also made clear that an operation would do no good and would more likely kill the patient.

Though the medical team had said that Grace had been in "high good spirits" at the start of the week, the ordeal of twice moving the patient had taken its toll. By Wednesday the doctors agreed that Grace was "sinking." The *New York Times* reported that death was no more than 24 hours away.[5] That afternoon the police were allowed in to Grace's room at the infirmary to take down his "ante-mortem statement." The *Journal* reporter at the infirmary was struck by the "impressive solemnity of the scene." Morris Prioleau, who was present, told the *Georgian* that Grace betrayed no emotion when told that his death was imminent. "He was a stoic. His manner was cheerful and business-like." Though the small room was crowded, the only sounds were Gene's rasping voice and the "energetic sound of the typewriter" taking it all down. The public was told Grace's statement would not be released until after his death. Still, the *Journal's* man claimed to have some knowledge of Grace's account of the events of March 5th and described it as "one of the most horrible stories I have heard or read."

Daisy was described as "visibly moved" by the news accounts of Gene's x-rays. She asked the reporters, "Why don't they operate?" Asked if she would want to see him before he died, she eagerly said yes. That, however, was highly unlikely. At the infirmary Gene had made it plain to all: "I won't see her. I want you people in charge at the hospital to see to it that she is not brought here."

Meanwhile, Judge Ridley had re-set Daisy Grace's court date for the following Tuesday, March 19. J.W. Moore, her attorney, did not object to the delay, and he asked to relay his client's sincere concern for her husband's condition. Out of respect, the defense would not seek bail at this time. Ridley asserted that Mr. Grace's fate would determine all. If Mr. Grace lived, then Mrs. Grace might request her bail at some future time. But if he died, murder was not a bailable offense in Georgia. So the defense and the prosecution (and, in fact, an entire city) would be forced to endure a grim vigil.

Not that the daily newspaper onslaught would be placed on hold. The *Journal's* Monday afternoon edition headlined Gene Grace's newest claim: "Daisy shot me for the insurance." While that claim made a great newspaper headline, the life insurance policies were not three months old. Could any reasonably intelligent person think she could insure her husband's life in December, mastermind his murder in March, and walk away with the insurance money?

If that was her "diabolical plan," however, she was to be very quickly forestalled. Over the weekend the Pennsylvania Mutual Life Insurance Co. had gone into Atlanta federal court to ask to have their policies on the life of Eugene Grace ruled invalid. P.C. McDuffie, the local attorney for Penn Mutual, told the court that in 40 years of doing business in Georgia the company had almost never taken such an action. In December 1911, Gene and Daisy had gone to the offices of Penn Mutual's local agents, Bagley and Willett, in the 4th National Bank building at Five Points. The two policies were issued on December 16: policy number 572482 was made out for $10,000, and policy number 572483 for $15,000. In the event of Eugene Hamilton Grace's death, the named beneficiary on both policies was Daisy Grace. According to McDuffie, the young couple had actually tried to purchase a third policy, but Penn Mutual had declined for reasons of "moral risk." Insurance companies are loathe to insure a person's life or property for more than that person or property is worth. "This is due to the effect of insurance upon the mind of the insured. An honest man may become less careful in protecting his property; a dishonest man may even seek to destroy his for the sake of obtaining the insurance. The danger of the loss through the carelessness or misconduct of the insured is commonly referred to as 'the moral risk.'"[6] Even with just the two policies, McDuffie charged that Eugene Grace had "fraudulently stated he had assets worth between $30,000–$40,000, including considerable property in Atlanta and Philadelphia." Clearly those assets did not exist. Issues of net worth aside, McDuffie stated that Penn Mutual would invalidate the policies "owing to the felonious conduct on part of the beneficiary [i.e., Daisy]." Of course, she had not been convicted of any felonious conduct at this point.

At the Tower, Daisy now agreed to voluntarily surrender the policies as requested. J.W. Moore said his client wanted it made clear to all that the policies were taken out by Mr. Grace at the explicit request of his mother, who had pressed them both to get insurance. Mrs. Hill had said it was a husband's responsibility to plan for his wife's future in the event of his untimely death. In his letter to Penn Mutual, Moore explained, "These six week old unpaid for policies which were procured without Mrs. Grace's knowledge or participation and without any representation whatever on her part to any insurance agent are personal matters between your company and Mr. Grace." Daisy Grace's decision to turn the policies in, Moore wrote, clearly demonstrated that she had no interest in any pecuniary gain. Her finances were well in order.

A major shift in public perceptions of the case was underway. This began with a series of reports from the *Journal's* "Special Correspondent" in Philadelphia. The *Journal's* city editor, Ralph Smith, had been up there for a few days talking with many of the people who knew the story of Daisy's first marriage and her hasty leap into a second one. He even got the first interview with little Webster. (The lad told the reporter that Gene was a "very nice man" who brought him toys, but he really missed his daddy.) The "specials" were spread over several days in the *Journal* but will be combined here for convenience.

The reports began with some news of the ill-fated Mr. Opie. Charles Huff, of Huff, Barnes and Opie, remembered his late partner as a very successful road salesman, well-liked but with a penchant for living beyond his means, spending extravagantly. Though he did not think Opie would have been called "rich," Huff knew that the man had spent a good deal on the house in West Philadelphia and dressed his wife in the latest styles and fine jewelry.

William Carr, partner in the Philadelphia law firm of Hepburn, Carr and Krause, was more than willing to share his gossip. He was Daisy's lawyer. It is very possible from Carr's apparent antipathy to *both* Opie and Gene Grace that he may have simply been jealous. Carr was the source of the story that Opie drank too much. He stated that on the day of Opie's fatal injury cranking the car, the man was "well-saturated." The cause of Opie's death was erysipelas. The injury that Opie had suffered was not one that should have killed him. But, as all the medical textbooks of the day made plain, erysipelas is a great danger to those who indulge in "the free use of alcoholic liquors."

It was at Opie's funeral that Carr first met Gene Grace. The best that Carr could say about the fellow was that he was good-looking and sober; despite the café life, he had helped Daisy control her drinking from the Opie years. According to Carr, Daisy seemed to be afraid of Gene, as if he had some unusual influence over her. From Daisy, the lawyer had also heard about that supposed 10,000-acre plantation Gene's family had in Georgia, and she had added that Gene's mother had promised to make him a gift of $10,000 on their wedding day. Still, Carr was skeptical. If Grace had all this family money, why was Daisy paying all the bills? Grace was always after her to pawn this, sell that, and cash out everything. It was no doubt upon Carr's counsel that Daisy had placed some of Opie's money in stocks.

Carr revealed that the Opies' home at 4246 Spruce Street was known in West Philadelphia as "the House of Mystery." Opie had something of a diamond fetish — he collected them. In December of 1910, Daisy filed an insurance claim for $10,000 worth of diamonds that had been stolen from Spruce Street, she claimed, by a burglar. She had seen the thief but he ran off, dropping only his red bandanna in flight. The police had looked into this heist but, for whatever reason, decided not to pursue the case. According to Carr, Opie had gotten drunk one night and been suckered into paying $2,000 for some paste stones. When the insurers — Fidelity and Casualty — saw them, they refused to pay, believing all the "diamonds" were inferior. Of course, Opie had since died. But Carr insisted that Daisy's claim was legitimate, and had she chosen to fight the action, she would have gotten her money. When the insurers offered just $250, Grace told her to take the money. She did. He spent it.

Carr had not seen Daisy since she left for Georgia the previous fall. Of course, he was dubious when Daisy told him that she was going south to invest in Gene's new construction business in Georgia. This was *after* she had discovered his plantation fantasy. Carr warned her that Grace had yet to display any aptitude for business, and she would no doubt lose her money. With a rueful smile, Carr told the *Journal's* "Special Correspondent," Ralph Smith, "She didn't listen to me." Carr, to be sure, would have been one of those "rotten Philadelphians," in Gene's opinion, anyway.

And Mother Ulrich was more than willing to say her piece. "Special Correspondent" Smith also sat down with Daisy's mater in the living room of her home on South 60th Street. "I am now convinced that man wielded an evil influence over my daughter. I believe he had her hypnotized and I think he was only after her money." She acknowledged that Daisy's first marriage had not been perfect, but maintained that Daisy and Opie would have managed to stick together — had Gene Grace not come along. Gene fascinated Daisy, and she would do anything for him. She paid for everything, even his cigarettes. Mother Ulrich was sorry to have now been proven right. "I told her a man like that is worthless." Yet she thought her daughter was still in love with the man. "It's a woman's way."

For all the ink that was used to detail the Graces' lively social life while in Philadelphia, it seems odd that no associates came forward with information about them. Perhaps they felt it impolite to gossip. But the *Georgian* reported that Atlanta police had requested the assistance of their Philadelphia brethren in locating two people said to be estranged friends of the Graces. One was a chap named George B. Morris, a telegraph operator who — according to the sources talking with the *Georgian* — had pre-dated Grace as Mrs. Opie's extra-marital dance partner, if not more. Meanwhile, there was a Mrs. Yates, who had been seen running around with Mr. Opie back in the day. The belief was that this Mrs. Yates might have information — perhaps even letters — that would reveal that Daisy and Opie had "an understanding" about such things. Nevertheless, Daisy was said to be extremely jealous of Mrs. Yates. And George Morris was described as "gravely disappointed" at Daisy's marriage with the interloping Grace. The *Georgian* breathlessly egged on the police in their search for these two people, as they no doubt held the key to the "innermost secrets" of the strange triangle of the Opies and Gene Grace. But in the end, if the police ever did track down one or both of these individuals, there is no record of their providing any information of value to the case.

Gene Grace's entire life was now under "microscopic inspection," the *Georgian* reported. Detectives employed by Daisy's lawyers had canvassed Philadelphia for information. A source at Fitkin and Co. laughed at a report that Grace had earned as much as $15,000 a year as a bond salesman. The truth was that Grace worked solely on commission and had rarely sold anything. The *Georgian* summarized the Philadelphia findings: "He was a lavish spender but small record is found of his having been an earner of much money. He met Daisy while her husband was on his death bed and he knew the embryonic widow would shortly come into a comfortable fortune."

All of these reports, special or otherwise, were having their effect on the still evolving Atlanta opinion. The *New York Times* reported that there had been "a reaction in favor of Mrs. Grace."[7] Lawyers for Daisy backed up Ralph Smith's report that it had been almost the last of her money that had gone into the Grace-Lawrence Company. They displayed a stack of cancelled checks to prove, they hoped, that Grace had been "virtually dependent" upon his wife. Such dependence would have reflected badly on Grace's manhood among chivalrous Southerners. An Associated Press report, carried in many papers across the country, said the new information from Philadelphia had caused support in Atlanta to "veer" in Daisy's direction.[8]

The opinion change does beg the question: just because a woman financially supports her husband, does she have the right to shoot him when her money runs out? Nevertheless, the wind had definitely shifted. J.W. Ball, the former police chief, went so far as to say that absent any direct evidence of her involvement in the shooting, her acquittal now seemed certain. The *Journal* also published a letter of support for Daisy signed by some of her fellow inmates in the Tower. "Mrs. Daisy Grace — We are prisoners like yourself, some of us innocent as we believe you to be. We can't help you but we sure do hope you may beat them to it." The scrawled, almost unreadable note had been signed by the inmates of "Fourth East," the nearest cellblock to hers. The signers were listed as "dips, dopes, yeggs and several blind tigers." (For the help of modern readers, the criminal argot can be translated as pickpockets, drug users, burglars and several bootleggers.)[9]

The legal team watching the case for Eugene Grace had taken note of all this "bad press" and moved swiftly to challenge this newly found sentiment for the lady in the Tower. Reuben Arnold made plain that the delay in the court proceedings was only a procedural matter. They were ready to go now. He went so far as to release to the public the contents of Grace's now unusable ante-mortem statement. Gene had told police that on the morning of Tuesday, March 5, he awoke feeling somewhat stupefied and in considerable pain. Daisy had ignored all his pleas for help. Call a doctor, he pleaded. She told him he did not need a doctor. "Pray for me, Daisy," Gene entreated. She responded, "I can't pray." She left the room and locked him in. Grace stated:

> I thought I was paralyzed when she left the house. I discovered I was shot by feeling my nightshirt was wet. I found myself getting weaker and weaker and made my way to the phone by the bed. I found it muffled ... stuffed with a boudoir cap and other cotton material.

With great effort he was able to make the phone call to the police, but it was "an eternity" before they arrived.

Arnold stopped in mid-story to declare that he had never read a tale of greater cruelty. The "crowning bit of evidence" he would now reveal — that on the night before the shooting, in a casual but sinister conversation with her unsuspecting husband, Mrs. Grace had asked Gene directly, "Where is a man's heart?" To Arnold, the point of the question was obvious: Daisy wanted to be sure the bullet was fatal. "This mercenary woman," the lawyer fumed, was motivated solely by her greed for the proceeds from her husband's life insurance policies. She had so drugged her husband into a defenseless stupor that she was able to approach him and fire a bullet from a very close range. He had even given her the target to aim at. All of this, Arnold promised, would be made clear in court.

The back and forth cut and parry continued in a quest for public support. The betting portion of the public watched the odds change almost daily; they were now running slightly for acquittal. It all seemed to swing based upon which side controlled the day's front pages. Daisy would have a good day in the papers, and then Grace's forces would surge back with new claims. Grace took another hit when Maier and Berklee, the Whitehall Street jewelers, repossessed a $700 diamond brooch and sunburst pendant he had purchased for Daisy's birthday in February. The jewelers required 20 percent down and the rest paid over 10 months at 6 percent interest. Grace had as yet made no payments on the bauble. A sheriff's deputy came to Daisy's cell to take the brooch, which she gave up without a squabble, adding disingenuously, "I didn't know you could make a gift until it was paid for."

This incident led to the "great jewelry exchange." Gene now demanded that Daisy return to him his Shriners ring and matching cufflinks, as well as his Alpha Tau Omega fraternity stickpin. Daisy riposted with her insistence that Gene give back to her his wedding band, with three diamonds, that had been Opie's and was to eventually be little Webster's. When lawyers for the respective disputants met for the handover, Daisy's team made clear that, once again, she had to put up the $85 to retrieve Gene's jewelry from the pawn shop where he had left them. According to the *Constitution*, "Neither has anything now that was given by the other." It was a mean little affair, but the public seemingly could not get enough of it.[10]

Almost passing unnoticed amidst such pettiness was a small item in the *Journal* announcing that Luther Z. Rosser had joined the defense team. Rosser, now in his mid-fifties, was a former city judge and a larger than life legal character reputed to be "the most-dreaded cross examiner at the Georgia Bar." Steve Oney, historian of the Leo Frank case, called him "the embodiment of Atlanta's fierce moneyed might."[11] On March 14, Rosser spent an hour in conversation with Daisy in her cell at the Tower. Ironically, Rosser's office was on the same seventh floor of the Empire Building where the Grace-Lawrence Building Company had its rooms. The *Journal* suggested that bringing Rosser aboard on behalf of Daisy Grace "means we are likely to see one of the most sensational and hard fought legal battles ever staged in a Fulton County courtroom." The *Valdosta Times* salivated at the prospect of "the most thrilling trial this part of the South has seen since the days before the Civil War."[12]

CHAPTER 12

To Philadelphia

Thursday night and on into Friday, March 15, Atlanta received more than five inches of rain in a terrifying 12-hour thunderstorm. The Chattahoochee River and Peachtree Creek washed over their banks. In the lower areas of downtown Atlanta the water was knee deep in the streets. The deluge caused hundreds of thousands of dollars in losses in north Georgia. During the day on Friday, one of Daisy's lawyers, J.A. Branch, ventured out on Daisy's behalf. He was allowed to go back into 29 West Eleventh Street to retrieve her clothes and personal items. Branch was accompanied by two Atlanta detectives and Lamar Hill, representing the interests of her husband. Daisy had now been held in the Tower for more than a week, and she had been wearing only the few items she had packed to take with her to Newnan.

The visit to the crime scene caused a "mild sensation" between the Peachtrees. The *Constitution* reported that among the items removed from the house was the now celebrated "coat of leopard skins, which Mrs. Daisy Grace made famous here and in Philadelphia." Not that she would require such a remarkable garment in jail. Everything removed from the bedroom and bathroom upstairs was taken below to the drawing room to be inventoried. Most of Daisy's finer clothes were to be placed in storage. The newspaper estimated that the "handsome clothes" that had been carried off for safekeeping were worth "many hundreds of dollars." Only toilet articles and "necessary clothing" were brought to Daisy's cell. The house was then locked up once again; the police guard remained in place.

"Of all the weird tangled mystery cases with which the police of the South have had to deal, the case of the shooting of Eugene H. Grace is the most weird, the most tangled. Love and hatred and avarice and hypnotism and nightmares all enter into it; all help to make it more extraordinary, more unfathomable."[1] This report in a Midwest newspaper was typical, even as the case entered a second weekend.

The Atlanta clergy was not pleased at this unsavory distraction. The Central Presbyterian Church, across from the state capital, hosted one of the city's largest congregations. The pastor, Dr. Dunbar Ogden, was one of the city's leading religious voices, and he "never sounded an uncertain note." He expressed his distress over what he called the "unwholesome publicity" the Grace case had engendered. There was an ongoing debate in 1912 about the purity of the food Americans were eating. Dr. Ogden submitted to his congregation that they must be every bit as concerned about what goes into their souls. The amount of attention being given to this unseemly matter was entirely improper:

> It is wrong to parade the most personal and sacred things of life simply to satisfy the curiosity of the public. It is perversive [sic] of the best interests of law and justice to hold the trial of a case in the public prints. There is a tremendous psychological evil in centering the thought of an entire community for weeks upon one domestic tragedy.[2]

The newspapers, continued Dr. Ogden, were wallowing in the scandal and had become as much a threat to the home as disease:

> The policy of unwholesome publicity makes the daily papers a menace to the home ... as perilous to a home as though they were covered with smallpox germs. I appeal to our editors to not use their freedom for an occasion to the flesh.

The Reverend E. Dean Ellenwood of the Universalist Church, at East Harris and Peachtree, had similar thoughts. But he had concluded that Eugene and Daisy Grace were not so much immoral as they were unmoral. "I have never met either of these two deluded, abnormal and morally incompetent children of earth." Nevertheless, he had found reason to conclude that they "lack the moral equipment necessary to the truly successful, wholesome, profitable life."[3]

The clerical commentary seemed not to trouble either Daisy or Gene. However, there were the first signs that Daisy's customary good humor was not limitless. She had become a bit cranky in the Tower, complaining about vermin and the food. The menu was unvaried: cornbread, chuck steak and rice. This was not the fare to satisfy the palate of one who frequented the "lobster palaces" of this world. Over the weekend, Mrs. Sanders, who ran a fish wholesale business *cum* restaurant at 114 Decatur Street, close by the jail, sent up a meal which, if not lobster, was greatly appreciated.

Daisy remained alone; there was a little stir when another white woman was brought in on March 14. Ruby McGinnis was booked for larceny but immediately bonded out and so never had the opportunity to be Daisy's first cellmate. For entertainment, Daisy was said to be reading a novel left with her by one of the visiting clergy. It was *Weaver of Dreams*, the newest from Myrtle Reed, a then popular "romance novelist" whose books generally involved a woman disappointed by a man.[4] The book Daisy was reading had been published posthumously; Myrtle Reed (Mrs. James S. McCullough) took too many sleeping powders in the summer of 1911.[5]

The *Journal's* inmate-forger-reporter Bert Walmsley was back with some more cellblock psychology. He began to wonder if the solitude might be getting to Daisy: "Alienists assert such confinement is destructive of the nerve centers and can lead to phantasmagoria. Given her personality, if Mrs. Grace is innocent, her current life is a Torquemadian torture." Goodness. But alone Daisy would remain; even her request that faithful "Nig" be allowed to share the quarters in "Third West" was rejected by Sheriff Mangum.

J.W. Moore told reporters that he too had grown concerned over Daisy's "restive state." He would be asking Judge Ridley for bail. The updated news on Gene's health was encouraging, to a point. The man had rallied from the near-death collapse which prompted the ante-mortem interview. The weekend papers had reported that he "passed his best day Saturday" since he was shot, but "his case is as hopeless as ever." Those who had seen him at the infirmary brought word that he was as "courteous and genial" as the man they knew. His "Emperor William" moustache—named for the Kaiser's upswept waxed curls—had been shaved off. Gene scoffed at reports that he had the moustache removed to spite Daisy, who had urged him to grow it. He said he had to give it up for infirmary rules.

However, again on Tuesday, March 19, Judge Ridley postponed the hearing on the charges against Mrs. Grace. He now reset the case for Thursday week, the 28th. The decision was made in consultation once again with Gene's doctors. There was a wrangle over bail: Moore argued that there was "no actual reason for her incarceration for a long period while her husband is ill." She cannot be held in what amounts to solitary confinement indefinitely while Grace's condition seems to have stabilized. The defense was willing to pay any reasonable bond for her release and assured the court that Daisy would attend when her presence was demanded. Ridley said he was not yet ready to consider a request for bail.

Thus it came as a shock when the following morning—Wednesday, March 20—readers of the *Constitution* awoke to learn, "The gates of the Tower [had] swung open to Mrs. Daisy Opie Grace at 11:25 o'clock last night." It was the first of a series of moves, involving the courts and attorneys for the two parties, to attempt to give the slip to the press and public. When Judge Ridley had said he was "not yet ready," he apparently meant to say, "Give me a couple of hours." Ridley set the bail at $7,500. Again the money was put up by Clark, the saloon-keeper. The papers were signed at 7:30. The actual release was delayed until 11:25 in hopes that Daisy might get away with as little attention as possible. Not so much. When the Tower gates opened, the chase was on.

So much for secrecy. A *Journal* reporter was there to witness Daisy sign the release papers, observing that "her fingers shook." She had been held at the Tower since March 7. As she emerged from the jail, an eruption of flashlights from the photographers stunned her, and she gave a slight cry. The *Constitution* took time to describe her parting outfit: Mrs. Grace wore a "natty blue velvet suit which clung close to her petite figure." She also wore a wide black hat with ostrich plumes, "sitting at a saucy angle." She said very little in response to the barrage of shouted questions: "Oh, I am so happy, me and my heart." Moore cut the reporters off: "I want to be fair to you boys but Mrs. Grace is going to Washington. There is nothing more to say."

Daisy climbed into the red Sultan taxi, accompanied by her attorney, J.A. Branch. As the vehicle pulled away, there was a "follow that car" melee outside the Tower. Reporters piled into anything with wheels and gave chase. The *Constitution* claimed one of their reporters actually jumped on the rear bumper of Daisy's cab and clung to the frame for the wild ride to the terminal. "Regardless of speed limits [the center city speed limit was a modest 12 MPH!] and honking through the crossings, the procession of machines raced through the darkness. Up Butler Street, across Hunter Street, onto Fraser Street, onto Capitol Place and then on to East Mitchell for the straight run across Whitehall Street six blocks to the station."

The Southern Railway Train number 36, the "United States Fast Mail," was due to leave Atlanta at 12:15 A.M., bound for the nation's capital and then, via Philadelphia, on to New York City. The Southern ran three trains daily to New York City. The night train offered electric-lighted sleeping carriages, coaches and "Southern Railway dining service."[6] There was a ticket office, conveniently enough, in the lobby of the Kimball House. A ticket had been purchased for Daisy in the Cammack car, a Pullman sleeping car, and she was given lower berth number 7. Branch, her lawyer, was to accompany her throughout the journey and berthed nearby. The station master had posted railway guards to keep all but ticketholders off the platform.

At 12:29 A.M., in the "inky darkness," the train steamed out from beneath the huge shed. Those fortunate reporters who were able to get a ticket had clambered aboard. They were joined by two Pinkerton detectives hired by the bondsman, just in case. Beyond the terminal, the train turned to the northeast at Brookwood, crossing Peachtree Road. The Southern Railway tracks followed the Peachtree Ridge into Dekalb County and on towards Gainesville.

Just over a year previous, the same train had been held up by "masked bandits" who stopped the train in the darkness at White Sulphur Springs, beyond Gainesville.[7] Nothing that eventful took place on Daisy's journey. It customarily took some thirty-six hours to travel from Atlanta to Philadelphia, including the time change. Until 1941, Atlanta was in the central time zone. This trip would be longer than normal. There was a delay of several hours in Greensboro, North Carolina, because the heavy rains mentioned earlier had washed out a rail crossing. The delay gave Britt Craig the time to file his first report for the *Constitution*. The "Staff Correspondent on Board Train" described the mad scramble to make the departure. Things had since settled down. After getting some sleep, Daisy had gone to the Triola breakfast car, appearing quite refreshed. She did make a complaint to the conductor that she was sure that there had been a "peeping tom" in the Pullman. The conductor regretted any intrusion and promised that a better watch would be kept on her privacy. As always, her clothing would be worthy of mention: at breakfast she wore "a black broadcloth suit with v-shaped white linen collar, black pumps, black silk stockings and a large black hat." She ate heartily, pronouncing the breakfast fare to be greatly superior to the morning offerings at the Tower. The *Journal* helpfully printed the menu, a breakfast board featuring poached eggs, German fried potatoes, corn muffins, griddle cakes, etc.

The kitchen aside, she did not mean to be critical of her jailers; the jailers at the Tower had treated her "exceptionally well." Still, she complained that "ugh, the mice and roaches" kept her busy, and the bathing facilities were insufficient. The people, however, were "typical of southern people whom I have grown to love with a keen devotion.... Atlanta has some of the finest families I have met in my extensive travels." For the moment, she remained unsure whether she would remain in Atlanta "once the trouble is over."

The conversation was limited to such desultory pleasantries, since attorney Branch sat nearby and dourly indicated that any questions about the shooting would not be answered. Daisy wistfully gazed out upon the passing Carolina scenery. Reporter Craig presumed that just about everyone on the train knew they had a celebrated fellow traveler. At breakfast she was the "subject of mingled stares and sympathetic eyes," but no one approached her. Surrounded by reporters, Daisy laughed and said, "It does look like you newspaper folks would get tired of writing about me."

Meanwhile, back in Atlanta, Reuben Arnold did not have such a pleasant breakfast at his home on Ponce De Leon Avenue. The *Constitution* headline infuriated him: "He Is Dying: She Is Gone." By the afternoon papers, Arnold made the flat statement that "Mrs. Grace has fled; she will not return." His co-counsel, Lamar Hill, admitted that they had agreed to bail, but they did that believing that Mrs. Grace had only wanted to leave the Tower for some quiet place near Atlanta. They had never countenanced any rail journey of nearly 1,000 miles. Chief of Detectives Lanford compared it to a kidnapping and grudgingly allowed it was "the slickest move" he'd ever seen. She won't be back, he glumly concluded.

J.W. Moore presented himself to the reporters to put out the fires. He tried to reassure everyone that Daisy had not run off to escape prosecution or flee to Timbuktu. She will be returning to Atlanta after a very brief stay in Philadelphia. She will attend to some matters vital to her defense and also have the occasion to visit with her blind son and her aged mother who has been unwell. The defense had given their promise to Mr. Dorsey and Judge Ridley that should Mr. Grace die, Mrs. Grace will return to Atlanta immediately. Judge Ridley, who was under some fire himself, also defended his decision to grant bail: the law must allow her bail — it is a bailable offense. He reminded his critics that Mrs. Grace is accompanied by her respected attorney, Mr. Branch, and also enjoys the omnipresent attentions of reporters. "I am as sure that there is a God in heaven that she will return for her trial."

Aboard the train, beyond Greensboro, there were more delays caused by flooded track beds. When the train finally emerged from the tunnel under Capitol Hill to arrive at Union Station in Washington, there would be little time to halt. The Atlanta reporters handed their copy out carriage windows to messenger boys who dashed off to the telegraph office. A reporter from the *Washington Herald*, who had come aboard in Culpeper, Virginia, thought that Daisy looked "bedraggled."[8] When more reporters poured onto the train in D.C., she greeted them with an "air of indifference." They shouted their questions — had she heard that no one expected her to ever return for her trial? She smiled, wearily, and assured everyone, "As soon as I can straighten out money matters in Philadelphia I will immediately return to Atlanta to face my accusers. I am innocent." The conductor's warning sounded, and the local writers decamped. The train pulled out, heading north, and Daisy returned to her berth for a "much needed rest." There was no repeat of the "peeping Tom" disturbance.

The Southern Railway train reached Philadelphia on Thursday morning, March 21, arriving during a sleet storm. Crossing the Schuylkill River, the tracks followed the old elevated viaduct known as "the Chinese Wall" into the enormous train shed at Broad Street station near City Hall. For some reason the gaggle of Philadelphia reporters and the curious had been expecting Daisy to arrive at the next station, at 32nd Street in West Philadelphia. They would wait in vain. Daisy and Branch, followed doggedly by the Atlanta press pack, got off at Broad Street. They went by taxi directly to the St. James Hotel, ironically one of her favored café venues from those halcyon nights. Whether it was the tariff, the service, or perhaps because Mr. Branch did not want to give the appearance of overdoing it, they left the St. James and went instead to breakfast at the more modest Colonnade Hotel on Chestnut Street.

Refreshed and fed, Daisy Grace began her morning at the Girard Trust Bank.[9] She entered the Pantheon-like building at Broad and Chestnut, and crossed the lobby of white marble beneath the great domed ceiling. She discreetly nodded to those employees she recognized. She headed directly for the safety deposit vault. It is unlikely she took reporters along with her into the vault, but the *Constitution's* Britt Craig reported that she "ransacked" her box. The *Journal's* Harrlee Branch claimed she filled a blue envelope with a stack of bonds; how many he could not say. He could report that the bonds were valued at $1,000 apiece. In all, Daisy spent 40 minutes in the vault. The securities retrieved were to be used to pay for her defense. The *New York Times* suggested that, by now, Daisy well knew she was in for a "hard fight," and it would be a costly one.[10]

The Philadelphia reporters had, at last, tracked her down. Leaving the Girard Bank, the local scribes fell in with their Southern colleagues, and something of a "press mob" followed her to City Hall. Though the sleet had abated, it remained a cold morning, but Daisy had come north prepared for the weather. She was wearing "magnificent furs." No reporter mentioned "leopard spots," so we must conclude that she had not gotten that celebrated garment out of storage for the trip. She helpfully played tour guide for Mr. Branch and the Atlanta press. She pointed out the various Center City landmarks, including the famous 37-foot statue of William Penn atop City Hall. More than 500 feet below "old Billy," at street level, Daisy entered the building seeking the south corridor and Room 154, the Recorder of Deeds, to clarify her ownership of the property at 4246 Spruce Street.

It was noon when Daisy gave the cabman outside City Hall that very address, and she went by taxi (followed, of course) back across the Schuylkill River into West Philadelphia. She did not remain long inside the former "house of Mystery" but left after collecting "many private papers and documents." Her stay in Philadelphia was to be short; the business done, Daisy raced to spend as much time as she could with her family. She claimed that she had received numerous invitations from friends, but she had been forced to decline them all. "It is highly mortifying for me to face my Philadelphia friends with this blot on my reputation but I am sure they all will believe my innocence." Instead, she remained with "Mother Ulrich" at her home a little west of Spruce Street in a more modest row house at 900 South 60th Street.

The reunion of mother and daughter, Britt Craig told the *Constitution's* readers, was "dramatic to the extreme." There was the expected sobbing: "God bless your little soul," blubbered the old lady. The ordeal of her daughter had obviously affected Mrs. Ulrich. "Her voice was thin and monotonous and also most lifeless. Her gray sunken eyes were bottomless pools of grief." They had much to share with each other.

Of course, the reunion would not be complete without little Webster, who was summoned from the Overbrook Institute. When the blind boy entered, he reached out to touch a feminine arm. His grandmother whispered to the child, "Do you know who that is?" He cried out, "Is that you, Momma?" She "crushed the child to her breast in a fond embrace and mingled her tears with his." Even reduced to newsprint, the story brought tears to the eyes of countless readers. Craig of the *Constitution* described the scene as "pathetic in the extreme."

Daisy remained closeted with her family in her mother's home for two nights. She was to make the noon train on Saturday in order to be back in Atlanta by Sunday night, as promised. She did not leave the house at all on Friday; the slushy street outside was crowded with cold and stamping reporters, and the ubiquitous "morbidly curious." The Atlanta reporters were favored with brief audiences. Craig broke the news that Daisy had slept with the envelope full of bonds and documents safely beneath her pillow. How he got that bit of information we shall not ask. Harllee Branch, the *Journal's* man on the scene, was struck by the change in Daisy's entire aura as she stood in her mother's small but respectable drawing room. She now displays a "dainty femininity amid an atmosphere of womanly luxury." She even had the occasion to flash a rare smile. "The blue kimono fell away to reveal a fine column of throat, and the loose folds somewhat accentuated the full ripe figure of a woman in her mid-thirties." Daisy Grace had claimed another conquest.

There were more convulsive scenes at the inevitable parting on Saturday. Little Webbie promised that he would be a good boy at school. He asked his momma if he should pray for Gene. Daisy told him, "Yes, Webbie, pray that he gets well." To avoid the (non–Atlanta) reporters and onlookers who kept their wintry watch on South 60th Street, Daisy and her entourage slipped out the back door of Mother Ulrich's home, across an alley and through a friendly rear neighbor's house for a short walk to a streetcar that took them into the city center. There was just time for a bit of shopping at Wanamaker's, where Daisy purchased a dress suit and a spring hat. They made their way to the B&O's Chestnut Street station for the train to Washington. They arrived in the capital well before their connection with the Southern Railway train for Atlanta. Daisy rested at the New Willard Hotel near the White House, while attorney Branch did some unrelated legal business in the District.

After dark, Daisy and Branch caught the Southern Railway's number 37 train for Atlanta. As the locomotive smoked into Virginia on that Saturday night, heading south, with Daisy Grace lost in her thoughts and the reporters refining their copy, another train was pulling out. This was an Atlanta and West Point train, leaving Atlanta's Terminal Station. Among the stops would be the Newnan Depot. Aboard the train was Eugene Grace. He had been released by the doctors at the St. Joseph's Infirmary. He was going home to die.

CHAPTER 13

Gene Grace in a Bad Light

Eugene Grace was released from St. Joseph's Infirmary in the late afternoon of Saturday, March 23. It was said that the release was granted "at the solicitation of Mrs. S.L. Hill." The Infirmary's Dr. Goldsmith admitted that they had done all that they could for the wounded man. The bullet was still lodged in his backbone. He remained "dead from the wound down." Surgery was an option, but at what risk? You are supposed to leave the hospital when you get better; the infirmary was not a long-term care facility. Eighteen days after he took a bullet in the side, Gene was as "better" as he would ever be.

A Patterson ambulance carried him to the Terminal to catch the 5:30 train. With most of the "media" attention still focused on Daisy's stunning dash to Philadelphia, only one reporter made the journey home with Gene Grace. Angus Perkerson, the new editor of the *Atlanta Journal's Sunday Magazine* (he would keep the job for 44 years), said Grace was moved very gently. "Be careful, boys," he cautioned the bearers.

There were non-stop trains from Atlanta to Newnan; that journey took one hour. Perhaps the doctors thought the speed and rocking of the carriages would be too much for the suffering man. Still, it seems rather cruel that he left Atlanta on the A&WP's "milk train." Gene's stretcher was secured to the floor in the baggage carriage. With him were Sam Hill and Sam's brother Lewis, Dr. Bailey of Newnan, Angus Perkerson and the unidentified milk man. Train number 41 made calls at College Park, Red Oak, Stonewall, Fairburn, Palmetto, Coweta, and Madras before reaching Newnan at 6:55 in the evening.[1] It was an "extraordinary and solemn trip," wrote Perkerson. At each stop the milk man would exchange full pails for empties. The empty cans then rattled and chimed like some doleful carillon as the slow train gently swayed south. Asked repeatedly how he was doing, Grace said he was fine and felt no pain. The reporter thought the man on the stretcher looked pale but still seemed to be alert to all that was going on around him.

That Friday evening was thick with clouds and damp as the locomotive halted for Newnan. Friends were at the depot to meet the train, and Gene's cot was carried to a waiting "covered wagon." The wagon, alas, was not quite long enough, and the tall man's feet protruded from the rear. He was covered with several blankets to protect him from the chill. The horses bowed their backs and moved off slowly, directed by a roundabout way in search of the firmest path with the least mud. His mother was waiting for Gene on the front porch at 112 Greenville Street. Gene Grace's cot was carried into the very room he had had as a youth. Readers of the *Journal Sunday Magazine* pondered the sad story. "So Eugene Grace came home to die."

Gene's return to Newnan was reported in Newnan's only newspaper, the weekly *Herald and Advertiser*, which to that point had not deigned to even mention the great sensation of the hour. Newnan readers were tersely informed that Eugene Grace, "who was shot in his home in Atlanta some time ago,"

The home of Gene Grace's family, 112 Greenville Street, Newnan, Georgia. The lines of the home today appear remarkably unchanged from the newspaper photographs of 1912. The detailing at the peak of the roof (right) is as it was then (author's photograph, September 2011). The house was at the time under a City of Newnan order to either be restored or removed.

had been brought to his mother's house. The report suggested that Gene's condition was grave and no operation was likely.[2] The local paper may not have given the story much play, but Atlanta reporters found that the Grace shooting was on everyone's mind in Newnan. At all the usual places around the courthouse square it was all that was being talked about. A former mayor, Colonel Albert Reese Burdett, called it a heinous crime and noted, "I don't suppose there's a man in Newnan who doesn't think that Grace was shot by his wife." Mrs. W.Y. Atkinson, widow of the former governor, had known the Hills and thought Gene was a delightful boy and very good to his mother.[3] As one would expect, the sentiment in Newnan was strongly pro–Gene.

Gene Grace's melancholy departure from Atlanta would be contrasted with the return of his wife 24 hours later. Daisy's train number 37 was expected at five P.M. but arrived at seven. "No royal ruler was ever greeted by such crowds," proclaimed the *Journal*. The *Constitution* estimated the crowd at more than 2,000 people, mostly made up of "idlers who pass every Sunday on the streets." What seemed more troubling was the interest that had been taken in this whole affair by Atlanta's young women. The crowd was more than half female, "young women who are anywhere that there is a promise of excitement, and well-dressed women well in the prime of life, gathered at the Terminal station." This troubling theme would become a frequent topic in the weeks ahead.

No matter their reason for being there, the waiting hordes would get very little opportunity to catch a glimpse of the woman of the hour. Again the station's railway guards kept the platforms clear. Daisy Grace would not have to continue her journey in a buckboard. Attorney Moore had arranged with the stationmaster to have a waiting cab pulled up directly alongside the tracks. Daisy was able to leave her Pullman and take but a few steps to the vehicle and be whisked away at "fast and dangerous" speeds. The driver almost lost control as his wheels spun out while climbing the "badly paved incline of Madison Avenue" leaving the Terminal.

It was then just a short ride to the Kimball House. Security had closed off all the hotel entrances. She was met and escorted by a cordon of house detectives through the rotunda to the elevators. Reporters were told that "owing to her fatigued condition, Mrs. Grace is to retire early." Nonetheless, to observers, Daisy seemed to be in "buoyant spirits" and declared herself delighted to be back in Atlanta and looking forward to clearing her name. "I am innocent," she cried, as the elevator doors closed. The elevator climbed only to the fourth floor. Daisy was given suite 411; there would be no more talk of the "hoodoo" vibes of room 613. Louise Wilson, a local private nurse, had been employed by Daisy's defense team and would be en suite with this most celebrated individual.

It had been a weekend of movement and excitement, with Daisy's travels north and Gene's return home. Yet, legally, all stood still. At the solicitor's office, Dorsey was facing a fairly common prosecutor's dilemma. Should he move speedily and prosecute Daisy "for a particular offense based upon the facts known at the time?" Or should he wait until the "ultimate result of her conduct became known?" In other words, should he wait until Gene Grace dies. The longer he lingered, the greater the difficulty for the State. Mrs. Grace could not be held in custody indefinitely. She would have to be bailed; this gave rise to a flight risk. The more time it takes to bring a case to court, the more other issues come into play, such as preserving the evidence, keeping the witnesses within reach and, most importantly, keeping their memories intact.[4] For the time being, Dorsey opted not to press the matter forward. He was comfortable with saying that "so long as the present status of things exists, no bill will be presented." He was keeping an open mind on the case and claimed to know only what he had been reading in the papers. Whatever legal reasons Dorsey may have had for sitting on his hands, the delay was felt cruelly by the two leading actors. Their pent-up emotions could not be so easily shelved.

On Daisy's return train journey, while her legal escort, Mr. Branch, was either dozing or adding up his billable hours, she made her first admission that she knew more about the shooting than she had previously let on. The *Georgian* broke the story with the headline "New sensation: Mrs. Grace claims 'Eugene knows who shot him and so do I.'"

The *New York Times* had been reporting that private detectives had been trying to track down a divorcee that Gene supposedly had known in Atlanta and who had lived with him at least briefly in Philadelphia. The theory was that Gene had thrown the woman over for the ravishing widow with the late Opie's fortune, and thus this "Madame X" had a very good motive for revenge.

The theory was bolstered when, soon after Daisy returned from Philadelphia, those copies of several of Gene's letters to Daisy somehow found their way to the in-boxes at each of the Atlanta newspapers. Though their provenance was not clearly established, it stands to reason that the letters were in that envelope kept beneath Daisy's pillow. The letters revealed a darker side of Gene's personality. "Sensational letters," headlined the *Constitution*, "they are directly opposite to Grace's own statements that he was a moral man, never drank, knew nothing of women and that he was not dependent on his wife financially." The *Georgian*, with typical verve, printed the letters fully, highlighting in bold-faced capitals the choicest revelations — e.g., "my only curse has been women" and "the finis to such fast living is death," etc.

In the first fortnight following the shooting, Eugene H. Grace had been clearly viewed as the more sympathetic figure. His wife was a flashy stranger from up North, a dangerous outsider. The *Milledgeville News* had gone so far as to paint her as a modern day Cleopatra or Semiramis, "ancient queens who loved and then slew their lovers."[5] Gene, on the other hand, was a local man who had attended college in the city. He was young, of powerful physique, and now lay near death or faced a life of paralysis. The publication of these letters began to mitigate much of that early sympathy. Gene Grace, for the first time, was being seen in a "bad light." In addition to the "other woman" theory, the letters added more credence to the earlier reports that Grace had been sponging off his wife's money. He had made "repeated and persistent demands" for her support.

The mood in Atlanta continued to shift to Daisy's side. Lamar Hill denounced the letters as a "simple effort to blacken a dying man's character and to create public sentiment for the woman who shot him." The allegations pertaining to drink and women "are absolutely untrue. We are absolutely at our ease on the question of Mr. Grace's character." Reuben Arnold rejected the idea that these spurious letters might insinuate the involvement of some third person in the shooting. It is "mere bosh. There are only two principals in this case."

Angus Perkerson, meanwhile, who was still in Newnan, reported in the *Journal* that when Mother Hill read those letters in the paper, she was brought to tears. Someone (and she did not have to give that person a name) was trying to blacken her son's character. In one of Gene's letters, not quoted, he had written to Daisy that his folks had gone to church but he stayed home to write a letter. The *Georgian* wanted to know whether Gene was a church-goer. Mother Hill brusquely replied, "Gene has made his peace with God and does not consider membership in a church as essential to Godliness."

As for Gene, he let others call the letters forgeries. True or not, all the talk about his past was beside the point. "Before I married I did things I am ashamed of. Who hasn't? But I was always on the level with my wife. I never even flirted with any woman after I married her. There is no other man or woman in this case." He admitted that they had gotten married too hastily. "I was unwilling to marry as soon as we did after Mr. Opie's death. I told Daisy it would seem heartless and naturally would arouse criticism, but she insisted." He soon discovered that his marriage was a mistake. The reason they had gone out to Hot Springs was so she could get the cure for "tippling," as she drank too much. "I discovered that her society had been that of the cafés, and her friends [were] the loose and fast livers." When his friend Olen Teate came down to Newnan for a visit, Gene told him that if anyone reads the letters closely, they'll see that they're actually quite endearing. "But it does not matter what those letters contain, she had no right to shoot me." A valid point, it seems.

Grace was now showing more bitterness than ever before. He told Perkerson that he still remembers waking up about seven that morning and smelling the "sulphury fumes of powder smoke." But he had no idea that he had been shot. When he did discover the wound, he begged for her to send for a doctor. "I said to her, 'For God's sake, there's the telephone.' But she said she would go out for the doctor. She left the room and locked the door and left me there to die. I have been absolutely on the level."

He admitted that his marriage had been under some strain, but Daisy was the cause of that. "She had grown tired of me. I had noticed that for several weeks before she shot me. I wasn't interesting to her any longer." She didn't like Atlanta or Southerners. She was "always knocking" Atlanta. Now she says she loves the South. He even took on "Webbie"—accusing Daisy of using Webster for sympathy. "She was always ashamed of the boy and used to pull the tam-o-shanter down over his eyes so people wouldn't know he was blind." In his rant, Gene became so overwrought that his doctors had to order that no more reporters, even the omnipresent Perkerson, be allowed into the sickroom.

At the Kimball House, Daisy was doing more interviews again in room 411. She insisted the Philadelphia letters were all legit and had been written to her by her husband. Of course, she had "nothing to do with making them public." Daisy believed someone may have stolen them from her mother's house. The *Constitution* reported that their interview took place while Daisy was "seated in a rocking chair so her long beautiful hair could dry over a radiator. Apologetically, she touches the folds of her blue silk kimono." For all the talk of the coat of leopard spots, Daisy's "robin's egg blue" silk kimono got its fair share of ink as well. For the record, in one of Gene's letters begging her to come join him in Atlanta, he'd advised Daisy, "If you can come down, bring your furs." But this interview at the Kimball House was brief; nurse Wilson, now Daisy's ubiquitous companion, gestured with a "quick little jerk" that it was time for the scribes to leave.

Daisy remained at the Kimball House, seeing only her lawyers. Though she was still in legal limbo, she was certainly not under any house arrest. On March 26 she gave the lobby loungers of the press the dodge by eschewing the elevator and using the stairs to a side exit where she met K.T. McKinstry, a local auto dealer, for a ride in his "big black Firestone Columbus." The outing had been arranged by her lawyers. The pressmen, alerted to the ruse, belatedly gave chase. On the way back to the hotel, McKinstry drove past 29 West Eleventh Street. There, Daisy asked him to halt. The papers reported that she seemed "slightly excited" as she gazed upon the house that had been her home for but seven weeks. Later that week, W.S. Witham, known as "the Man of a Hundred Banks," with branches throughout Georgia and the southeast, and owner of a huge mansion (Bideawee) in Buckhead, sent his driver and limousine. The driver left the city to the north via Peachtree Street, the only smoothly paved road leading from downtown to the growing "suburbs" to the north. "It is greatly congested for this reason." Daisy's driver negotiated the infamous "Dead Man's Curve" at St. Andrew's Church out to where the new trolley line stopped in the "famous Buckhead section." Beyond that point, even Peachtree was unpaved, and the drive was slowed by the condition of the roads.

This second journey quickly degenerated into a "veritable hare and hounds affair," exclaimed the *Thomasville Daily Times Enterprise*. The limo was pursued by cars hired by the papers. The speed limit, which beyond the city's inner fire zone was all of 15 mph, was ignored. Now this was a brand of "rough-neck journalism" not previously seen in Georgia. The police thought the public was being endangered by all this dashing about and warned the pressmen to back off. The reporters put the blame on Daisy's lawyers; after the Philadelphia flit, the papers had to be ready for any sudden moves. If Messrs. Moore and Branch would just keep them better informed, they would stand down their chase teams. Instead, Daisy took no more drives up Peachtree.

Another motorist became a brief figure in the Atlanta mystery. There was a good deal of excitement at the news that a traveling salesman named Abe Steinberg had given an affidavit to a notary in Jacksonville, Florida. Steinberg claimed that he happened to be in Atlanta on March 5 and had been driving down West Eleventh Street. It was nearing noon, and he heard a gunshot. Then he saw a white woman and a black man come quickly out of number 29. The woman especially was very agitated. Steinberg must have been driving very slowly. Steinberg stated that he was then on his way to the Piedmont Hotel for a business meeting, and when he got there he saw Mrs. Daisy Grace at the hotel. He knew both of the Graces from Philadelphia. He swore that Daisy was definitely not the woman he had seen leaving the scene of the shooting only a few minutes earlier. He also swore that later on that same day he took a train to Macon, and who was on that train but the identical Negro man he had seen on West Eleventh Street. He confronted the fellow, who said his name was Gibbs. (Remember the letter from Mattie Gibbs?) Steinberg said the man Gibbs did give him "information which he has deemed expedient to hold in reserve."

The whole story seems comical in its string of coincidences. Yet word of this great "break" in the case was picked up in papers across the country.[6] It combined both of Daisy's theories in one convenient bundle: another woman and a Negro. It is important to establish that there actually was an Abe Steinberg who traveled the eastern seaboard selling varnish. Eugene Grace had sold paints. It is possible they knew each other. However, the *Journal*, by "long distance telephone," tracked down this Abe Steinberg making sales calls in Hendersonville, North Carolina. The man said he was acquainted with the Graces but knew no more about the case than what he had read in the papers. The *Journal* pronounced the Steinberg affidavit "exploded." But where did it come from?

While dousing one sensation, the *Journal* offered a brand new headline: the Graces had never gotten married in New York City. The Atlanta *Journal* gets credit for the most productive legwork in the early days of the shooting sensation. Daisy and Gene, it was generally believed, had been married at the Little Church around the Corner in Manhattan. But a New York reporter had decided to toddle down to the Manhattan records office and wrote up the story that he could find no registration for any marriage between Eugene Grace and Daisy Opie. The *Journal* decided to then send wires to "reputable newspapermen" in all the various cities Eugene and Daisy had visited prior to their arrival as Mr. and Mrs. Eugene Grace in Atlanta. They were rewarded by a report from New Orleans: Eugene Hamilton Grace and Mrs. Daisy Ulrich Opie were married in New Orleans on May 10, 1911, by Judge Val Stentz of the first city court.[7]

Judge Stentz even remembered the couple. He told the *Journal* they drove up to the courthouse on Royal Street in a big touring car on a bright sunny day. He thought them to be quite a handsome couple. She gave her age as 31, he said he was 27. They gave their address as the Grunewald Hotel, Baronne Street. They swore under oath that there were no impediments to the marriage. She said her first husband had been dead for some time (actually it had been three months). Stentz thought they seemed "quite wrapped up in each other," and he would not have thought them a runaway couple. The groom seemed to have considerable funds on hand, and he tipped the witnesses liberally. Nice people.

Neither the partisans of Gene nor Daisy chose to make too much out of this new information. The only important fact that needed to be established was that Gene was legally married to Daisy; it mattered not where it had taken place. If Eugene Grace knew he was not the lawful husband of Daisy, setting aside whatever moral censure that might have brought down upon his head, he would have been in an entirely different legal status. A man may certainly testify against his mistress![8] In Newnan, Sam Hill said Gene had told his mother all about the New Orleans wedding. Gene had wanted to be a married man before he brought this woman home to meet his mother. The net winner, again, was Daisy. As her lawful husband, he was now legally silenced in a Georgia courtroom. The fact that Gene had traveled around the country for some weeks, registering as "Mr. and Mrs. Grace," with a woman not yet his wife added fire to those who thought him a womanizing cad.

A court date had been set at last — Tuesday, April 16. The date was set after still more delays while Gene's doctors again dithered over the possibility of an operation. "To the utter surprise of his doctors," Gene had gotten somewhat better while resting in Newnan. Dr. Bailey said that his patient continued to amaze him: "Any other man would have died from pure hopelessness." The plan, which Gene had enthusiastically supported, was to return him to Atlanta for an operation to remove the bullet. Then, only days before that planned movement, there was another relapse. It was toxemia, the dreaded blood poisoning. The doctors now gave him only a few days. There would be no operation. The latter decision no doubt disappointed the numerous correspondents who had written offering to purchase such a celebrated bullet. Dr. Bailey "disdained" all such offers.

Fortunately, Gene rallied yet again! The death watch on Greenville Street was cancelled. The idea of an operation, however, was now off the books. Still, quite plainly, this could not go on. The *Athens Banner* wise-cracked, "If Eugene Grace does not hurry up and die the Atlanta papers will run out of sensation news."[9]

CHAPTER 14

Hearst Stirring Up Atlanta

There were 28 newspapers in Atlanta prior to the Civil War, including the curious *Georgia Blister and Critic*. Only one survived the war, *The Intelligencer*. It was in 1868 that the *Atlanta Constitution* first appeared, giving voice to those who opposed Reconstruction and all those Carpetbaggers in their midst. The *Atlanta Journal* was the *Constitution's* first serious competitor; the *Journal* brought out its first afternoon edition in 1883. That was the year of the great Kimball House fire. The little newcomer grabbed attention by putting out an unheard-of Extra the afternoon of the blaze, and it was a "phenomenal success." For most of two decades the morning *Constitution* and the afternoon *Journal* were the unrivalled papers of choice in Atlanta's better homes.[1]

In the early years of the twentieth century, William Randolph Hearst was indisputably the "King of All Media." He was so powerful a figure that he launched a presidential bid late in 1911—too late, perhaps, and he withdrew from the race to concentrate on his nationwide newspaper empire.[2] Nationwide, that is, but for the South. He had purchased the *Atlanta Georgian* in early 1912, only a few weeks before Eugene Grace was found shot. The *Georgian* was a relatively young paper, having been started in 1906 by F.L. Seely. Following the Atlanta race riots in late September of that first year, the *Georgian* (along with the even more racist *Atlanta News*) was harshly criticized for its coverage.[3] Throughout the summer of 1906 the *Georgian's* editorials had ranted about the "hellish lust" of "Negro fiends" that had created a "reign of terror under which the noblest race of women on earth live in fear and sleep in apprehension."[4] Castration was the answer. J. Max Barber, the sub-editor of Atlanta's *Voice of the Negro*, believed that the *Georgian's* editor, Colonel John Temple Graves, was "one of the most vitriolic enemies of the negro race."[5]

The *Georgian* purchased the *Atlanta News* in early 1907 and merged the mastheads. The combined *Georgian and News* had since won some grudging acclaim for its exposé of Georgia's brutal convict lease system, campaigns against Atlanta vice, liquor and crime, and for establishing the Atlanta holiday tradition of the Empty Stocking Fund. But by 1912, unable to keep pace with the morning *Constitution* and its afternoon rival, the *Journal*, the *Georgian and News* was a "doddering and decrepit" newspaper.

Hearst settled for buying the failing *Georgian* (dropping the *News*) after his earlier offers for both the *Constitution* and the *Journal* had been spurned as inadequate.[6] But F.L. Seely took Hearst's money and left Atlanta for Asheville, North Carolina, where he built the Grove Park Inn. Hearst had finally "invaded" the South, his critics declared, and they warned that southern journalism would never be the same.

The *Constitution* and *Journal* both published polite, boilerplate, welcoming wishes for Hearst. The *Constitution*, for instance, acknowledged that there is "no discounting the influence for constructive publicity that characterizes his publications." Colonel Graves, who had left the *Georgian* to work for the *New York American*, a Hearst paper, was expected to return to the city. Instead, 33-year-old Keats Speed was sent south. He had risen from drama critic to city editor of the *New York Evening Journal*. Born in Kentucky, he had the reassuring Southern heritage for his new assignment. He was gifted a wonderful story.

> The Grace murder [sic] occurred only a little while after Speed had reached Atlanta, completed his reorganization and was praying to the Hearst gods for a story with which to dazzle the town. He did it with the Grace case. Both Grace and his wife, who was accused of murdering him, were prominent socially, and the *Georgian* played the story for all it was worth, and more. Pictures and more pictures, sob stories and scholarly dissertations by Beatrice Fairfax on the amorous aspects of the case. Everything in the Hearst menagerie was trotted out and paraded before wondering Atlanta. The town gasped, but bought the paper.[7]

Herbert Asbury had been a reporter for the *Georgian*. He recalled that the Hearst methods, and the *Georgian's* resulting circulation surge post–Grace shooting, "soon had the *Constitution* and the *Journal* teetering on the verge of insanity."[8]

"The advent of a Hearst newspaper in a city often resulted in the adoption of Hearst methods by rival papers, in the belief that they could thus meet the competition," warned one of the many Hearst-haters of the day.[9] Let it not be said that the *Constitution* or the *Journal* were boring broadsheets; they had the resources and the writing talent to take up the *Georgian's* challenge. As seen, whether it was a *Constitution* reporter hanging onto a speeding cab to get a story, or the *Journal's* "Special Correspondent" traveling hundreds of miles to interview an 8-year-old blind boy, the game was on. Soon the *Montgomery Advertiser* was claiming that the *Journal* and the *Constitution* had "out–Williamed" Hearst:

> The Grace case gave these papers the first real opportunity to go wild since Hearst struck Atlanta. All of the Atlanta papers have been loaded daily with overdrawn details of this case. Hearst has had a bad effect on Atlanta and its newspapers. In many respects they were already daring enough, but now they recognize no limit. We are sorry to see the dear old *Constitution* going back on its raising in any such manner as this.[10]

To its credit, the *Constitution* published this sharp critique from "the esteemed *Advertiser*" prominently on its editorial page. The lead writer cheerfully admitted that "the three Atlanta papers are competing in a tidy little Marathon to see which shall get the news first and which shall 'play it up' in the most fetching style, e.g. an exclamation point where previously only a semi-colon grew." This heightened activity was much more typical of a big and fast-moving city than, well, Montgomery. "Bless your sweet and reposeful soul, neighbor," the *Constitution* twitted.[11]

Closer to home, in-state papers were every bit as fascinated with the attention the Grace case was receiving in the Atlanta dailies. "It is another case of the utter willingness of the public to be fed on details of anything of this nature, anything sensational, involving prominent people, whether it be sweet or bitter, modest or obnoxious."[12] *The Athens Banner* thought something new was happening: "Never before has Atlanta been regaled with the minute details of a crime."[13] The *Macon Telegraph* simply opined that the Atlanta newspapers had "gone dippy." The paper's Atlanta correspondent reported, "This town is literally mad over the Grace case ... lashed by the frantic play of the Atlanta papers with frequent extras and screaming headlines to stir the populace still more."[14] Having said all that with a frown, the Macon paper had also made sure to run its own daily front page updates and the required photographs of the mysterious Mrs. Grace.

It has already been seen that leading voices among the Atlanta clergy decried the ceaseless attention afforded the Grace case. Within the legal community, as well, there was the concern that too much was being played out in the press. But this was the Hearst method, according to the British critic Charles Whibley, who called it "trial by journalism":

> A thousand reporters, cunning as monkeys, active as sleuth-hounds, are on the track. Whether it is the criminal that they pursue or an innocent man is indifferent to them. Heedless of injustice, they go in search of "copy." They interrogate the friends of the victim, and they uncover the secrets of all the friends and relatives he may have possessed. They care not how they prejudice the public mind,

or what wrong they do to innocent men. If they make a fair trial impossible, it matters not. They have given their tired readers a new sensation.[15]

Whibley might get more credit for his insights — if not for his statement that such tactics are "happily strange on our side of the ocean."

The *Georgian* insisted that the newspapers were not entirely to blame. In an editorial printed on March 14, the *Georgian's* Keats Speed asserted that it is the lawyers on both sides who are "talking the most amazing statements ever permitted to go before enlightened people in a sane community." It was Rube Arnold and John Moore who met the press daily with a charge or a denial. "The *Georgian* respectfully submits that there is no need for lawyers to give such an extraordinary display of illegal, unjudicial and unwarranted statements that can only inflame public opinion and do a great deal of harm in the end."[16]

For this and many other reasons, Solicitor Dorsey was anxious to somehow get the Grace case moving toward a trial. There was a new grand jury about to be empanelled in Fulton County, and Dorsey wanted to present them with the charge against Mrs. Grace. There was first the legal formality of an official charge. On the night of March 5, Daisy had been arrested on the charge of "assault with intent to murder." She was bonded out on that occasion and remained free on bond still.

On April 16, 300 people managed to wedge themselves into Judge J.B. Ridley's modest magistrate's court on Auburn Avenue. When Daisy entered the room for the 10:00 session, the flashbulb explosions left "the air as murky as a thick fog." She wore a black dress with white lace stuff at the wrists and neck, a black hat with fluffy trim, and a thin veil. In another ruse, Ridley postponed the hearing until 3:00, hoping to thin the herd in the sweltering room. The tactic was only modestly successful; at three, it was still standing room only. The *Journal* thought the people came merely out of "thoughtless curiosity." The onlookers, by and large, did not know nor really care anything about Eugene or Daisy; the pair of them were simply "characters in a mysterious love story" that they hoped to follow to the finish.[17]

To avoid repetition, since most of the witnesses will appear again at the great trial still ahead, I will keep the details of the hearing brief. The witnesses went over the already well-covered ground of the day of the shooting. The only new evidence came from Detective Bullard who testified that on that day, after Mr. Grace had been removed by the ambulance to the infirmary, the police had discovered a piece of oilcloth on the bed. It had been placed under the sheet, and on top of the oilcloth was a towel. Mr. Grace had been found lying above where the oilcloth had been found. The highlight of the day, for those who stuck around to see it, was the presentation of said oilcloth, removed from a "gruesome bundle of bloodstained articles" and held aloft. The oilcloth was a piece of material about 4 feet by 5 feet.

The other witnesses at the hearing were "the Negress" Martha Ruffin, Mrs. Samuel L. Hill and Dr. Goldsmith. The attorneys for Mrs. Grace were present and followed it closely, taking copious notes but asking no questions. Judge Ridley decided that the evidence was sufficient to sustain the charge which must now be presented to the Fulton County grand jury for an indictment. Daisy would have to return to the Tower.

The reality was that Daisy was about to lose her room at the Kimball House, anyway. Atlanta was bracing for the annual influx of visitors for the performances of the touring New York Metropolitan Opera at the auditorium. Excitement was especially high this April because Enrico Caruso, breaking his personal rule, was going to sing in three performances in one week. The previous year the great tenor had been *hors de combat* in Atlanta with a throat issue, and that had "occasioned much regret." All the hotels in the city were sold out.

But even the approaching opera could not budge the Grace story from the front pages. Only one story could push aside the news that Daisy Grace had been sent back to the Tower. The *Titanic* elbowed the Grace hearing to a side column on the front page of the morning *Constitution*.[18] The rest of the page was given over to coverage of the disastrous sinking of the great liner. Major Archie Butt, a popular, debonair, Georgia-born officer, and a former war correspondent for the Atlanta papers, was among the missing. "Is Butt safe?" everyone wanted to know. He was not among the survivors. Nor was Isidor Straus, who ran the Macy's department stores. He had come from Germany as a boy and settled in south Georgia, where he got his start in retail by running a general store in the town of Talbotton, southwest of Macon. As the liner was sinking, Straus' wife refused to get in a lifeboat and leave her husband. Thus, she too went down with the ship. In the Tower, Daisy avidly read all the grim coverage of this terrible tragedy. She told her jailers that she had seen many icebergs herself while on her honeymoon voyage to Newfoundland. She could not imagine a worse death than to be thrown into the icy waters of the north Atlantic.

Daisy would remain in the women's ward, alone, for another three weeks. Georgia is a state that requires a grand jury to indict any person accused of a felony. The prosecutor presents the evidence supporting the charge to the grand jury. There are no witnesses; the defense does not have a role. On May 6, the Fulton County grand jury returned a "true bill" against Mrs. Daisy Grace, charging her with assault with intent to murder her husband, Eugene H. Grace. The fact that the 23-member panel had taken almost three hours to make their decision was seen to indicate that there was a good deal of debate in the room. It seemed clear that the prosecution's lack of direct evidence was going to be a problem. Unless Grace died, his statement of events would remain inadmissible. Hugh Dorsey assured the jurors that the State was ready to go ahead with the case and had now closed "the chain of circumstantial evidence" to where he was confident of a conviction. The jury, finally, agreed.[19] No date for the trial was set. As long as Gene lived, Daisy was eligible for bond. If convicted of the charge of attempted murder, Daisy faced a sentence of two to seven years at the newly established state prison farm for women in Milledgeville.

The grand jury decision to indict came as a blow. Her first reaction was to put a brave face on it. To have the case dismissed would have been wonderful news, but at least the indictment meant the trial was finally at hand and she would have the opportunity to clear her name. That night, however, she collapsed in her cell.

Was it possible she was pregnant?

CHAPTER 15

An Operation

The *Constitution* reported on the morning of May 7, the day following the grand jury's indictment, that Daisy had "created a sensation last night by announcing she expects soon to become a mother." The *New York Times* also carried the report.[1] If true, this was certainly a remarkable turn of events. The reproductive arithmetic was authenticating; she had only been away from her husband for nine weeks. She might well have only just realized that she was carrying his child. What would it mean? The pregnancy possibility "further complicates one of the most remarkable cases which have ever been recorded in the criminal annals of the South and adds another angle to a many sided story which was for a time the first page feature of practically every newspaper in the country." The *Constitution* speculated freely: Has Mr. Grace been told? What will he do if this is true? Will he drop the charges?

The following day, the *Constitution* retreated (and without explanation) from the earlier claim. The paper now reported that Daisy was being treated only for a "nervous collapse," and she would remain under a doctor's care for several more days. The true story behind Daisy's collapse was less sensational than a pregnancy but quite macabre. The deputy jailer, sensing Daisy's boredom, offered to take her on a tour of the Tower. The tour included the "death chamber" on the fifth and top floor of the institution. The gallows were then being readied for the hanging of a black man named Ben Green, a man of some notoriety among the Atlanta criminal set. Down on Decatur Street, in fact, he was known as "Ben Green, the King of the Cocaine Fiends." On the night of March 21, a young barber named Aaron Morris, living in Gilmer Street, heard a neighbor's cries for help. Mrs. Cohen told Morris that a "drunken Negro" had just assaulted her as she was walking home. The young man gave chase, confronting Ben Green near Boys High School. Green pulled a knife and stabbed him. Morris died at the scene, leaving four daughters and a fifth child on the way. The violent crime shocked the city. For several days the Morris murder and the Grace mystery shared front page prominence in all three papers. The most bloodthirsty depictions of the "horrible stabbing" were printed again and again. A fund for Morris' widow was established, and donations flowed.[2] The murder had taken place only two weeks after the Grace shooting. Plainly, in the case of black-on-white crime, Atlanta justice moved much more swiftly. Ben Green had been tried and sentenced to hang in a space of about six weeks.[3] The preparations were underway on the fifth floor, the rope having been fastened to the great cross-beam. The jailer-cum-tour guide even demonstrated for Daisy the workings of the "fatal trap." With just the flip of a lever the trap dropped open, and a weighted bag of sand dropped into eternity at the end of the rope. No woman had yet been hung from these gallows, but should Gene Grace die, and daily the doctors were expressing their opinions that it was a likely possibility, Daisy might have been looking at the fate that waited her upon conviction. She collapsed in a fit, screaming, "I can't stand it. Get me out of here." The tour of the Tower was over.[4]

Nevertheless, the news that Daisy Grace was pregnant had gotten out and would occasionally appear in many of the out-of-town stories, even during the trial, but it seems clear Daisy was never pregnant.

Daisy remained in the Tower for two more weeks. Her bond had been reduced somewhat to $5,000. Apparently there had been a falling out with the cooperative saloon keeper who had provided bail on the two previous occasions. He had not been paid. On May 22, Daisy left the Tower, the bond money this time having been provided by Chess Lagomarsino. The son of an Italian immigrant who had launched a profitable produce business, Chess was "in real estate." He owned a shop in the lobby of the Peters Building where Daisy's lawyers (Moore and Branch) had their offices. He did not know Daisy but he knew her lawyers, and if they said she was innocent, it was good enough for him.

Daisy left the Tower, stepping once again into the ever-present burst of flashbulbs. She was wearing a dark blue silk coat suit, a small black hat and veil, black suede slippers and gloves. She told the reporters, "I'm as happy as a schoolgirl." She was going to be staying with her faithful nurse, Louise Wilson, who lived at 270 Ashby Street, near Oglethorpe Street, in West End. "The pretty little suburb," at that time, had been developed in the late 1800s and annexed into the city of Atlanta. There was a streetcar to downtown, allowing Daisy to meet easily with her lawyers in the run-up to the trial. But for now her thoughts were on her regained freedom. On a previous visit to West End, Daisy said the laughter of the neighborhood children had reminded her of her happy childhood back in Pennsylvania. In the suburbs Daisy hoped that the seclusion would allow her to regain her strength for the approaching trial. "I hope people will let me alone so I can go out on the streets.... I would like to have a little pleasure after all the trouble I have been in."

Daisy was, for the moment, off-stage. But she was still to be talked about. Bob Jones, the 29-year-old Alabama evangelist and future founder of his eponymous university in South Carolina, came to Atlanta for a women-only prayer meeting on June 2. His chosen subject was the passage from the book of Timothy: "She that Liveth in Pleasure is Dead while she Liveth." At no time did Jones ever mention Daisy Grace by name, but certainly his audience would have identified her as one of that growing number of "fast women" (or, as Jones called them, the modern "decorated" women). "She walks with an air as much to say 'How do you like me? Don't you think I am unusually attractive?' Such women in their dress and lasciviousness are a torment to decent men. Manhood is being cursed by women's fashions," he declared. The newspapers have given far too much attention to such women, asserted Jones, and as a result, society's barriers Jones asserted, have been dangerously relaxed. "The tendency to overlook (there is no suggestion of forgiveness in the custom) the actions and well-known reputation of women in society — women conceded to be 'under a shadow' and to continue to extend to such the same recognition accorded to good and pure women puts a premium on sin, the dangers of which cannot be estimated." He warned the mothers of Atlanta to be watchful of their daughters and the influences of the modern world. "One crooked society woman can do more to damn pure young girls than all the outcast women in the earthly hells of immorality."[5]

Whether it was the legal authorities, newspaper critics or the mothers of Atlanta, many forces were moving together to get this case to trial. And Gene Grace desperately wanted to be there; in fact, he dreamed of walking into the courtroom and looking Daisy right in the eye. His only hope of that happening was an operation. It seems there was an old black man in Newnan named Level who had been shot and left paralyzed in a very similar way. But Level's doctors had cut on him right away and removed the bullet. Level survived the surgery, and he was still seen hobbling in some ungainly manner around the streets of Newnan. In fact, he had even been out to visit Gene, and the two men had talked medicine.

Spring had now come to Newnan. With the warmer days, the windows in Gene's back bedroom had been left open. Friends passing by would hear him idly whistling, and they would approach the window for a conversation. The Hill farmhouse property ran down almost to the A&WP tracks, where beyond the rail line stood the Coweta Cotton Oil Mill. The Hill homestead was a pleasant place with the warming sun, the smells of the barnyard (at least some of them), the view of the fields and trees where he once romped as a boy, and the swimming pond beyond. It had all helped to restore Grace's strength and his determination to have the surgery. The doctors had tried to impress upon him that no operation would likely restore to him the use of his legs. They would do it solely to remove the bullet. The toxicity of the slug, they knew, would eventually kill him.

On Wednesday, June 12, at four in the afternoon, Gene Grace was operated on at his home. It is impossible to imagine the agony of waiting all those hours on a June day. Dr. Bailey was assisted by a Newnan surgeon, W.A. Turner, Jr. The reporters kept a respectful distance. When the two physicians emerged, Dr. Bailey read their statement. They had operated in an attempt "to restore animation" to the lower body of Eugene Grace. The operation had confirmed that the spinal cord had not been severed by the bullet. The bullet, however, could not be removed owing to its inaccessibility, although they believed that the pressure on the cord had been reduced. "The enlodgement of the bullet in the ninth dorsal caused a severe bulging of the internal left posterolateral wall causing paralysis. They removed the posterior arch of the ninth dorsal and the spinous process and laminae of the seventh and eight dorsal vertebrae." Dr. Bailey reported that "as perilous as the operation was, the patient had showed no fear." Grace had recovered consciousness quickly, and when they left him he seemed cheerful. The doctor concluded, "It was a very dangerous operation and we must watch him very carefully."

Two days later the doctors reported that Gene had had "no bad effects" from the operation and should recover normally from the surgery. The patient was now experiencing some "spasmodic jerks" in his legs. This was a normal development, the medical men believed, and one that did not offer any new hope. The patient, however, was "much encouraged."

On June 23, the Fulton County court calendar was released for July. The case of the *People versus Mrs. Eugene Grace* would not begin until Monday, July 29. Solicitor Dorsey was meeting regularly with his witnesses. The best witness, of course, was Gene Grace, but he had not died. His "dying declaration" was still in Dorsey's desk, but it was now useless. It seemed ridiculous to so many people that the man who knew exactly what had happened in that bedroom had his lips sealed by the law. The Georgia Legislature was then in session. State Representative G.Y. Harrell of Stewart County introduced a bill in the Judiciary Committee proposing to change Georgia law to "make the husband or wife a competent witness upon the trial of either for any criminal offense when the charges amount to a felony."[6]

Harrell insisted that the need for a change was not simply prompted by the Grace case. Only a few months prior to the shooting on West Eleventh

Street, Lizzie Ector, a Griffin woman, had been convicted of stabbing her husband — on his testimony. The Georgia Court of Appeals threw out the conviction and re-affirmed the ban, which has its roots in historic common law. "The law shuts the husband's mouth, whether he wishes to speak or not, in every case where his wife is charged with crime; and it makes no exception, even if the crime is charged to have been committed upon his person." Judge Richard Brevard Russell (the father of the future Senator) conceded that the public might not understand why this curious provision of the law is on the books. Though it had been challenged many times, it remained Georgia law, for which Judge Russell felt that credit was partially owed to the "innate sense of chivalry" of which all Georgians could well be proud. But the justice also warned the public of the consequences of changing the law:

> Attacks upon husbands by wives were very rare, and that, even if they sometimes occurred, the right to testify on the part of the husband might in some cases be abused, and used as a means of getting rid of a wife of whom the husband had tired.[7]

J.W. Moore, of "team Daisy," was seen to be "mingling" with the members of the legislature's judiciary committee during their debates. Harrell's bill never got out of committee.

It was just another setback for Gene Grace. Angus Perkerson of the *Journal* returned to Newnan to interview Grace in the wounded man's "cool bedroom, looking out a drowsy street [while] a canary trills in the window." Gene seemed frail and his formerly brilliantined hair was now streaked with gray. But Grace assured his visitor that he would be in Atlanta for the trial:

> I have prayed day after day to get back my strength, even just enough to be carried into the court room on a stretcher. I want to face her and to tell my story to the jury.... I know she did it and I want to tell the jury just how she shot me and left me to die. I want to put it to them how it happened. I want to let them know how she took away the best part of my life.

For the first time, Grace questioned his medical care. "If I had been a Decatur Street n****r, they would have taken me to Grady and cut the bullet out and I'd be fine today." If the doctors had not been so careful, he surmised, the bullet would have been removed and he would be better off.

> Instead [placing his hand below his chest], I am dead from here down. I've been here nearly four months flat on my back but I'm not seeking retribution. I guess it sounds as though I'd like to take the same pistol I was shot with and bang away at my wife. [He smiled and shook his head.] That isn't the way. But I want her punished. I want justice done.

Daisy, in the meantime, had the chance to enjoy some rustic relaxation of her own before the trial, and she did not have to leave the city to do it.

William Zimmer, who owned the Kimball House, had a large piece of land he called Kimballville Farm in what is now the Morningside section of Atlanta. Originally, Zimmer had hoped to raise some chickens and cows, and grow some vegetables for the hotel kitchens. Those plans expanded to the point where "Farmer Bill from Kimballville" had established a "high class stock and dairy farm."[8] Four miles from Five Points, the farm boasted prize-winning Jersey cattle, Berkshire hogs ("unquestionably the hog of the day"), the "finest flock of Pekin ducks in the South," plus pigeons, geese and the famous "white Orpington chicks." All that's left of the farm today is a street sign for Zimmer Drive, but at the time, people would come out for the day. Daisy Grace, a frequent guest at the Kimball House, was one such visitor. The *Constitution*, including a picture of Daisy at Kimballville, reported that the accused woman "took her requisite exercise and did little chores around the inviting southern farm home to amuse herself. Trimming flowers, and feeding the strained white Orpington chicks."

The woman expected to be the central focus of the most sensational Atlanta trial in years certainly seemed unconcerned. "She is no more worried over the approaching trial than she would be over attending a party, and her fearlessness is evinced in her conversation." Daisy was untroubled by the reports that she would have to face her husband again. "I love that man as I love life itself. I could no more hurt him than I could hurt my mother. He's nearly all I have in the world to love. On the brink of a trial which I know will not end in my conviction, I again say, Gene cannot face me in court and say that I shot him."

In Newnan, Gene told reporters, "I've accused her and I'm game to face her."

At last, the trial was at hand.

CHAPTER 16

"A deathlike stillness"

The trial of Daisy Grace was to be held in a rented meeting room in the Thrower Building at 33 Mitchell Street, on the southeast corner of Pryor Street. The new "Temple of Justice," more prosaically to be known as the Fulton County Courthouse, was then under construction only a block to the north, at Pryor and Hunter Streets. In the meantime, the various courts, agencies and offices of county government were forced to find temporary space scattered about downtown Atlanta. It had not gone well. "If it was not for the prospect of some day having a brand-new courthouse to work in everybody connected with the courts and the various offices of Fulton County would resign forthwith."[1] Since June of 1911, the criminal court operations had been based in the Thrower Building. Solicitor General Dorsey's office was on the second floor. On the fourth floor, opposite the temporary offices of the county commission, was Judge Leonard S. Roan's criminal courtroom.

The Thrower Building, named for the local developer Marvin L. Thrower, was built of reinforced concrete and had only been finished in the spring of 1911. With the new railroad viaducts in place, growth was moving to the "other side of the tracks" in downtown Atlanta.[2] The Thrower Building, in modern terms, was multi-use. The Pryor Street frontage was commercial, with the main tenant being Max Kutz's Wholesale Millinery, one of the largest hat purveyors in the country. The Mitchell Street side was primarily office space. On the top floor "nested" the meeting room of the local Owls Club — that is, if by meeting room you meant barroom. Though Atlanta was officially dry, a person could lawfully keep any amount or type of liquor in his own locker at his own club. So-called "locker clubs" were everywhere in the city and, with few exceptions, were known as "boozing dens."[3] The county battled with the Owls, but the club won an injunction to keep pouring drinks two floors above the criminal courts.

Judge Roan's fourth-floor "courtroom" was ill-suited even for its tem-

The M.L. Thrower Building, at Mitchell and Pryor streets, circa 1951. The courtroom entrance was on the Mitchell Street frontage, left. The building beyond is
the Atlanta City Hall (Lane Brothers collection; Special Collections and Archives,
Georgia State University Library).

porary purpose. It was nothing but a large open room with low ceilings supported by pillars. An L-shaped railing had been erected to separate perhaps
400 square feet for the "participants." Deputy Sheriff Plennie Minor handled
the seating arrangements for the Grace trial. Judge Roan had an elevated
bench in one corner to the right. The prosecution and defense tables sat parallel in the middle of the space, facing the witness box. The "box" was actually
a small raised platform with a wooden arm chair. The jury sat to the right of
the witness stand. The press table was wedged in between Judge Roan's bench
and the defense table. Photographs taken during the trial show as many as
thirty people crammed into that space. The remainder of the room was given
over to seating; the number of seats, supposedly, was 123, many with
"obstructed views." There were windows against only one wall, and they
looked out over a narrow alley between the Thrower Building and Nunnally
and McRae's overall factory on Mitchell Street. The *Constitution* called it a

"dingy" room. The *Journal* thought it had the feeling of a "Turkish bath"; the ventilation was very poor, and even during routine business the occupants had "suffered intensely."

Built up by frenzied reports for almost five months, the interest in attending "the great Atlanta shooting trial" had been overwhelming. The sheriff's office began fielding offers to purchase advance "reserved seats." The Atlanta press had fanned some brief interest in the idea of moving the trial to the new Auditorium Armory at Gilmer and Courtland streets. Built after the race riot to house a better equipped National Guard battalion, the auditorium had since been the venue for poultry shows, auto shows, religious revivals and the annual visit of the Metropolitan Opera. President Taft, Teddy Roosevelt and Woodrow Wilson had all spoken there within the previous year. The auditorium seated 7,500 people. It boasted a $40,000 Austin organ with 6,000 pipes (to entertain the audience during lulls in the trial?).[4] Luther Rosser, who was now leading the defense team, blasted the idea: "They have no more right to hold it there than on top of Stone Mountain." Solicitor Dorsey did not favor the move either. In the end, the Auditorium proposal was dropped as being "beneath the dignity" of the courts.

The sun that Monday morning in July foretold the hot day ahead. The *Journal's* weather column predicted that the city was in for a "siege of hot weather." The Thrower Building had but one small passenger elevator, but it was in constant use by the various county bureaucrats toting their ledgers and records between the floors. The jurors, spectators and reporters had to climb the switchback concrete steps to the fourth floor. Court was to open at nine, but long before that the available public seats were taken. The hallway outside was crowded with those who could not get in; they milled about, "sweaty and fuming." Policemen on the street limited entrance to the building; court bailiffs let one person in for every one that came out.

Judge Leonard Roan entered the courtroom at nine. Roan had been appointed to the bench in 1902 by then governor Joseph Terrell. "It fell to his lot to preside at the trial of more celebrated criminal cases than perhaps any other judge who has ever sat on the bench in Georgia; and it was conceded by the bar and the people that he was one of the best trial judges of criminal cases that the State had ever produced. He was fair and firm, but lenient and kind-hearted."[5] As he did almost every day, the judge had taken the train that morning from his home south of the city in Fairburn, (then) Campbell County. He was 63, a small balding man with a full brush moustache that accentuated his unusually high cheekbones.

It was Solicitor Dorsey's plan to give everyone in court the impression that this was just another Monday morning by disregarding the tumult in the hallways and the fully occupied press table. Dorsey began the day with routine court business. "Ten burly Negroes shackled together" were marched into the room for their first appearances before the bench on charges ranging from burglary to murder. In fact, there were four murder cases scheduled to be heard after the Grace trial. In contrast with the drawn-out Grace preliminaries, the four killings had all occurred in Atlanta since June 24. The *Journal* reported that Mr. Dorsey was dealing with "crimes of violence galore," and these were "some of the quickest indictments and trials" ever seen in Fulton County. But all these defendants would have to sit in their cells in the Tower until the great shooting case was heard. The formalities were concluded, and the guarded chain-line shambled out. The crowd shuffled uncomfortably in their seats. How much more of this was there to sit through? Where was Daisy Grace?

Daisy had begun this important day in conference with her lawyers. At about 8:45 they left the Peters Building for the quarter mile walk to the courthouse. The Whitehall Street viaduct carried them over what *The Atlantian* monthly called "the Amazonian river of smoke" that was the railroad cleaving the downtown in half. The upper end of Whitehall Street, even so early on a Monday morning, was always an active place. Several streetcar lines used the viaduct; employees were arriving to open the great "department stores" of Messrs. Rich and High. Those on the sidewalk parted to allow Daisy's entourage and the trailing knot of reporters and photographers to pass along. At Hunter and Mitchell streets, at McClure's Ten-Cent Store, one of the lawyers stopped in to purchase several palm fans which, at three for a nickel, were a wise investment indeed. Reaching the Thrower Building, Daisy et al climbed the four flights of stairs to Judge Roan's court. During Mr. Dorsey's preliminaries, however, Daisy waited with seeming calmness in the county commission offices across the hall; the *Journal* said the scene "suggested an actress waiting for her curtain call." The call came at 9:35.

The defendant entered the room, accompanied by her attorneys, Louise Wilson, her nurse, and her security man, Captain Charles Burke, who was described as a "Special Agent of the Southern Railway." Also in attendance was Daisy's mother. Mrs. Ulrich — "a little white-haired lady" — had been in town since Friday, arriving by train from Philadelphia. Everyone in Atlanta was quite disappointed that Mother Ulrich had come South without little "Webbie." The blind boy had remained behind at his school; Daisy's sister would keep him on the weekends. The boy was only told that his grandmother was going off to a convention.

All eyes in court, of course, were going to be on Daisy Grace. What would she be wearing? There were rumors that she had purchased several new Parisian gowns for the trial. Each day of the trial the crusty newspaper men would struggle to describe her outfits. On this opening day, Daisy wore "a dress of white Irish linen, hand embroidered, eyelet worked, covered with Irish lace; she wore white kid gloves, a small straw hat with a large ostrich plume, brown satin slippers, brown silk stockings and a brown silk parasol." A "well known woman writer" told the *Journal* that the dress was "quite an appropriate gown for an afternoon tea." The defense, it seemed clear, had no strategy to tone down the legend of "Daisy of the Leopard Spots"—she would dress the part. But the reporters also noticed that Daisy seemed expressionless, with a hint of pallor, as if the actress had a case of first night nerves. Nonetheless, when asked to rise and answer how she would plead to the charge, in a voice heard clearly throughout the room, Daisy firmly replied, "Not guilty."

The process of selecting the jury was lengthy and tedious. Three panels of 36 men each had been summoned. The best known name on the list was Asa Candler, the pharmacist turned Coca Cola magnate and "reputedly the city's richest man." Candler was not chosen. Given the intense newspaper coverage of the previous four and half months, finding anyone who had not heard about the shooting or formed a conclusion was going to be no easy task. There was also the fact that the jurors were told in advance that those selected would be sequestered and fed nightly at the Kimball House. No slur, certainly, on the comfortable rooms or the *table d'hôte* of the Palm Garden Grill Room, but "a reluctance to serve was manifest." Some of the excuses offered were so flimsy that outright laughter was heard throughout the room. The prosecution and the defense went back and forth with their usual challenges; Dorsey had ten, the defense had twenty. The process seemed never-ending. Time and again Daisy was instructed, "Prisoner at the bar, arise and look upon the juror. Juror, look upon the prisoner." Yet few of the sweltering spectators, entrapped in these legal doldrums, were willing to give up their seats. For the word had been whispered among them that "Grace is coming."

Eugene Grace had been carried from his home on Greenville Street in Newnan in time to make the 9:00 train to Atlanta. His doctors, Bailey and Turner, had signed off on the trip; the latter called Gene "a man of remarkable will power." The story of Grace's last ghastly ride on the milk train had so moved the members of the Newnan Elks Club that they agreed to handle these arrangements. The *Constitution* had a picture of the five smiling Elks, including the "exalted ruler," T.G. Farmer, Jr. The *Journal* reported that Grace was cheerful and said "it felt good to get out." He was wearing his usual night clothing (pajamas) and a golf cap he had purchased in Newfoundland. Also making the journey was Grace's tireless Negro nurse, identified only as "Bob," who seemed to have been tasked with the continual massage of the wounded man's legs and feet.

Once again Gene Grace would have to make the journey while resting in the baggage car of the A&WP train. Despite the best intended arrangements of the Elks escort, Gene would travel north this time sharing the carriage with the coffin of a dead man. Though a bit gloomy, it certainly was a quieter journey minus the clanging milk pails. The train reached the Terminal Station at about ten in the morning, where a crowd of 200 people had gathered. There was an ambulance waiting from Patterson's, the morticians, and Grace was driven to the Thrower Building. Police had to force the crowds back to allow the Elks to carry the stretcher into the building; Grace covered his face with a newspaper against the stares and the flashbulbs. The Elks carried him up the four flights of "narrow winding" stairs. At times it seemed that Grace's litter would pitch over at any moment. But at last the fourth floor was reached. To allow Grace (and the sweat-soaked Elks) some time to recover from the journey, the stretcher was placed in the Fulton County commission offices, the same room that his wife had occupied an hour earlier.

At 11:30 word was received in the courtroom that Grace had arrived, and, having been refreshed, he now wished to attend the proceedings. There was some discussion over where the injured man could be placed. J.W. Moore thought it politic for the defense to be seen to be accommodating in every way and said he hoped that Mr. Grace might be placed wherever he would be the most comfortable. A space was cleared against the small railing, immediately to the right of the jury box and with a fine view of the witness chair.

The small door behind the judge's rostrum opened a few moments later. The *Journal's* Bradford Byrd described the scene:

> Four attendants pushed back the dingy door to the court room in the temporary hall of justice and, tugging at the four corners of a cot, carried the inert form of Grace into the room, while spectators, attorneys and principals in Atlanta's greatest sensation in years, gaped and whispered in astonishment.

Other than the tread of the litter-bearing Elks, there was not a sound in the room. The *New York Times* noted that "a deathlike stillness" reigned.

For the first time since she had left him coughing and spitting blood in a room at St. Joseph's Infirmary 146 days before, Daisy Grace was again in the presence of her husband. As Gene was carried in, as "a coffin into church," she grew pale and seemed to swoon. Nurse Wilson, at her side, produced a prepared hypodermic and injected some restorative "white fluid" into Daisy's right arm. The nurse spoke a few soothing words to Daisy. The two women seemed to be as unconcerned as if they were in a private nursing home.

Gene Grace, meanwhile, seemed to beam from his stretcher. Solicitor Dorsey walked over to shake his hand and welcomed him back to Atlanta. Grace acknowledged some familiar faces at the press table and assured them,

"I am feeling fit as a fiddle." The Elks had brought a small electric fan into the room, which was plugged in to provide the man some slight relief. Grace pointed toward the defense table and told the Elks, "Watch me close, boys. I don't trust her."

With Grace now settled in, and the defendant bolstered in spirits, the process of selecting the jury could resume. It was nearly noon before the panel of a dozen men was sworn. They truly came from "all walks of [white] life." There was a house painter, a butcher, an ad salesman, a bill collector, etc. Eleven of them were married men, the twelfth a bachelor.

Hugh Dorsey rose to tell the court that the State planned to call 31 witnesses, and he read the list of their names. The defense declined to present the list of their witnesses. Dorsey called that unsatisfactory, to which Luther Rosser fired back, "Well, we ain't going to call their names so you might as well be satisfied." It was the first of dozens of occasions for legal bickering between the two men, providing amusement for those who knew that Dorsey's sister was married to Rosser's son. Rosser's refusal also suggested the possibility of surprise witnesses and "sensations to come."

Hugh Dorsey was 40 and slight in build. Like Grace, he was a newlywed, having married Miss Adair Wilkinson, a Valdosta beauty of some renown, only a few weeks after Gene and Daisy were married in New Orleans. With his "cowlick plastered on a high, eggish forehead, [Dorsey] bore a striking resemblance to a shrewd young owl."[6] Dorsey was from a longtime and prominent Fayetteville family, and he had been solicitor general (a position later happily renamed "district attorney") since 1910. He had been appointed to fill a vacancy and was — concurrent with the Grace trial — involved in a contested Democratic primary to keep his job. His supporters pointed to the fact that "convictions in the criminal branch of the superior court of Fulton County have doubled since Hugh M. Dorsey, solicitor, has been on the job, a period of one year. This is a remarkable record!" For this case, Dorsey would be assisted by Lamar Hill. Reuben Arnold had withdrawn from the case a few weeks before the trial. That was taken as encouraging news for the defense, as the redoubtable Arnold knew what's what and saw trouble ahead for the prosecution. But cynics thought for sure that Arnold had turned his nose up at the fee.

With or without Rube Arnold's costly assistance, Dorsey seemed altogether confident in his case. During a break in the jury process, he had sidled over to the press table to whisper confidentially but with emphasis, "We have our line of prosecution complete. Every link fits the chain." The consensus on the street was that the trial would be over by Tuesday. The chosen jurymen could only hope so.

CHAPTER 17

The Bloody Bundle Redux

Daisy Opie Ulrich Grace was being tried on the charge of "assault with intent to murder." In the grandiloquent phrasing of Georgia law, the exact charge was that

> Mrs. Daisy Grace, being then and there a person of sound memory and discretion, with a certain pistol, the same being a weapon likely to produce death, in and upon one Eugene H. Grace, a human being, in the peace of said State, then and there being, did make an assault, with the intent, the said Daisy Grace, to kill and murder, and with the said certain pistol which the said accused then and there held and had, did then and there unlawfully, feloniously and with malice aforethought shoot at and towards him, the said Eugene H. Grace and shoot him through the left side etc.

For a conviction, then, the State of Georgia would have to prove that she shot Gene Grace, that she had a motive for doing so, that she intended to kill him and that she took the action with malice aforethought. If convicted of the crime, the Georgia code called for a sentence of two to ten years. To get that conviction, Hugh Dorsey had welded together his chain of circumstantial evidence. There was no direct evidence, that which "immediately points to the question at issue." There was no one else in that bedroom when the gun went off but Daisy and Gene. Gene Grace — if indeed she had shot him — could not testify against her. There was only the circumstantial evidence, defined in Georgia's code as evidence "which only tends to establish the issue by proof of various facts, sustaining by their consistency, the hypothesis claimed."[1] But it is a misconception to simply dismiss "circumstantial evidence" as insufficient. Few people commit crimes when other people are watching; prosecutors every day rely on the much-maligned circumstantial evidence and win many a conviction.

In his opening remarks Dorsey told the jury that the State was prepared to show that the only person who might have shot Eugene Grace was his wife, Daisy.[2] Only she had the opportunity to do the shooting in the likely time period; there was no sign of a burglar or intruder. Only Daisy had access to the gun that was used in the crime. Only Daisy had a motive — the insurance policies. Dorsey said the State would also detail for them the evidence of prior planning — the "malice aforethought" — including the alibi letters, the drugs, and the presence of a mysterious "mourning dress" she had packed for her trip to Newnan. The prosecution opened their case by calling Police Officer Robert Wood to the stand.

Wood was a former detective who had briefly lost his badge after a brutality charge.[3] He recalled arriving at 29 West Eleventh Street at about 2:30 on the afternoon of March 5. He described the scene as he entered the bedroom to find Eugene Grace with his head hanging off the bed. It was a now familiar story, and Wood told it well. But, when given his chance, Rosser attacked the policeman for presenting some newly elaborated details not heard during the officer's earlier appearance at the hearing before Judge Ridley in April. Rosser was "merciless" in pressing the officer for details on the blood. Where was it? How large were the stains? How did he know the blood was dry? Observers thought Wood seemed to get rattled a bit, but overall he made the points required for the prosecution.

Wood's partner, Patrolman James Dorsett, was next, and his appearance was the cue to bring in the bloody bundle. Dorsey held the bundle up for all to see; The *New York Times* observed that "the sight of [the bundle] caused Mrs. Grace to grow pale." One by one Dorsey pulled the items out of the sack and held them aloft for the officer to identify: a blood-stained Turkish towel, pillow slips, and, finally, Mr. Grace's "baby blue silk nightshirt stained crimson." Given the nightshirt to hold, Dorsett dramatically pushed his right index finger through the bullet hole. The puncture was found about two inches below the pocket on the left breast of the nightshirt. Dorsett also testified about the gun and how he concluded that it had been quite recently fired. Rosser had that professional defense counsel's disdain for police officers as witnesses. Dorsett was unclear about where the phone was found, on the bed or on the floor. The call officer admitted that he had not personally collected the bloody items, and the Turkish towel was something he had not seen before. Rosser also established that Dorsett was not, by any means, a firearms expert.

Judge Roan called for an hour's recess for a late lunch — if the bloody nightshirt had not put everyone off their feed. Regardless, all those who were packed into the stifling, smoke-filled courtroom appreciated the respite.

The first witness in the afternoon session was Detective James Doyal. Dorsey used the opportunity to have the plainclothesman clarify anything left uncertain by the sometimes shaky testimony of the two "uniforms." Doyal testified that the phone had been found on the floor; it had been stuffed with a cotton boudoir cap. That cap, Doyal was sorry to say, had since been lost. Doyal also identified the oilcloth that had been found under the sheet. The large rubber cloth was brought over to the jury box for their inspection. Dorsey wanted to know if the detective had searched the bathroom medicine chest. Rosser was on his feet. This was a rented house, rented furnished, and thus there would have to be evidence presented linking Mrs. Grace to anything that might have been left in the bathroom cupboards. The jury was sent out of the room. Doyal told Judge Roan that the police had found three bottles of interest: a 4-ounce bottle of "Radway's Ready Mixture," a 3-ounce bottle of "Dr. King's New Discovery," and a 2-ounce vial of paregoric. Rosser's objection was sustained; Dorsey would have to find another way to get that information to the jury. Rosser was also able to get Doyal to admit that when the police left 29 West Eleventh Street, they had locked the bedroom and locked the house and given the keys to Lamar Hill, who was at that time acting for the Grace family. Hill was now sitting at the prosecution table. The detective could not say whether Mr. Hill or anyone else had since been in that bedroom unbeknownst to the police.

  J.C. and Martha Ruffin, respectively, testified against their former mistress. J.C., of course, was well aware by now that Daisy Grace had tried to suggest that he might have been the shooter. On the morning of March 5, Ruffin said he found a note, signed "Mrs. Grace," when he entered the house: "Don't wake me up until nine. Don't make any fuss downstairs or disturb us. When we want to get up, I will come downstairs and let you know." He threw the note away. But Mrs. Grace had come down to the kitchen at eight and said Mr. Gene was sick and she would take his breakfast up to him, which she had never done before. She later came down again and told them, "Hurry up with the dishes, the sooner you're away, the longer your holiday." Dorsey wanted to know about Ruffin's relationship with Mr. Gene (of course, the wounded man was lying there only a few feet from the witness box). J.C. said that he had never quarreled with him. Mr. Gene had been very kind to him and had given him one of his old suits only a few days before the shooting. Again, Rosser attempted to befuddle the witness with rapid-fire questions, primarily dealing with the time. What time did this happen? What time was that? Ruffin admitted that he threw out the note because Daisy was always leaving notes — about the laundry, the grocery shopping, etc. Finding a morning note was not anything unusual.

  A final question for the servant: Do you know a woman named Rebecca Sams? He could not say. Wasn't she at the Grace home on many occasions, including the night before the shooting? He could not say. The mention of a woman's name unheard before in connection with the mystery caused a murmur through the courtroom. Had the defense found the "other woman" at last?

The murmurs and whispers may have been the only breath of air that moved in the fourth floor cauldron. The *Constitution* reported that conditions had become "suffocating" and estimated the temperature inside the room at 98 degrees. Judge Roan, in the interests of their comfort, said he would allow the jurymen to remove their coats *and* straw hats. Rosser, with the sweat glistening on his bullet-headed pate, asked if the lawyers might also be granted the bench's favor. The robed judge declined: "I think you can suffer along with me, Mr. Rosser." One slight factor in Rosser's favor: he never wore a tie, even in court. No other Atlanta lawyer would dare challenge the dress code.[4] Admittedly, however, it provided only scant relief.

When Martha Ruffin took the stand, the *Constitution* described her as "looking like she had just stepped from a comic supplement." Cruel aspersions aside, Martha Ruffin was perhaps the most important witness of them all. She was apparently the last person to see Gene Grace, other than his wife, until the police broke into the bedroom. Martha was clearly intimidated by the presence of her mistress, now sitting only a few feet away. She made no eye contact with the prosecutor, and Dorsey had to repeatedly ask her to speak up. Martha testified that Daisy came into the kitchen at eight that morning and asked for two soft-boiled eggs and some coffee. She sat in the kitchen to have her breakfast. Then she told Martha to fix a tray with some eggs, toast, coffee and a glass of ice water for Mr. Gene. Daisy took that tray up herself. Martha heard nothing more until nine, when she was called up to the bedroom to light a fire. When she entered the bedroom she saw that Mr. Gene had eaten none of his breakfast. He was lying in bed, groaning. Rosser objected, "Your honor, she's giving a medical opinion. How do we know she knows what a groan is?" Dorsey asked her to make the sound she heard that morning. The poor woman said she could not imitate the sounds. Martha did recall Daisy telling Mr. Grace, "You ain't sick, Gene, you sleepy." Significantly, Dorsey never asked Martha questions such as, "Did you look at Mr. Grace? Where was he on the bed? Was he under the covers?" These would seem to have been quite important pieces of evidence. If Gene had been shot before nine o'clock, Daisy would surely have covered the man up with blankets before any servant was called into the room. Giving Dorsey some credit for being a polished prosecutor, it would appear that he did not ask the questions because he either knew the answers would have been unhelpful or because Martha had told him "I don't remember."[5] Prosecutors hate to hear those three words from one of their key witnesses. If the prosecution did not broach the subject, the defense wisely did not go there either.

After lighting the fire, Martha had returned to the kitchen until being summoned again at about ten o'clock to button up her mistress' dress. The servant stated that Daisy then hurried her out of the room. Daisy later came downstairs to say that if Doctor Cromer were to come, send him away. The mistress said that Mr. Gene was now feeling much better, but still they should not disturb him. They should make as little noise as possible and then take themselves away. Dorsey finished his questioning by asking Martha if she regularly made the bed. She did. Had she ever seen the oilcloth? Never. Martha had also worked for the Graces during the time they lived on North Boulevard. Was there a typewriter in that house? Martha recalled that there was.

Mrs. Ruffin would have to suffer next through a five-minute barrage of Rosser's staccato questions, and he scored some points as she floundered in confusion about the time. Martha told Rosser that Mrs. Grace was standing facing the bed while she stood behind her to do up the dress. So, therefore, Martha was also facing the bed. The implication for the jury was that Daisy was not trying to divert Martha's eyes from the groaning Gene. Martha also admitted that nothing on the morning of the shooting, as far as her duties were concerned, had been out of the ordinary routine at 29 West Eleventh Street.

J.C. and Martha Ruffin were important witnesses for Dorsey. By now, the married servants had been well-coached to tell their familiar story of being hushed and hurried away, etc. But again it was all circumstantial evidence. The Ruffins were never asked, for example, if they had heard a shot. By implication, we can assume they did not. Still, Daisy Grace's great effort to seemingly rush both of them out of the house was a problem for the defense.

The next witness was Hardaway, the cabman who took Daisy to the Terminal Station. He picked her up at 11:00 at West Eleventh Street and dropped her off at 11:45. The Newnan train was not until two.

Hamilton Hill was the last witness to take the stand on day one. Gene's stepbrother was 14. He recalled being sent by his mother to meet the carriage bringing Daisy from Newnan station for her visit to Greenville Street. When he told her what had happened, she answered, "I don't believe it." Dorsey then showed the lad the gun found at the scene, and Hamilton identified it as one he had seen before at West Eleventh Street. Hamilton had been at the Grace's home on many occasions and stayed overnight there while in the city. It was Dorsey's plan to use the youth's testimony to clarify the purpose of the sinister oilcloth. He asked Hamilton, as someone familiar with the Grace home, if he knew who slept on what side of the bed. Rosser erupted from his chair, convulsing the courtroom with his objection. What would this 14-year-old country boy know about the sleeping arrangements of adults?

It was a highly improper question, he blustered. Dorsey's query would have to go unanswered. Martha Ruffin made up the room each day; perhaps Dorsey should have put the question to her? Dorsey handed Hamilton an envelope and asked if he had ever seen it before. The boy said the envelope had arrived in Newnan addressed to Mrs. Grace, but by that time she had already gone back to Atlanta. Before leaving Newnan, however, she had told him that she was expecting some mail, and it should be forwarded to her in Atlanta immediately.

With that, Judge Roan adjourned matters for the day. It was only 4:30 but the heat in the room was intolerable. All of the news accounts of the trial's first day made that point (the reporters wanted their editors to know the conditions under which they were forced to work). The *Journal*, racing to get the news into the late editions, told their readers that the trial was being held "in a tiny overcrowded courtroom in which the heat is intense.... The air became close and stuffy, and the humidity was increased by steam that poured from the cement floors and the walls which reeked of tobacco." There were a few electric fans around the room, but they merely circulated "an odor that was sickening."

Beyond the heat, the main focus of the first day's interest was the remarkable reunion of Eugene and Daisy Grace—"the one dramatic moment of six tiresome hours," according to one report. Photographs of the trial reveal the close quarters shared by all the parties within the rails. Gene and Daisy were only a few feet from one another. Reporters were able to watch closely for any gestures or body language that might indicate the emotions being held below the surface. Even professional eyewitnesses, however, told different stories:

The *Washington Herald*: "All during the day Grace stared

Eugene Grace, sketched in court by P.A. Carter ("How Grace Listens to Testimony in Court," *Atlanta Georgian*, July 31, 1912).

steadily at his wife as though he would hypnotize her and Mrs. Grace returned the stare with a sort of wistful look."[6]

The *New York Tribune*: "Never once, however, did he glance in his wife's direction."[7]

Rallying from nearly fainting when Gene arrived in court, Daisy had otherwise tried to maintain her composure. She read the newspaper during much of the jury selection process. During the testimony she appeared to follow it with interest, occasionally shaking her head or pursing her lips. On one occasion she let loose a loud scoffing laugh, which drew a censorious glance from "the staid judge." The *Constitution* thought that Daisy wanted to appear as unconcerned as possible, but made a "feeble and pathetic effort" at best.

There was a "mild sensation" coming late in the day. Daisy, in a whisper to one of her lawyers loud enough to be overheard, said, "Look at Gene's legs, they're moving." She was not alone in making such an observation. The *Macon Telegraph's* man at the press table thought Gene "raised his right knee nearly eight inches above his pallet." This played into Daisy's long held belief that her husband was "shamming." She had even told one reporter that if she were convicted, she fully expected Gene to get up and walk out of the courtroom. There had been other rumors that Grace had been seen about Newnan in a wheelchair or on crutches.[8]

While he was in Atlanta for the trial, Grace was to spend his evenings at the Piedmont Sanitarium on Capitol Avenue in the Summerhill neighborhood. Later becoming the first location of Piedmont Hospital, the sanitarium offered patients a "comfortable homelike setting." The facility occupied a 15-room stone mansion formerly owned by Charles T. Swift, who made his fortune peddling various nostrums, including "Swift's Syphilitic Specific," which boasted of providing a "certain cure" for that particular ailment.[9] The sanitarium's $50-a-day fee was being picked up by the benevolent Elks. Reporters followed Grace there from the Thrower Building to ask about this notion of shamming. Gene became quite angry and said he would allow any one of them to stick a pin in his legs, if they would like. Dr. Bailey, who was there with him, spoke up and explained that whatever people saw in court was merely a reflex twitching that they had earlier reported. There is no controlled movement in Gene's lower body.

With that, the reporters were ushered out. Mr. Grace needed his rest. It had been a long day. The *Constitution* summed it up: "The fear of death, swift, silent and relentless, clutched at the heart of Eugene H. Grace [Monday] as he lay helpless on a hospital cot in the tobacco-laden court room of the criminal division of the superior court, listening to the sordid details of the crime which he has charged to his wife."

CHAPTER 18

Mother Hill's Ordeal

The newspapers across the country, whose attention had perhaps wandered from the events in an Atlanta bedroom some months ago, were eager to pick up the story again in July. The trial had, at last, begun. The same old mistaken descriptions were brought out: Daisy had been "one of the numerous sirens of the Great White Way of New York," and Gene was still being labeled "the scion of an aristocratic Georgia family."[1] Theirs was the story of a madcap love affair between a wealthy widow and a young man of athletic physique who turned all the women's heads. But now, "The victim of the tragedy has displayed great bitterness against his wife since her arrest and has supplied practically all the evidence in the hands of the prosecution." The trial would be followed with great interest, of course, in Philadelphia. "Mrs. Opie Grace faces jury at last," headlined the *Inquirer*, with an odd choice for their front page photograph, captioned, "Mrs. Grace Fondling a Macaw."[2]

Daisy was again escorted through the crowds into Judge Roan's courtroom shortly before nine on Tuesday morning. Here is the *New York Tribune's* descriptive reportage: "Mrs. Grace wore a black silk dress, a new Parisian 'pompadour pannier' creation. Her head was almost completely hidden from the curious crowd, mostly women, by an expansive Panama hat." The *Georgian* noted her earrings, observing how the "diamonds flashed." She fanned herself vigorously but seemed in unusually good spirits, and "chatted gaily" with her lawyers.

There was to be some delay in getting day two underway. The Newnan train was running late, carrying the day's star witness, Mrs. Sam Hill. And then there was the unfortunate elevator incident. Gene Grace had come over from the Sanitarium with the Elks, who decided on this occasion to forsake the stairs and use the freight elevator. Grace's "cot" was well over six-feet long, and with his escorts, whether from the accumulated weight or the size of the stretcher, the elevator became stuck between the third and fourth floor. It took several anxious minutes to get the lift running again.

During the delay the crowd sat panting and fanning. In the hallway a "little negro boy" was selling fans for a nickel apiece. "Cold dopes," or Cokes, were also for sale. Again, inside the fourth floor courtroom all available space was taken. There was one narrow entrance for spectators, and "those that push hardest" got in each morning. But there was a good deal of turnover; many of the women stayed only briefly. They left with a sense of accomplishment: "Well, I've seen her." In fact, the public turnout was overwhelmingly female. Some women, if the published reports can be believed, had even brought small children with them. Many of the women were "handsomely gowned," and the Atlanta writers noticed several young ladies from prominent "society families." But the writer in the *Georgian* thought they were mostly "just ordinary women who view it as a 'big show' to vary the monotony of their daily lives." They sat there "dull-eyed, chewing gum incessantly."[3]

Once Gene had been extricated from the elevator and brought into the courtroom for the day, Mr. Dorsey called "Mother Hill" to the stand. The

The prosecutor: Fulton County Solicitor General Hugh Dorsey (1871–1948).

"sweet faced old woman" from Newnan exchanged a smile with her son, who raised his head to her as she passed. She told the court that on Tuesday, March 5, she had been waiting on the porch when Daisy arrived from Newnan depot that afternoon. She said Daisy appeared greatly upset at the news of the shooting. Mrs. Hill knew her son had a gun and wondered if it might just have been an accident. Daisy did not think so and suggested that maybe the "negro butler" had done it. Quoting Daisy, she said, "Yesterday, he nearly beat Martha to death and Gene told him if he touched her again, he would wear his cane out on him." Daisy had described J.C. as a "mean Negro." Daisy told her that Gene had been feeling poorly of late and she had given him some Radway's. He had awakened that morning very drowsy and complaining of some numbness in his legs. But Daisy went on to tell her that when she left the house, Gene was sitting up on the side of the bed and planning to make his train for Philadelphia. Mrs. Hill testified that the wire she had received from Atlanta indicated that Gene had been shot through a lung, and Daisy asked her twice, "How is it possible that a man can survive being shot through the lung?" When Daisy was told that the police had to chop through the door, she fretted, "That will cost money." Daisy asked her if she knew whether the police had been in the bathroom because

The lead defense counsel: Judge Luther Z. Rosser (1858–1923).

she was worried about some of her "soiled things" lying about. That evening, when they were all getting ready to leave for the train to Atlanta and the infirmary, Mother Hill recalled that Daisy was insistent that any letters arriving for her should be forwarded to the city.

Dorsey closed by asking if Mrs. Hill knew whether the defendant had packed a black dress for her trip to Newnan. Rosser objected. Dorsey explained the State would show that Daisy had planned to remain in Newnan until Friday. Then, accompanied by Mrs. Hill, the defendant planned to return to Atlanta, where they would be "shocked" to find Eugene Grace dead in the locked room. The black dress was intended to be her "mourning gown." Mrs. Hill testified that Daisy told her she had the black dress with her, but she never actually saw it. Dorsey's hopes for the "mourning dress," if it was intended to show evidence of prior planning, seem dubious. If Daisy was notified in Newnan that her husband had been found dead up in Atlanta, it would have been curious for her to have then been traveling with a "mourning dress." A diabolical woman would hardly have done that. If, on the other hand, as Dorsey was otherwise suggesting, Daisy had planned to walk in upon the body of her dead husband where she had left him, it would have caused no comment had Daisy then found the proper "mourning dress" in her closet. Why carry it with her to Newnan? The black dress seemed to be a red herring.

Mrs. Hill was a comfortable witness. The *Georgian* reported that she spoke in the "soft soothing tones she might have used to comfort the son who lay helpless on a stretcher a few feet from her. [She was] a little woman, pleasant faced and pleasant spoken." Rosser would not be as solicitous as Dorsey. He went at her "hammer and tong," according to the *Washington Times*, focusing on the discrepancies from her earlier statements. She had never mentioned the Radway's before or the numbness, she had never mentioned Daisy's remark about the lungs, she had never said anything about forwarding the mail, nor had she ever mentioned the black dress. This was all new information, according to Rosser. Mrs. Hill explained that in her earlier statements — at Judge Ridley's court in April — she was still too overcome with anguish over her son's condition and could not possibly remember everything that had happened that day. But these were some remarkable new facts, said Rosser. Mrs. Hill was becoming "excited and nervous." Rosser asked whether it was true that Mrs. Grace often brought dresses of many colors to Newnan because she liked to give her old dresses to the Hills. Rosser asked her how many dresses and other articles of clothing Mrs. Grace had given to Mrs. Hill and her daughter. The woman snapped, "I don't know, I'll get you a list." Rosser backed off a bit: "Please don't get impatient. I only want to get at the truth."

The $27,000 in insurance policies, with Daisy as the sole beneficiary, was the stated motive for this plot to murder Gene Grace. Isn't it true, Rosser asked "Mother Hill," that she was, in reality, the moving spirit in Gene's decision to get all this life insurance? Didn't you sit with Gene and Daisy "under a sycamore tree" on the farm and suggest to him that it was a husband's duty? Mrs. Hill recalled telling them "it was a duty they owed to each other. Had I known it would have caused such trouble I wouldn't have breathed a word of it." Rosser produced a letter that Mrs. Hill had written to Gene reminding him of that prudential conversation. He handed her the letter but she did not have her reading glasses. Rosser offered her his. She declined the ocular assistance and merely admitted the letter was hers. The simple fact that Gene initiated the purchase of the policies does not rule out the possibility that Daisy planned to kill him for the proceeds. Nonetheless, Rosser returned to his seat well pleased.

The Hill family was well represented in Tuesday's witness list. Ruth Hill, Mother Hill's sister-in-law, had made a telephone call to Daisy from Atlanta on the afternoon of March 5. She told the jury that, down the phone line, she got the sense that Daisy was more worried about the axe-chopped door than her wounded husband. Preston Hill said he was present at the Marion Hotel on Pryor Street on March 7 when a letter arrived. The letter had been addressed to Mrs. Eugene Grace at 112 Greenville Street in Newnan. The letter had been forwarded to Mother Hill at the Marion, where she was then staying, arriving in Atlanta on March 8. This was the piece of mail that contained the so-called "alibi letters." Although it was clearly addressed to Daisy, Preston Hill said he brought the letter to Gene at the infirmary where the wounded man opened it.

The last witness of the morning was Dr. William S. Goldsmith, for more than two decades an Atlanta physician associated with St. Joseph's Infirmary. The doctor recalled the day of the shooting. Grace had arrived at the hospital in shock, with a pulse rate approaching 120. He was cold and blue, the result of difficulty in breathing. Goldsmith began describing the wound to the jury. Dorsey stopped him and asked if the doctor might like to step over to where Mr. Grace was lying to indicate exactly what had happened. This does not happen in a courtroom every day. There was a loud scraping of furniture; people stood on chairs, on radiators, anything to get a vantage point. The bailiffs, with difficulty, restored order: "Return to your seats and stay seated!" Goldsmith walked the few paces to Grace's cot and was greeted with a cheery "Howdy, doc." Grace raised his shirt to reveal his still scarred chest. Goldsmith pointed to where the bullet had entered Grace's left side and described the path that it took between the sixth and seventh ribs, passing through the lower lobe of the left lung and lodging then in the vertebra. The bullet had narrowly missed Mr. Grace's heart, preventing the wound from being instantly fatal.

Returning to the witness box, Goldsmith was asked by Dorsey what he knew about Radway's Ready Remedy or Dr. King's New Discovery. The doctor knew they were patent medicines. Did they contain opium? Rosser jumped to his feet, but the question was allowed. Goldsmith admitted that he was unaware of the formulae for these mixtures. By way of information, and relying on contemporary sources, Radway's was recommended for everything from female complaints to wind. An analysis had described it as "a watery alcoholic solution of oleoresin of capsicum (cayenne pepper), camphor and ammonia."[4] Dr. King's was a more sinister sounding concoction of morphine and chloroform suggested for consumptives, asthmatics and cough sufferers. A critic called it a "diabolical concoction to give to anyone ... the opium drugs the patient into a deceived cheerfulness."[5] Lastly, there was the paregoric. The drug carried a warning label, but the amount of opium in it was so small that by 1914 it was re-categorized as an "exempt narcotic."[6]

Dorsey moved on to what was a much more vital area of questioning.

Was Dr. Goldsmith present when Mrs. Grace had come to the infirmary the night of the shooting? He was. Did he hear their conversation? He had. Before Dorsey could go any farther, Rosser objected to such hearsay evidence being given to the jury. This vital point had to be argued out. The jury was once again sent to its holding area. Dr. Goldsmith then told Judge Roan his version of what he heard that night, beginning with Daisy's first question: "Gene, what does this mean, telling everybody that I shot you?" To this Gene replied, "You must have, if you didn't, I don't know who did?" Dorsey and Rosser thumbed through their law books, throwing out citations for relevant cases, but Rosser won the argument at that time. Judge Roan reserved his final decision and said Dr. Goldsmith might be recalled to give his evidence.

When court resumed after the hour for lunch, Gene Grace was not there. His doctors said the heat in the room had taken its toll. His temperature had reached 103, and he would have to return to the sanitarium to recoup his strength. Grace was certainly not alone; the afternoon *Journal* thought that anyone who stayed inside that room for no professional reason was "torturing themselves."

The hand-held fans fluttered in slight surprise when prosecutor Dorsey began by re-calling Mrs. Sam Hill to the stand. Dorsey was intent on getting this hospital conversation admitted into evidence. Dorsey wanted to establish the point that no one had accused Daisy of being in any way responsible for the shooting, yet she walked right in to Gene's hospital room and said, first thing, "What are you saying, Gene, to make people think I shot you?" What people was she talking about? Dorsey asked Mrs. Hill if, during the journey from Newnan to Atlanta, there had been any discussion that Daisy might have been involved. There had not. She had been with Daisy all the time. Mrs. Hill's return to the stand meant another session with her "old friend" Rosser and his persistent questions. Mrs. Hill admitted that two police detectives met them at the station. She and her husband had gone to the infirmary in a separate cab from Daisy. "So," Rosser asked, "You misspoke when you said that you were with Mrs. Grace all the time?" Mother Hill's day in court had been a long one.

Morris Prioleau, who was described as "Gene's great friend," actually did ride in the cab with Mrs. Grace from the Terminal to the infirmary. He told the jury that Daisy was quite composed at the time, and he did not think she seemed overly upset. She talked more about the damage to the bedroom door than her husband's condition. Prioleau said he asked her who might have done it, and she suggested, "It could have been J.C. [Ruffin]." Prioleau never suggested to her that he or anyone else thought she might have been involved. He had walked with her from the cab into the infirmary and then to Gene's room. Dorsey asked the young man to tell the jury what Mrs. Grace had said upon meeting her husband. "Hold on here," bellowed Rosser. The jury went out again. Dorsey told Judge Roan, "We expect to show that Mrs. Grace faced her husband and upbraided him for accusing her of the deed when not a living soul had intimated to her that she was suspected or accused of the crime."

That was an interesting evidentiary point. Dorsey's goal was for the jury to hear from a witness who was present at the time that Gene Grace accused his wife of shooting him. Courts will almost never allow a witness to relate the details of an overheard conversation. That is hearsay, and the evidence is inadmissible. Georgia's rules were clear on this point, with the so-called *res gestae* exception.[7] *Res gestae* is the Latin phrase for "things done." Paul Milich, professor of evidence at the Georgia State University School of Law and author of the leading text on Georgia's Rules of Evidence,[8] explains that "a spontaneous statement in a stressful situation can be admitted despite the hearsay rules because the person is not as likely to lie." For example, the person who gets out of a car after an accident and blurts out, "I'm sorry, I wasn't paying attention." Ooops! Dorsey wanted Judge Roan to allow Prioleau to repeat the words he heard that evening in the infirmary. The meeting between Daisy and Gene was obviously a "stressful situation." Daisy had walked in and blurted out words to the effect of "Why are you telling people I shot you?" And Gene answered, "You did." As already made clear, the rules of evidence blocked Dorsey from ever being allowed to put Gene Grace on the stand to accuse his wife. However, the prosecutor could put other witnesses forward who had overheard Grace make that accusation. Judge Roan said he would only allow Prioleau to tell the jury what Daisy said and what Gene said in reply, nothing beyond that.

The jurors trooped back in and heard Prioleau's version of what was said. Prioleau testified that he heard the following:

DAISY: "What are these things they are saying about me?"
GENE: "Daisy, why did you shoot me?"

Like a bad game of "telephone," everyone's memory of that night was slightly different.

It was a victory, of sorts, for the prosecution. Dorsey might certainly have coached Prioleau to "remember" a more damning exchange. Rosser did trip Prioleau up during cross examination. With Rosser's "round little face" stuck close to his, the witness admitted that Daisy had been out of his presence for several minutes before he overheard her exchange with Gene. Prioleau also conceded that there were police everywhere that night, and one of the "final editions" of the afternoon paper, with the story of the shooting on the front page, was even in Mr. Grace's room. Daisy very well might have had the sense she was under suspicion.

Dorsey now turned his attention to the so-called alibi letters. To review, on the day after the shooting an envelope had arrived in Newnan, addressed to Daisy. This envelope, unopened, was then forwarded back to Mother Hill in Atlanta at the Marion Hotel, where the family was staying. Preston Hill then took it upon himself to bring the envelope — again clearly addressed to Daisy — and give it to Gene at the infirmary. There it was opened, and inside were two letters. One of the letters was typed — it was to be identified as Exhibit A. The other was written in pencil and was to be referred to as Exhibit B. The defense was prepared to fight the good fight to keep these letters out of court. Rosser would argue that since these letters came into the court's control from the hands of Eugene Grace, they were tainted and inadmissible. Dorsey had to show there was some reason to suspect Daisy was complicit in the preparation of these two letters.

Harry Ashe was called to the stand. Ashe was the manager of the Atlanta office of the L.S. Smith Typewriter Company in the Y.M.C.A. Building on Pryor Street. The witness told Dorsey that he was an experienced type-writer man and had developed the facility of telling what machine had been used to type a letter. He was "an expert witness." Exhibit A, Ashe testified, had been typed on a Smith Premier No. 2 machine. He was shown another letter, a business communication, known to have been typed by Eugene Grace. Had they been typed on the same machine? Ashe was certain that they had. Handed over to Rosser, Ashe admitted that Smith Premier No. 2 machines were everywhere.[9] The manufacturer was "one of the giants of typewriter history." Beyond that, Rosser loosed a volley of questions as to Ashe's methodology, the lawyer's skepticism imprinting every word. Finally, Rosser pulled a few letters from his pocket. Did Mr. Ashe recognize any of these that might have been typed on a Smith Premier No. 2? Ashe, unfor-tunately, picked a letter that Mr. Rosser said had actually been typed on a Remington 8. No further questions. [Later, contacted by the *Georgian*, poor Mr. Ashe tried to explain that he had come to court without his glasses (I presume magnifying glasses). "I am going to ask the judge to show me the two letters again."[10] He was not to be given a second chance to display his expertise.]

Paul Clement, a manager at the Atlanta Box Company, owned a home at 471 North Boulevard. He told the court that he had let the home to Gene and Daisy Grace in November of 1911, and they had resided there for two months. Clement had owned a typewriter, a Smith Premier No. 2. Did he still own such a machine? He did not. The witness claimed that the typewriter had gone missing. Dorsey then told the court that it was his belief that the typewriter's disappearance was all the handiwork of the defense. Tempers flared, and Judge Roan thought the heat might have been getting to all parties and called for an adjournment.

Several of the jurors groaned (not a medical term). That earlier talk of a two-day trial was going right out the window (perhaps the wrong phrase in the stifling room). One juror suggested a recess and urged that the judge require evening sessions to speed this whole thing along. But Rosser and Dorsey, in their matching wilted collars, came to a rare agreement. Dorsey told the judge, "Your honor, I am physically unable [to continue]." Roan agreed to end business for the day. The courtroom slowly emptied out, all and sundry trudging down the concrete stairwell to seek the relative fresh air of Pryor Street. The jurymen, meanwhile, hatless, coatless and perspiring freely, were escorted off for their dinner and another night on the county at the Kimball House.

In fact, the patience of all had been strained to the limit. The *Journal* called the conditions in the courtroom vile: "The heat was insufferable ... the ventilation was abominable and the fetid smell of the place was practically intolerable to a person of delicate nostrils."

The evening papers were on the streets. The *Georgian's* "final" headlined: "Sensational Letters in Grace Case relied upon to expose plot." In Philadelphia, The *Evening Item* stated, "Thus far it is the general impression that the prosecution has failed to fasten any damaging evidence." The next day the *New York Times* would also conclude that Mrs. Hill's testimony had done Daisy no harm: "It seems that the case against Mrs. Grace is about to collapse." Mother Ulrich thought things were going well: "Just as I thought, no evidence has been produced at the trial of my daughter which would tend, in any way, to substantiate the charge that she shot her husband."

A report on the events of Tuesday's session was sent as far away as New Zealand. In a story dated July 30, albeit not published until September 28, antipodean readers learned that "amid dramatic surroundings ... hundreds of women belonging to the best families in Georgia who shared the public eagerness to attend the trial were unable to secure admission."[11] The number of the residents of Poverty Bay who could find Georgia on a map (and vice versa) cannot be estimated.

During the long day, Daisy had sat in her place at the defense table, fanning herself. Fashion-sensible reporters thought her decision to opt for a shirt-waist ensemble was wise, given the heat. She appeared to take a great interest in the proceedings and was seen to be in close discussions with her legal cohorts. She was regularly and greatly amused by Rosser's formidable manner.

Her husband, meantime, having been removed to the sanitarium in mid-afternoon, was reported in the evening papers to be "in a state of collapse." T.B. Sherman, a writer for the *Georgian*, had been watching Grace during the hours of the long trial:

> If any disturbing thoughts have flashed across his mind ... there has been no reflection upon his face. He lies there as if he was suffering from no more than a petty inconvenience. He doesn't appear to be a wreck. His cheeks are rosy, his eyes are clear ... he might be a man of normal health thrown abed by some trivial disorder. What must he be thinking?

CHAPTER 19

The Alibi Letters

When Daisy Grace entered Judge Roan's courtroom on Wednesday morning, a slight undercurrent of disappointment swept through the crowd, as she had chosen to wear a rather subdued monochromatic outfit. The *New York Times* wrote that "Mrs. Grace was all in brown to-day, even to brown stockings and brown velvet pumps."[1] The *Journal* observer recognized the dress and hat as what she had worn on the night she returned to Atlanta from her late-March dash to Philadelphia. In fact, she had bought the dress at Wanamaker's. In the *Georgian*, the writer thought that seeing Daisy in the same dress twice might have saddened the female onlookers. "However, when she removed her coat in the morning, the women in the audience gave a gasp. A marvel in the shape of a peek-a-boo lace shirtwaist was exposed. The lacework was intricate in its creation." In the end, Daisy did not disappoint. The *Milwaukee Sentinel* reported, "The accused woman is astonishing Atlanta with her costumes."[2]

Her husband was not there, however, to either admire or sneer. Gene Grace was unable to leave the Sanitarium after what his doctors called a "nervous" night. He remained feverish. The question had to be posed: What if Gene died during the trial? Mrs. Grace was being tried for "assault with intent to murder." If Gene died, there would have to be a mistrial and the charge then elevated to homicide. There was also the issue of double jeopardy. The U.S. Supreme Court had only that previous February ruled on a case from the Philippines where a man had been *convicted* of assault and battery and then tried for murder when his victim died a month later. In *Diaz v. the United States*, the high court held that the protection against "double jeopardy" did not apply in that case.[3] Such potential arguments in Daisy's trial were quickly made moot, however, as Dr. Bailey assured everyone that Grace's problem was merely exhaustion. The doctor said Gene just wished to rest and recoup his strength so as to be ready to return to the courtroom if and when his wife testifies.

The third day began with the reappearance of witness Paul Clement, the erstwhile owner of the Smith Premier No. 2. The *Journal* had headlined, "Who has that machine?" Dorsey again established that the typewriter was in the house when the Graces rented the property. When the Graces moved to Eleventh Street, the typewriter remained in the Clement home. But the witness told the court that about ninety days previous, around the first of May, a young attorney named Clarence Bell came to him with a court order for the typewriter. The firm of Bell and Ellis was also located in the Empire Building, a few floors above Rosser's chambers. A messenger then came to their home, and Mrs. Clement turned the machine over and he had not seen it since. Dorsey asked if the court order still existed. It had been destroyed. Dorsey asked Clement if he had been promised that he would not have to appear in court. Rosser was quick to stand, proclaiming, "Your honor, the solicitor is incorrigible."

Dorsey told Judge Roan that the State would show that the typewriter was delivered to somebody, and they would also show the connection proving that that somebody had to be one of the lawyers for the defendant. The obvious intent was to frustrate justice. The typewriter that would tie Daisy Grace to these diabolical alibi letters had been made to disappear. "It is another link in the chain of circumstantial evidence." He considered this to be a matter of great importance, and, if need be, Dorsey vowed to call all the clerks in the offices of Messrs. Rosser, Moore and Branch. Judge Roan said he could not allow him to do that. Dorsey then called Luther Rosser to the stand.

Rosser aggressively took the step up into the witness chair but refused to be sworn in. The *Georgian* described him as being "as brawny as a blacksmith, his great round head thatched by reddish hair which stands out like a porcupine's quills." Dorsey, though a man of forty, seemed boyish in comparison.

DORSEY: Have you the typewriter, a Smith Premier No. 2 taken from the Clement residence subsequent to the shooting of Eugene H. Grace?
ROSSER to the judge: It is your duty not to let me answer this question, even if I should want to.

Judge Roan agreed.

Dorsey asked a few more questions — all of which Rosser refused to answer. "I decline to answer any question concerning the typewriter because it would be a violation of confidence with my client." Rosser was excused. Dorsey's exasperation was plain, but his displeasure might have been better directed at the police or even his own office; the State had been aware of the

"Where was that machine?" A Smith Premier No. 2 typewriter (courtesy Alan Seaver, proprietor of the website www.machinesoflovinggrace.com).

typed alibi letter since March yet failed to secure the typewriter, which had remained in the Clement home for several weeks. From where she sat, Daisy seemed delighted by the legal byplay; she was overheard to declare, "That's another point we've gained."

Dorsey calmed himself and summoned a new typewriter expert into the room. The disconsolate Mr. Ashe had let them down. Charles Beauchamp was manager of Atlanta's Remington office on North Broad Street. He may have sold Remington machines for a living, but he could recognize a Smith Premier No. 2. He was shown Exhibit A, the typed alibi letter, and the other letter known to have been typed by Eugene Grace. Beauchamp swore that both letters were typed on the same Smith Premier No. 2. Having remembered to bring his "glass," Beauchamp was able to explain the similar characteristics of the D, lighter at the bottom than at the top, and the "peculiar nick" in the A. Rosser opted to let this expert testimony go unchallenged.

Dorsey now asked the court to allow him to place in evidence several documents. He presented, without objection, a copy of the Graces' marriage certificate from New Orleans. Dorsey also brought forward the lease for the occupancy of 29 West Eleventh Street, signed by Eugene Grace and Mrs. Kiser on January 9. Rosser objected, telling the judge that neither Mrs. Grace's name nor signature was on the lease. Her husband had negotiated that lease, not her. But Dorsey said the details of the lease would explain why the defendant seemed more concerned about the furnishings and bric-a-brac in that house than her wounded husband. "This woman was so mercenary, that she put extra sheets and an oil cloth on the bed because the mattress was among the furnishings covered in the lease." For one of the few times in the trial up to that point, Daisy reacted to Dorsey's attack; the *Journal* reported that "her lips pursed, she flushed and shook her head." Roan said he would not allow the lease to go into evidence.

It was time at last to fight out the question of the alibi letters. The jury shuffled out of the room. The ensuing dispute would take four hours, not including the luncheon recess. Rosser went through a litany of reasons why the letters should not be admitted. "There is not a scintilla of evidence linking Mrs. Grace to those letters." He spoke for two hours. Returning after lunch, he admitted that he did not have the strength to continue. Rosser took a seat in the rear of the room near the lone open window and allowed his cohort, James Branch, to finish the argument. The points were several:

- The letter was postmarked in Atlanta at 4:30 on March 5. On that date, Daisy Grace had left Atlanta at 2:00, and, as everyone now knows, she was in Newnan at that time.
- Before leaving Newnan, she had only said, "*If* I get mail ... forward it to me."
- The envelope, when it arrived in Newnan, was addressed in Eugene Grace's handwriting. It was intended for her. She never received it. She never saw it.
- That the prosecution now has the letter means someone has violated the criminal laws of our state. In other words, it was stolen and inadmissible.
- Gene Grace had admitted writing the pencil note (Exhibit B). As for Exhibit A, that famous typewriter on North Boulevard was as accessible to Eugene Grace as it was to Daisy. It proves nothing.

Dorsey began his presentation to Judge Roan with a frank admission: Without the letters, the State's case was in some trouble. The letters were vital to the chain of circumstantial evidence. They exposed Daisy's "diabolical" plan to pin her husband's death on some entirely fictitious "Carolina bum." Dorsey insisted to Judge Roan that Daisy had most definitely indicated that she was expecting mail to arrive for her in Newnan. It was not "if" but rather "when" her mail arrived, and she gave very definite instructions that any letter be forwarded to her. As for the postmark at 4:30 P.M., Dorsey suggested the letter could easily have been left in a remote box to establish her alibi.

At about 3:45, Judge Roan, very softly, announced: "Gentlemen, I'm going to let those letters in." It was not an unexpected conclusion to the argument. A judge must give a jury all matters of fact. The judge rules on questions of law. In almost every case a jury will be allowed to decide if a document is forged or not. GSU Law Professor Paul Milich says that unless a judge feels that no *reasonable person* could believe a particular document could be authentic, then the question must go to the jury.[4] Hearing Judge Roan's words, Daisy Grace hung her head briefly in disagreement. Rosser almost left his seat to make a statement but said nothing. In the words of the *Constitution*, "It is the greatest victory yet for the prosecution."

Dorsey read the letters to the jury. He began with Exhibit A. The solicitor noted that it had been typed on stationery embossed with 4246 Spruce Street, Daisy's home in West Philadelphia.

My Dear Wife Daisy — After saying good-by to you at the station to-day, I run into a fellow friend of mine from Charlotte, N.C. He was down and out. My heart went out to him. He was dead broke. It is a pitiful story. He is out of a job. I am going to have him come out to 29 West Eleventh, give him a bath and let him sleep all night with me. In the morning, I will give him a suit of clothes as he is very tall and I think my clothes will fit him if he pulls his suspenders up.

Daisy dear, I am one day late getting away so I am going to be one day late getting back to Atlanta. O, instead of me coming to Newnan, you bring mother along up to Atlanta with you, and I'll send you a telegram when we may meet at the station. I hope you wrote to your mother to tell her I will be in Philadelphia, and to have your satchel ready packed so I won't have to wait for it.

All my love to you and a million kisses from your devoted husband. Gene.

Placing the typed letter on the table before him, Dorsey now picked up Exhibit B, the letter written in pencil:

My Own Darling Wife: After I put you on the train, I got talking to an old boyfriend of mine and got left, which will make me a day late in getting back. I am terribly sorry that this is going to keep me away longer but I shall hurry back dear girl and bring you back something real nice. My friend is here at the house with me now. I've been telling him what a nice sweet girl you are.

I am awfully sorry what I said and everything that happened Sunday, and I know it will not happen again. I hope you are having a fine time in Newnan and that you see lots of people. I shall think of you all of the time that I am away and I shall be as good as I know how. Be a good sweet girl and think of me lots.

With all my love and a billion kisses, Gene.[5]

The reader must remember that Gene had admitted writing the pencil note, saying he did it to please his wife, who was in one of her "teasing" moods. Still, it beggars explanation why he did it. Gene Grace, of course, could not take the stand to be questioned about the pencil note or any other evidence against his wife. Instead, Dorsey called Lewis Hill, Gene's step-uncle, who was put on the stand to identify the envelope and the two enclosures. He had been at the infirmary when the forwarded letter arrived. Hill then sparred with Rosser in a heated discussion about the handwriting used to address the envelope. The witness would only say that the handwriting on the envelope might have been Gene's. Rosser was insistent: "Isn't it true that you know that is Mr. Grace's handwriting?" For a change, it was Dorsey's turn to object, and the leading question was ruled out of order.

The final witness for the prosecution was Detective George Bullard. He was one of the policemen who met Mrs. Grace at the Terminal the night she returned from Newnan. At no time did he give her any reason to think she was under suspicion. At the infirmary he walked with her to Grace's room. Dorsey asked him to tell the jury what Mrs. Grace said. Judge Roan agreed to allow Bullard to answer the question — but only to repeat Mrs. Grace's first words. The detective recalled that Mrs. Grace walked in and said, "How did this happen, Gene? What have you been telling these people? They tell me you say I shot you?" Dorsey wanted to know if she kissed her husband. Bullard said she did not; she stood straight up beside the bed. She showed no emotion. With that the State rested.

No doubt to the continuing disappointment of the weary jurymen, Judge Roan said he thought it best to allow the defense to begin fresh in the morning. Both sides were weary and nearly breathless after a day spent mainly arguing with each other, with the jurors idling in an anteroom. The day — stormy and with temperatures reaching near 90 — had made the courtroom even more noticeably humid. Everyone (but the jurors) could return to their homes.

In the end, it had been a better day for the prosecution. The Associated Press flashed word that "the state played its big cards today and won." The *Constitution* marveled at Dorsey's patient development of the case against Mrs. Grace, "like a spider weaves its silken thread about the captive fly." That evening Hugh Dorsey's supporters held a rally on Marietta Street in the Fifth Ward to boost his candidacy for election to a full term as solicitor. Weary from the ordeal of the continuing trial, the candidate did not attend. Nonetheless, "Each mention of Mr. Dorsey's splendid handling of the Grace case elicited applause."[6]

As Daisy left the courtroom, she remained buoyant. Trailed by reporters, she stopped to say the defense would not need three days to prove her innocence. "It doesn't take long for the truth to be told."

CHAPTER 20

A Grocer Calls

The previous day's storm had brought a slight break in the heat as August arrived. The mercury would only just pass 80 on Thursday afternoon. The conditions in the Thrower Building were muggy, nonetheless, and, if anything, doubly disagreeable: warm and sticky. But nothing could keep people away from what was sure to be a memorable day. The word was that Daisy Grace herself would be in the witness box. The chairs were all taken long before any of the participants entered the fourth floor room.

The *Constitution* had hit the streets that morning with a scoop. The defense planned to "lay out the last sordid chapter of [this] unholy romance." The paper claimed that the defense would reveal what had led to the "dramatic denouement" in the mysterious house at 29 West Eleventh Street.

Daisy was in her position promptly. She had chosen to array herself in the same dress she wore on Tuesday. It was a shirtwaist suit of Parisian pompadour silk with a pannier. The latter is defined as "an adjunct of female dress intended to distend the drapery of the skirt at the hips." The style was "signally favored" in the magazines of the period.[1] It allowed a lady, should she choose, to engage in the now lost art of "flouncing."

Judge Roan looked about for Mr. Grace and asked if the gentleman was expected for the day. The word was that Gene had rallied somewhat but would not be present until the afternoon session. The judge then nodded to attorney James Branch to open the case for the defense. Branch, who it will be recalled, had chaperoned Daisy on her trip to Philadelphia, had also been dog-sitting Nig at his home on Twelfth Street. He acknowledged that the jurymen were now in their fourth day away from their families and employment. He assured them that the defense would be brief because "every fiber of the State's case is rotten." The solicitor's claim that he had established an unbreakable chain of circumstantial evidence was "utterly untrue and wholly ridiculous." Dorsey interrupted, objecting to the harsh language. Judge Roan directed the solicitor to take his seat, he had had his turn. The judge did instruct the jury that they should understand that Mr. Branch's remarks were not evidence.

So much for being brief— Branch spoke for more than an hour. He said that Mrs. Grace had found herself married to a "lazy and worthless man." He bled her fortune down to almost nothing. He had a "mania for society," and he needed all of Daisy's money to play that role. When she resisted giving him more of her money, they fought and he beat her. Dorsey popped up and down to object, but Branch was allowed his say. "Beyond merely destroying the State's case, Mrs. Grace is insistent that the jury know what really happened on March 5, 1912. We are going to show the whole miserable facts." Branch said that on that morning there had been one last argument over money. He grabbed a gun to threaten her, they struggled, it went off, and Mr. Grace was shot in the side. Everything that followed that day, Branch said, was done at Grace's specific instructions. Mr. Grace was obsessed with keeping the affair a secret. "[Gene Grace] said he would be disgraced if the world knew that he had been shot in a 'n****r row' with his wife."

The wire service reporters left to send out the word of "an entirely new and startling turn to the trial." For the first time, Daisy Grace was admitting that she was there when her husband was shot. The *Journal's* early edition that afternoon was headlined "Springing a new defense for the first time."

The defense witness list was short; the first four spent only a few minutes each in the box. However, by calling even just one witness, the defense gave up the right to go last in the closing argument to the jury.[2] In an emotional case such as this one, the defense had opted to surrender a significant advantage.

The first man called was M.O. Jackson, chief assistant to the general manager for Southern Bell in Atlanta. Some years before, prior to Mr. Jackson's now exalted position, Gene Grace had worked for him. He knew the man's handwriting and swore that the envelope and the pencil letter were certainly written by Gene. Dorsey made quick work of the witness. Jackson admitted that Grace had not worked for him in seven years. They had not stayed in touch — no letters, etc. "And yet you swear you are still certain you know his hand? No more questions."

Scott Todd of the Hillyer Trust Company on Peachtree was shown the check for $2,000 that had been found on the bedroom mantel. It had been cancelled on March fifth, and the handwriting was Mr. Grace's. When Judge Roan accepted the check in evidence over Dorsey's objections, there was a burst of applause in the courtroom. The judge said that that sort of behavior would not be tolerated and the bailiffs would remove anyone who disrupts the proceedings.

Dr. Chunn, a pharmacist at Jacob's Drugs, the well-known Atlanta chain, testified that Gene Grace came into the Whitehall Street store complaining of a cold and purchased a small bottle of Dr. King's New Discovery. That was on Monday, March fourth.

J.P. Sturgeon was one of Atlanta's leading realtors, with offices in the Empire Building. He had been the witness on March 2 when Daisy had signed the Power of Attorney giving her husband the authority to go to Philadelphia and dispose of her property, including the house at 4246 Spruce Street. J.W. Moore then submitted the document as evidence; Dorsey did not object, adding wryly, "I am delighted." Moore snapped, "Then why didn't you present it?!" The power of attorney was on a single piece of paper that appeared "crumpled and shows signs of having been pulled at."

The next witness was a gentleman whose name had never appeared in the thousands of words of news copy written on the case since March fifth. Charles Meckel was the proprietor of Meckel's Meats and Groceries at 493 Peachtree, near Linden Street. He was 55 and born in Germany but had been an Atlanta resident and U.S. citizen for many years. Charles Meckel told the court that he had reason to call the Grace residence that morning in March to discuss their bill. He called at ten, and a man answered the phone. A ripple of whispers went around the courtroom. There was only one phone in the house. It was in the bedroom. Gene Grace must have been the man who answered the phone. Dorsey immediately objected to this new evidence, and the jury had to be sent out.

The grocer's call, if true, undermined the State's contention that Eugene Grace had been shot hours before that time while he slept in a drugged stupor. The shooting, the prosecution had insisted, must have occurred before the servants came into the house, as neither J.C. nor Martha Ruffin had ever claimed to have heard a shot. This would have put the shooting at some time earlier than seven in the morning. With the jury absent, Meckel admitted that he did not know the voice of Eugene Grace; he had had no business with him. But the witness stated that the man who answered the phone that day handed the receiver to a woman. Meckel, who said he spoke regularly with Mrs. Grace, was confident that she was the woman he heard on the phone that day. Dorsey angrily complained that this eleventh hour surprise witness was entirely out of line. The reader will recall that Rosser had refused to provide his list of witnesses when the trial began. But Judge Roan said the defense could continue; if it could be shown that Grace was able to hold a business conversation at 10:00—a normal conversation free from excitement—then it was important evidence. The jury was instructed to return.

Meckel told the reseated jurymen that he did not know Eugene Grace nor recognize his voice, but Mrs. Grace was a regular customer with whom he had spoken many times. After dialing Ivy 469 that morning, Meckel identified himself to the man who answered the telephone, who then gave the receiver to Mrs. Grace. He heard the male voice say, "Here's a man who wants his money." Meckel said he and Daisy then discussed the Graces' outstanding bill. She asked him to send over an itemized account, but if it was not there by noon she would have to wait to deal with it when she returned to Atlanta on Friday. Meckel was all right with that and agreed to wait until then. The witness told the jury that there was nothing unusual about the call, and neither person on the other end of the phone appeared in any way excited, upset or in pain.

It was obvious that Meckel's evidence had caught the prosecution off guard. This was a witness who appeared set to take a serious bolt-cutter to Dorsey's circumstantial chain. Dorsey demanded to know why only now the grocer had decided to come forward with this story of a phone call. Meckel said he was the type of fellow who kept to himself, and he preferred to mind his own business. When he read about the shooting, however, Meckel said it struck him as unusual because he had called the Grace home at around ten and everything seemed fine. The witness insisted that his telephone call was made on March fifth; he had not mistaken the day. He couldn't say how many business calls he made that morning, but he had made several. Yet he remembered this one so clearly? Dorsey wondered why Meckel, if he was so struck by this bit of information, had not brought it to the police. The man said he had not gone to the police but, rather, mentioned it to a friend who then put him in touch with Mrs. Grace's defense team. Who was this friend? Meckel said the man was just an acquaintance. The solicitor was incredulous. In the last four months Meckel had only told the defense about this singular call. Dorsey made it plain: "Now, isn't it a fact that you did not hear the voice of a man on that morning?" Meckel "flashed angrily" and almost shouted, "I said I heard a man's voice and I meant it." Rosser joined in the fray, bellowing, "The solicitor keeps dogging on the witness." Judge Roan blocked the question. Meckel was excused and allowed to return to his accounts. If he was to be believed, he had given important new evidence that a man's voice, in no pain or confusion, had been heard on the Grace phone some hours after the time that Grace was supposed to have been shot. The *Georgian* said a lot in only a few words: "This is an important fact."

E.E. Lawrence, Gene Grace's erstwhile business partner, was summoned and wove his way through the cluster of principals to take the stand for the defense. Lawrence must have appeared with some reluctance, as he and Daisy had been involved in separate litigation over the future of the Grace-Lawrence Building Company — Daisy was trying to get as much of her $6,000 out of that business as she could.[3] On the stand, Lawrence said he too had called the Grace home that Tuesday morning at something around 10:30. He had called to tell Gene that he had just received a check for $500. On that morning Daisy had answered the phone, and he did not speak with his partner. Mr. Grace generally did the banking for the firm, and Lawrence suggested that Daisy send Gene round to get the check and deposit it before leaving for Philadelphia. Again Lawrence was quite clear that he did not speak to or hear the voice of Gene Grace.

Moore asked that the bailiffs bring in the next witness, Mrs. Rebecca Sams. Mrs. Sams entered the courtroom with "a quick step." The earlier rumors that she might have been "the other woman" had been very quickly debunked. She was about 45 years old and a mulatto woman with "very bright and sharp features." The *Journal's* observer thought "she could pass for a white woman." Mrs. Sams lived on Fort Street in the Fourth Ward with her husband who was a cabman. She was a dressmaker "with many patrons among the better class of whites." On the night of March fourth, the eve of the shooting, she had come to the Graces' home to finish work on some dresses that Daisy wanted to have ready for her trip to Newnan. Mrs. Sams recalled that she came in the back way, the servant's way, and through the kitchen. Martha Ruffin was cooking waffles. The witness said she saw that Martha's arm "was tied up" as if she had been injured. She did not question her about it, as she did not want to embarrass Martha. Rebecca then went upstairs to work on a pink evening dress that Daisy had planned to wear to a Newnan party. Moore asked her if she had ever made a black dress for Mrs. Grace. Mrs. Sams stated that she had, in fact, made Daisy a black dress of messaline silk. The men on the jury might not have known that messaline was a fabric most often used at the time in the making of petticoats. Mrs. Sams said the black dress was never designed for mourning attire, as it was cut low about the neck and shoulders. Such black dresses are a "fad out there"— meaning in Newnan— and Mrs. Grace wanted to have the dress with her. The witness said that she stayed behind at West Eleventh Street with her needles while the Graces went out to the theater. She had worked on the pink dress until ten that night but could not finish the job.

On the morning of the shooting, Rebecca was working at the home of another client, Mrs. Luther Williford, on Ivy Street. She had mentioned to that lady in conversation that Mr. Grace was going to Philadelphia that day. Mrs. Williford asked if Rebecca would call over there to see if Mr. Gene might bring back some chiffon from Wanamaker's. As everyone knows, the chiffon was better and cheaper in Philadelphia. Mrs. Sams placed the call a little after nine A.M., and Mrs. Grace answered. Daisy said to her, "You boogie, you didn't finish my dress!" According to the *Journal*, it was "You booger," and that seems more likely. Atlanta's Joel Chandler Harris (Uncle Remus) had been regaling Southern folk (and terrifying their children) for years with tales of the "boogerman."[4] The musical phrase "Boogie-woogie" did not come into widespread usage until a few years later. Regardless of whether it was Booger or Boogie, Mrs. Sams told Daisy that, if she wished, she would come out to West Eleventh Street later that day to finish the pink dress. When she mentioned to Daisy that Mrs. Williford wanted some chiffon from Philadelphia, she heard Daisy speaking to her husband. Daisy returned to the phone and said Gene would be glad to get the chiffon, and Mrs. Williford could pay for it when he returned. That was the extent of the phone call. Again, this was a third morning call made after the hour that the prosecution claimed that Gene had been shot.

Mrs. Sams was a uniquely helpful witness for Mrs. Grace. She seems to have been in all the right places at all the right times. Would you believe that she also turned up at the infirmary on the night of the shooting? She had been working at Mrs. Williford's when the woman's husband called in the late afternoon with the news of this shocking crime. Luther Williford was a bookkeeper at the *Atlanta Journal* on Forsyth Street. He said that the reporters were all saying that Daisy might have had something to do with it. Rebecca then scurried directly over to St. Joseph's, and she was there when Daisy arrived from Newnan. She testified that Mrs. Grace seemed very upset. Daisy's first words to her were "How's Gene?" Mrs. Sams said she did not know. But Mrs. Sams remembered saying to Daisy, "I am sure you are innocent." If this was true, this was the first evidence establishing that Daisy knew she was under suspicion *before* entering Gene's room at the infirmary.

Mrs. Rebecca Sams had been another solid witness for the defense. Dorsey had to go on the attack. He approached the witness and, placing one foot on the raised stand, leaned in toward her quite closely, as if inspecting her face. His first question was blunt: "Are you a negro?" Mrs. Sams answered affirmatively. Dorsey wanted the jury to understand that this seamstress was very much in Daisy's debt. Rebecca freely admitted that Mrs. Grace had always been especially kind to her. She was given a meal whenever she came to work at West Eleventh Street. Would you consider her to be your friend? Mrs. Sams said yes, she would. Dorsey was intrigued. "She called you booger over the phone, what other endearing terms did she use?" And then Dorsey asked her, "Did you ever call her 'Daisy of the Leopard Skin?'" Rosser demanded that the judge stop this line of questioning: "Mr. Dorsey represents the state and he really should be reprimanded." Dorsey turned to Judge Roan to explain that he was only trying to get at the unusual relationship between these two women of different races and classes. He wished to suggest to the jury that Mrs. Sams was a paid agent for the defense. The judge allowed him to continue.

As mentioned, Mrs. Sams did seem to get around. She admitted to Dorsey that she had also gone down to Newnan and made a call at Greenville Street to pay her respects to Mr. Gene. She insisted that it was not a special trip, as she had a sick relative at the time in Newnan. She certainly had not gone there to spy on Mr. Gene. Rebecca had also known Martha Ruffin very well. Dorsey questioned her vigorously. "Didn't you, Mrs. Sams, beg Martha Ruffin three times not to swear against Mrs. Grace? Didn't you tell her that Mrs. Grace had several houses and plenty of money and would take care of you? Didn't you ask Martha Ruffin to swear that the oilcloth was on the bed?" "Most emphatically no," was Rebecca's reply to each question. Although Rebecca did admit she once told Martha to go see Mr. Moore (Daisy's attorney), she explained that she did that only because Martha wanted to visit Daisy in jail. Dorsey quite directly asked her, "Are you being paid for this?" Again she replied, "Most emphatically, no. I am too honest in my poor heart to take a cent." The busy seamstress also acknowledged she had had a conversation with Mr. Prioleau. She had known him since he was a child. "I told him he was making it look strong that [Daisy] was guilty," and he was doing wrong to align himself with the prosecution.

Before releasing the witness, Dorsey asked her if Mrs. Grace had ever complained to her about being mistreated in any way by Mr. Grace. She had not. Had she ever mentioned money problems, abuse, or anything of that sort? She had not. In fact, Dorsey insisted to the witness, Daisy had always told you that Mr. Grace was good and kind to her, did she not? The defense objected, but the witness had already answered, "Yes, sir." He repeated the question, emphasizing the word *always*. Again Mrs. Sams answered yes.

When Dorsey had finished with Mrs. Sams, Moore stepped forward to ask her to name the many women in Atlanta for whom she worked as a dressmaker. Dorsey objected, and Moore said he merely wished to show that Mrs. Sams had no especial relationship with Daisy Grace. She had done work for several prominent white women in Atlanta, who also gave her meals and treated her kindly. Moore also informed the court that "Booger" is not a term of endearment.[5] On that important point of clarification, the court adjourned for lunch. Mrs. Grace would take the stand in the afternoon.

Among the spectators, almost no one departed. The *Journal* observed that the crowd, again made up overwhelmingly of women, "spent the time laughing, joking and munching on sandwiches, not wishing to lose their seats for the afternoon session." Anyone who left lost their seat immediately.

During the interval the Elks brought Eugene Grace back into the room. A day and a half of recuperation in the sanitarium had allowed the man to regain the strength he needed to return to the simmering courtroom. Amid respectful silence, the Elks gently placed Gene's cot almost directly in front of the witness stand. If Daisy was going to sit in that chair, she would be unable to avoid her wounded husband's gaze. The United Press report suggested that the prosecution made certain that Grace was installed in exactly that spot. The State is "banking on the pitiful spectacle of the half-paralyzed man breaking the composure of the defendant."

Before Mrs. Grace could be called, however, the defense presented, in rapid succession, a few more witnesses.

Sylvester Kenny was a black servant who was employed in the Peachtree Street home of Judge J.K. Hines. The morning of the shooting he had gone to 29 West Eleventh Street on an errand. He heard a piano being played. When he knocked, the piano playing stopped, and Mrs. Grace opened the door. It was about 10:30.

Nurse Louise Wilson had been caring for Mrs. Grace since mid–March. At that time she noticed a bruise on Daisy's right leg, above the knee. It was greenish-yellow in color, indicating an "old hurt," according to the nurse.

Dr. S.H. Green, the doctor at the Tower, told the court that he was called to attend Mrs. Grace on March eighth. She could hardly talk. It was then reported in the papers to be tonsillitis. But the doctor testified it was beyond hoarseness. She had bruises on her throat. There was also a deep bruise on each arm above the elbows and bruising on the forearms above each wrist.

Three more doctors followed, all claiming to be experts on gunshot wounds and paralysis. They agreed in turn that Grace's paralysis would not have been immediate unless the spinal cord had been severed.

An usher at the Atlanta Theatre on Exchange Place testified that on one evening that previous February, during a performance of the musical-comedy *The Pink Lady*, a blonde woman came to him in the lobby to ask if Mr. Grace was in the house. He told the woman that Mr. *and Mrs.* Grace were inside. He agreed, however, to go and ask the gentleman to come out. Mrs. Grace followed some minutes later and there was an argument in the lobby but Judge Roan would not allow the usher to discuss that overheard conversation. The blonde woman was not identified.

Lastly, Daisy's mother was called. Dorsey objected on grounds that Mrs. Ulrich had been in court all day Monday; witnesses were not supposed to do that. Judge Roan decided to allow her to testify. Mother Ulrich offered the information that Daisy always used an oilcloth on her bed.

The next witness was to be Mrs. Daisy Ulrich Opie Grace.

CHAPTER 21

"Gentlemen, I am innocent"

It was 2:35 on that Thursday afternoon, August 1, 1912, when Daisy Grace took her place in the witness chair, having adjusted her flouncy pannier skirt. A courtroom sketch shows that, despite the heat, she was wearing her hat *and* gloves. There was a brief kerfuffle over Daisy's security man, Captain Burke, who had moved his chair — inadvertently, of course — into the exact position where it would interfere with Gene Grace's view of his wife on the stand and vice versa. The captain was directed to shift his chair to one side. With his sincere apologies, Captain Burke slid over to his left.

There would be no Bible presented to Daisy Grace, and she would not have to swear to tell the truth, the whole truth and nothing but. In 1912 in the state of Georgia — and in most every other state that followed the common law — no criminal defendant was allowed to swear to tell the truth. It was presumed that a defendant would lie. Of course he would say he did not do it. What is a perjury charge to a guilty person? The jury was instructed to listen to the statement with an open mind. The Georgia statute read:

> In all criminal trials in this State, the prisoner shall have the right to make to the court and jury such statement in the case as he or she may deem proper in his or her defense, said statement is *not to be under oath*, and to have such force only as the jury may think right to give it. The prisoner shall not be compelled to answer any questions on cross-examination, should he or she think proper to decline to answer such questions.[1]

The unsworn statement provision was even then under review by the Georgia courts. *The Georgian*, in an editorial published October 11, 1911, called it an "absurdity.... The defendant, if he chooses to testify, should be treated in all respects as any other witness." Georgia did not change its code for another fifty years. In 1961, Supreme Court Justice William Brennan would write: "The State of Georgia is the only State — indeed, apparently the only jurisdiction in the common-law world — to retain the common-law rule that a person charged with a criminal offense is incompetent to testify under oath in his own behalf at his trial." In *Ferguson v. Georgia*, the high court struck it down.[2] And not so much because these unsworn statements hurt the prosecution, but rather because so many defendants botched their opportunity so badly and their attorneys could do nothing but look on in horror.

But that looks ahead to 1961. This was 1912, and Daisy Grace was not likely to be one of those defendants. J.W. Moore told the press at the lunch break that "Mrs. Grace will make her own statement, just as she pleases, she can talk as long as she pleases and can stop when she pleases."

In a voice described as "clear but low" she began. "Gentlemen, I am innocent. I did not shoot my husband and he knows it." The eyewitness accounts all agreed that Daisy paused after these opening words and "looked directly into the eyes of her husband." He lay no more than twelve feet away from her. They held each other's gaze for several seconds. She then turned back to the jury seated to her right and continued. Her statement, in its entirety, follows, uninterrupted as she gave it[3]:

Gentlemen, I am innocent. I did not shoot my husband and he knows it. As God is my judge, it is the solemn truth. Mr. Grace and I took an oath over the Bible that we would never tell how this trouble happened, and not until I was indicted did I even tell my attorneys. Week after week I lay suffering in jail trying to decide upon the right thing to do. I knew I was innocent and knew that I was being unjustly punished, but I also knew that I had taken an oath never to tell how Mr. Grace was shot. Finally, I decided I owed it to the name of my old mother and my little blind boy that, regardless of an oath, I had to tell the whole truth about this difficulty no matter whom it might disgrace.

In order that you may be able to decide whether I am telling you the truth about the shooting, it is necessary for me to tell you some things about our lives before the shooting. To me Mr. Grace was the most fascinating man I had ever met, and without shame and without strength to resist it, I have made for him every sacrifice in this world that a woman could make for a man. From the time I met him until the fifth of last March, I gave him $15,000 in cash. I was as true to him as any wife could be to her husband, and I always have petted him like a spoiled child. I dressed him in the height of fashion; I cooked his meals for him when my servants could not please him, and I ceased to correspond with my widowed mother and sister in order to please him. I took his abuse and beatings time after time because of my devotion to him.

Our first serious quarrel took place in Philadelphia while we were living in the Esmond Apartments [12th and Spruce]. We had been entertaining some of his friends and after they had left I complained to him about bringing men to the apartment and drinking to excess. This infuriated him and he slapped me repeatedly and threw me across the bed. On another occasion, while we were living in these apartments, we were riding in my automobile, with Mr. Grace driving. He drove so fast that I became alarmed. I was afraid that he would injure someone and asked that he reduce speed. This made him very angry and he tried to push me out of the car. As usual, I made up with him. On another occasion in Philadelphia, Mr. Grace asked me for a sum of money which I thought was too much and told him so. He then threatened to pawn a diamond ring and scarf pin that he wore (they were gifts from my first husband). I finally compromised by signing a check which he drew for me.

Mr. Grace had been employed by Fitkin and Co. for about a month at a salary of $25 a week, but one day he came to me and said we had to go to Hot Springs, explaining that he was obliged to go there for an old chronic trouble, and I once again complied with his wishes. He told me that he had explained to Fitkin and Co. that he was going there to meet his ailing stepfather. He handed in his resignation and wrote to his mother that he was going there on a business trip. He told friends in Philadelphia that we were going to Europe. We left Philadelphia on April 9 and traveled via Buffalo, St. Louis and Memphis. We stayed in Hot Springs long enough for Mr. Grace to take a course of baths which are 21. From Hot Springs we went to New Orleans. We were in the elevator at the Grunewald Hotel and we met a man he introduced as an old Tech school chum. This was about 8 pm. Mr. Grace excused himself and said he would be back in a short while, but he did not return until 1 am and his breath was heavy with liquor. After a quarrel in which he slapped me, he finally admitted he had been to the Tenderloin. [Storyville, the red light district] Shortly after this we went to Mobile but stayed only one day, as I did not like it. We then moved on to Atlanta and registered at the Piedmont Hotel. One night, while dining at the Piedmont with Mr. Prioleau, the old sweetheart called. My husband took the call and then boasted about her. He said she had called to congratulate him on his marriage. He said he would have nothing more to do with this woman, and I don't believe he did until I gave him the money to get into business in Atlanta. After he got into business, my husband began to abuse me and treat me cruelly, and seemed to be very indifferent.

A day or so later we went to Newnan where I met his family. Mrs. Hill received me at her home in a tender motherly manner as only a good woman can. I was very much impressed with her, and we became good friends. My husband had led me to believe that his parents were very wealthy, but before we reached Newnan he admitted he had misrepresented their condition and they were in very moderate circumstances. This deceit on his part made no difference to me, in fact their condition only served to draw me closer to them. I wanted to do anything in my power to help them, and if this trouble had not come up I would never have mentioned to any living soul that I had been of financial assistance to them, but as matters now stand I think I should state for my benefit as well as your own that I loaned Mr. Hill $500 on his note and made many presents to other members of the family which runs into hundreds of dollars. I was very much impressed by the hospitality I received at Newnan, but my husband would not permit me to be entertained and after two weeks there we went on to Savannah.

At Savannah we stayed at the Desoto. My husband said he didn't want to go back to Philadelphia without my having an engagement ring, and he told me to buy one for myself. We went to a jewelry store and purchased one for $1475; in payment, I wrote a draft on my account at the Girard Trust. We remained in Savannah one week and then went to New York by steamer. We stayed at the

Plaza Hotel for two days. Then we returned to Philadelphia and stopped at the Bellevue Stratford for two weeks. Then back to New York where we stayed at the Hotel Astor. Then we took passage on the *Florizel* for Newfoundland. We purchased our tickets at the Red Cross line office. My husband said something might happen on the trip, and if I should die or get killed then he would be left penniless, and if I loved him as I said I did I should make a will in his favor. If I died without a will, he would have a hard time getting the money. Mr. McClealand—whom he described as a friend and attorney—drew up the will. Two strangers were called in as witnesses and I signed as directed.

Once on the *Florizel*, one night about 8:30 my husband came to me and suggested that we take a promenade on the deck. We went to the stern of the ship when he suddenly picked me up and sat me on the railing and pretended to frighten me by pushing me backward. He became so persistent in his efforts that I was much alarmed, and I clung to his neck and threatened to scream. When we got to our cabin I accused him of trying to push me overboard, and I demanded that he return to me the will I had signed before leaving New York. He told me that he had only been playing with me, but I was satisfied that he intended to drown me.

At St. John we took a buggy to drive around the city and look down over the famous fisheries.[4] We walked along the cobbled path, along a cliff. He became exasperated with me for picking up pretty little rocks to bring home. While I was bent down near the edge, he pushed me. I stood up and he pushed me down. I scraped my knee. I can show you the scar. He begged me not to tell anyone. He was always anxious that I tell no one of his meanness. This time, however, I was in a white suit and the blood on my knee had badly discolored my gown. He bought a magazine and ordered me to hold it over the bloodstain.

Then we went back to Philadelphia, once again to the Bellevue Stratford but soon to Spruce Street. On July 3rd—his mother and kin came for a visit. I had given him $200 for their expenses. He deposited that in his account and sent his family $100 or $125. They stayed two weeks, including a trip to Atlantic City. My husband had his pistol with him and shot quail along the way, which was upsetting to all of us. We stayed at the Haddon Hall hotel [North Carolina and Boardwalk] and I paid all the expenses. Before they left Philadelphia, my husband asked that I make his mother a nice present and I purchased her a $250 diamond pendant which she was very proud of. I often heard Mrs. Hill mention to my husband that he was too mean and cross to his wife. We had talked of all going to Europe but Mrs. Hill was too afraid of the water so we abandoned the plan and the Hills returned to Georgia.

Mr. Grace still wanted to go to Europe, and when I declined he became very angry. His language was so bad in front of my child I told him the boy would have to be sent away—he sent the boy out on the porch and became more furious than ever. He took his pistol out of his chiffonier [tall chest of drawers] and told me he would put an end to it all. I snatched the pistol out of his hand and ran upstairs. On my flight I threw the pistol among some pillows in a bay window. When he found I had disposed of the pistol he took his knife out of his pocket and I grabbed his hand, and in the struggle he stabbed me in the face which has left a scar as you can see for yourselves.

That September we went to Niagara Falls, Toronto, Montreal and New York for ten days. When we returned to Philadelphia, I suggested it was time he looked for some way to earn a living. His mother had said the same thing. Instead of going to work, he suggested selling the house on Spruce Street; I flatly refused and we argued. He hit me repeatedly, slapping me and striking me in the nose with my first husband's ring. I fell back against the wall with blood streaming down my face. I started to cry. He grabbed me and pleaded with me not to make a fuss. He said he would call a doctor and explain that some bric-a-brac had fallen off a shelf. Dr. Codman wanted to put a stitch in my nose but I refused and he used an adhesive plaster. I was compelled to remain indoors for many days owing to the discoloration of my face and eyes.

We decided to lease the house on Spruce Street and went to Atlantic City at the Hotel Strand [Pennsylvania and Boardwalk] where we had another violent argument over his finding employment. He threw me across the bed and held his revolver to my head and said he would kill me if I didn't stop haranguing him about going to work. I began screaming, he pleaded with me to stop. I ran from the room and went downstairs to the writing room. I wrote my mother saying Mr. Grace had threatened to kill me and I could stand it no longer and was coming home. I told him what I had done. I had given the letter to a hotel clerk, and Mr. Grace retrieved it, read it and tore it up. I said we were going back to Philadelphia immediately. We went back by train; I went to my mother's house, he went to the Colonnade. After a day, we reunited and went to the St. James. We went to New York where he thought he might try to work for Fitkin again. While there, we met a Mr. Slicer who suggested my husband should go to Atlanta and by putting up the money he could set up business with Mr. Lawrence, a practical and successful building man. Mr. Grace agreed, saying that in New York he would be a little fish in a big pond but in Atlanta he would be a king among men. I went back to my mother while he went to Atlanta to make the arrangements with Lawrence. He sent word that all he needed was $6,000 which I sent him. I came to Atlanta and we took lodging on Boulevard and the Grace-Lawrence Company opened an office in the Empire Building. We lived on the Boulevard, until January 15th when we moved to 29 West 11th Street, and it was at this address our present trouble took place.

In Atlanta, it became evident that my husband was neglecting me. He would stay out late, and if I said anything we would have another big quarrel. There would be phone calls, sometimes several a day, from a woman asking for Mr. Grace. I would ask her why she called but she would never say. I demanded to know who she was and she laughed and hung up. When I asked Mr. Grace about it he would get angry. He mocked me: "Sure all the ladies are calling me up. They are all crazy about me." He said what if I found out he had met a lady for lunch. I said as long as it was a lady it wouldn't be too bad, as long as he wasn't neglecting his business and spending lavishly. He went into a rage, cursed and beat me and warned me never to interfere with his lady friends.

A short time later, at the Atlanta Theatre,[5] an usher told my husband that a party outside wished to see him. He went and remained ten minutes. When I returned and asked him who it was, he became angry. Finally, he said it was a man who wanted to talk some business. I did not think he was telling the truth.

When the play was over, I sought out the usher and asked him. My husband tried to silence the man but before he could the usher said it was a lady. He described her as a handsome brunette about my height and stylishly dressed. Of course, we quarreled off and on about this for several days, and I threatened to go to Newnan and tell his mother. She was my only confidential friend in Georgia, and I knew she would scold her son, as she had many times before.

My husband said the business was not doing well — he became clamorous for money. He prevailed upon me to sign a Power of Attorney so he could go to Philadelphia and sell the Spruce Street property or dispose of my remaining stocks and bonds. It was against my wishes and my mother's. The house had been left for my use but the property was intended to be for my son. On March 2, he prevailed upon me to sign the Power of Attorney. He said the house must be sold so he would have the money to make a showing in Atlanta. He needed to join clubs and run in society and that cost money.

For several weeks, he had been talking about how I should go to Newnan while he went to Philadelphia. He was insistent upon my leaving on Tuesday. On Monday, I begged him to let me stay another day as my dress had not been finished. At first I did not suspect why he was so anxious for me to go to Newnan on that particular day, but I finally began to suspect that he was either planning to take a woman to Philadelphia with him or that perhaps he intended to get me out of town and have her come to our home and carry on his disgraceful conduct; and I believed it was either the woman who called him out of the theatre or the one whose picture he was carrying in his watch when I first met him and whom he had confessed that he had ruined and had taken from Atlanta to Philadelphia and had lived with her and at one time was very much in love with him. This is the same woman who telephoned him at the Piedmont when we were having dinner there.

On Monday the fourth he complained of a severe cold. He said he might not be ready for the next day's 11:00 train. But nevertheless, I must be ready to go the next day. I asked for more time for my dress but he refused, so Rebecca came that night. She stayed until ten.

On Tuesday, March fifth, he woke claiming he felt ill and said he might have to delay his trip. I had the fire lit and I carried up his breakfast with such little things as he wanted. He said he would probably be able to get the 11:00 train. He suggested I leave early, do some shopping on Whitehall Street, have lunch at the station and then get my train to Newnan. About 9:00, Rebecca called and relayed a request from Mrs. Williford. She wanted Mr. Grace to bring back some chiffon from Wanamaker's. My husband said yes but she would have to send the money. I told him to pay for it. He agreed to do that.

I told Mr. Grace that he needed to dress if he wanted to make the 11:00 train. He told me to just hurry up and get going and don't be telling him what to do. I saw he was in ill humor and decided to be quiet. Martha came up at 10 to help me buckle. At 10:00, Meckel called. Gene told me, "Here's a man who wants some money, you'd better talk to him." Gene had decided he would take the later train. He suggested that I go downtown and shop and then he would meet me at the station for lunch at 12:30. I suggested if he was not feeling well; why don't we both put the trip off until tomorrow and I can have my dress finished.

He told me to do as I was told. I was determined not to go. His manner was very suspicious. I made up my mind that he was trying to get me out of Atlanta so he could take a woman with him to Philadelphia or worse still. I thought he had no intention of getting the 11:00 train.

Mr. Lawrence called the house about 11:00 and said some money had come in and things were looking up. He wanted my husband to come to the office and get the money and put it in the bank. Lawrence thought that the business' financial affairs were looking better. I said to Mr. Grace, "I am so glad things are looking better," and asked him if he could not wait awhile before selling my home. At this suggestion he raised his voice very loudly, cursing and abusing me, and told me if I did not hurry up and get out of the house and do as he had told me to do he would break my damned infernal neck, at the same time looking as though he intended to make good that threat. It was plain that he would allow nothing to change his plan of getting me off to Newnan on the 2 o'clock train, and his actions so aroused my suspicions that I was convinced there was a woman at the bottom of his strange manner, and I decided that I would not permit him to send me off while he went away on a pleasure trip with some other woman on my money and sell my home and probably spend a great portion of the proceeds on the woman and on his own dissipation. And I told him as much.

As I said this Mr. Grace was still lying on the bed, grunting and rubbing his stomach. His coat was hanging just behind where he was lying. As he spoke, I walked to the coat and took out the Power of Attorney along with other papers. It was my intention to throw the Power of Attorney into the fire. He jumped from the bed and he grabbed me by each wrist and bent me over a bureau twisting my wrist so violently that I dropped the papers. Then he let go of that hand and grabbed my throat with his right and he reached in a small drawer in the bureau and took out his revolver. He was cursing in a low, hushed voice, and his face was so distorted with rage that I was badly scared, and when he made a motion to hit me with the pistol and then tried to shoot me, I threw all my weight and strength against him, grabbed him around the arms, backed him over the bed, and as soon as his legs came in contact with the bed he fell over backward, with me on top of him, and I was pushing, pulling and shoving and doing all in my power to keep him from hitting me with the pistol or shooting me, when suddenly the pistol went off and I screamed and jumped up. At first I thought I was shot, and then, when I did not feel that I was, I threw my arms around his neck and said: "Oh, Gene, what have you done? Are you hurt?" He said it was only a scratch. "No, I am not hurt, but for God's sake don't make so much noise or you will have the whole neighborhood in here. I have only a scratch; it doesn't amount to a damn, and all I want you to do is hush and get ready and get out of here.... It's damn lucky that one of us didn't get badly hurt or killed, and if I was not so stuck on that infernal piece of property in Philadelphia it would never have happened."

[She dressed as fast as possible.] I did everything that he wanted me to do and kept on begging him to let me call a doctor so we would both know how much he was hurt. "To hell with a doctor, pick up those papers as I told you and call a cab." I suggested that he might be hurt worse than he thought he was, and I told him he could tell the doctor that he was handling his pistol and dropped it and it went off and shot him, and he said if I had any sense I would not make any such damn fool suggestions and that he had as much experience with wounds as most doctors and could tell as well as any of them when he was hurt. He then told me the thing for me to do and to do quick was to go out of the house and leave the rest to him, and he said if this damn thing should get out in a neighborhood like this we would never be able to live it down and all his business and social prospects would be gone forever. He told me to go to Newnan at once. He told me to take the pistol away in a hand satchel and when I got to Newnan to hide it. He told me to lock the door so the servants would not know that he was in there; he said he would remain there until dark, and then he would go out and see a doctor and go out at the other door. I judged from the way my husband talked that his wound must certainly be only slight and that probably his plans were all for the best, and I know that he did not think the wound at all serious. When I picked up the phone book — he told me to call the Cox Cab Co. and ask for Charlie Sams,[6] but he was not available and I got cab 133. All this time he was continually giving me instructions. He told me to take the keys with me, as I would get back from Newnan before he would arrive from Philadelphia. The fact is, gentlemen, he told me to do so many things and hurried me so that I cannot remember all his instructions. This I do know. I tried as honestly as any human being can to carry out his instructions just as he gave them, although I was very much excited and frightened of him. I always tried to obey Mr. Grace in all things, and if I disobeyed any of his instructions in this affair that I can recall it was when I placed the pistol on the window sill in the hallway. I had put it in my handbag as he told me to do, but when I got downstairs I found I could not close the bag, as it was too full. I kissed him good-bye and he made me kiss the bible that was lying on the table and swear I would never tell what happened.

As soon as I got out of the house and in the cab I decided I would call a doctor as soon as I got to the Terminal station and have him go to the house and see Mr. Grace. I had made up my mind that I would not go away unless I knew he was all right, and as soon as I got to the station I went to a 'phone, and it occurred to me that perhaps I had better call up Mr. Grace first before I called a doctor. He would be angry if I sent a doctor out to the house against his orders. But when I got to the station I could not get our number. I tried again and it was busy. I presumed if he was on the phone he was all right. I had no friends. I could go to no one for advice. In fact, the only friend I knew in Georgia was Mother Hill at Newnan, so I decided I would follow out Gene's instructions and go to Newnan and call Eugene from there, and if I could get no word from him I would tell Mrs. Hill about it, and bring her back to Atlanta with me, but before I got to the house it was reported that Mr. Grace had been shot. So I then decided I had better keep my promise and do as Mr. Grace had told me to do — say nothing about it to anyone.

Gentlemen I have told you the truth of this most unfortunate affair and God above me is my judge. I never shot Mr. Grace. I loved him far too much to injure him. All I did was struggle with him and try to prevent him from beating or killing me.

At the hospital, I begged Mr. Grace to tell the truth, but from his manner I could see he didn't want to. So I remained silent. I asked him in the presence of all if I had shot him, and he replied that I had not and said that he took back all that he had said about my having done so.

I wanted to tell the detectives the story, but Mother Hill, Mr. Sam Hill and Preston Hill, who were with me all, insisted to the chief that I knew nothing of the affair. Mrs. Hill was very indignant with the chief because he seemed to think that I did, and they had some pretty sharp words. They all assured me that they believed in my innocence, and they all urged that I find an attorney. Mr. Preston Hill said that attorney John W. Moore would come in the morning to take charge of my case. He urged me not to say a word to the police until then. I am satisfied now that if I had been less devoted to Mr. Grace and thought more of my own interests that the chief of detectives would not even have detained me at the police station.

I hope I have made my statement so that you can understand it, as I have told you the truth and tried not to forget anything that you should know.

Daisy's statement, running more than 8,000 words, took a full hour to deliver. She did not read from a script but spoke her own words. Her voice was "steady throughout." Her face displayed the proper emotions, be it surprise, horror, or shock. When she described the bedroom struggle, she accompanied her words with gestures that were as "perfect as a consummate actress."

As she spoke, the 200 people in the room were completely still. The atmosphere may have been just as stifling as always, but the *Philadelphia Evening Item* reported that all "discomfort was forgotten in the eagerness of the public to press within hearing distance of the witness box." Several of the jurors were hunched forward in their seats to observe and listen. At the finish, Daisy sat there for some moments, as if not knowing what to do next. Finally, she stood up, smoothed her dress and returned to her seat at the defense table. No one spoke in the room for over a minute.

The silence was interrupted finally by Gene Grace's harsh whisper: "It's all a damned lie." Grace had followed Daisy's statement intently but without any outbursts or evidences of emotion. His head was supported by a bolster to allow him to watch it all from his "pallet." It appeared to observers that Grace had weakened as the trial dragged on. The cheerfulness of his Monday arrival had left him. It had been an effort to return to the Thrower Building, and he seemed quite pale and weak that afternoon. During Daisy's statement, Gene's Negro nurse held one of his hands. With the other, Gene fidgeted with his blankets or wiped the sweat from his face.

When Daisy finally moved to return to her seat, Dorsey was on his feet; he tried to begin swearing in Eugene Grace as a witness. "Mr. Grace, hold up your right hand." Everyone stood up to see, as did a furious Rosser, who bellowed, "Hold on, Mr. Dorsey. You can't do that. Judge, it's a trick of the prosecution. It's not fair to say this before the jury." The place was in turmoil. "For a moment pandemonium reigned," no doubt, in part, simply in release of the tension-filled hour of silence. Judge Roan hammered for order. It took several minutes. Grace lay quietly on his cot, for the first time that day displaying a "playful smile." The jury was forced to leave while the lawyers squabbled anew for half an hour. In the end Roan said he appreciated the skill of the solicitor's argument, but "he wants me to change the law and reverse our state Court of Appeals. I can't do it." Gene Grace could not speak.

Dorsey was given permission to call three quick rebuttal witnesses: J.C. Ruffin, his wife Martha, and "pretty Miss Ida Daniel," a nurse from Newnan. All three testified about the alleged witness-tampering machinations of Rebecca Sams. With that, the case was closed. Judge Roan told the jury that, following final arguments from counsel for each side, he expected the case would be placed in their hands by the following afternoon.

Daisy's statement, all the papers seemed in agreement, had made a "profound impression." No one could remember a performance anything like it in an Atlanta trial. It was the general consensus that she had won herself an acquittal. The *Constitution* thought the case for the prosecution "will now require all the logic and reasoning" of Hugh Dorsey to win a conviction. Yet a few points can be made in regard to this singular narrative. Again, she was not under oath. Not a word of it was necessarily true. Was it really possible that she was willing to spend most of four months in jail for a shooting that she could have explained away that first evening as the accidental result of a squalid domestic quarrel? Daisy failed to explain why, if the shooting had been an accident, she felt the need to try to throw suspicion on J.C. Ruffin. In her desire to carry out all of Gene's instructions after the shooting, did she ever stop to think how this doctor she was "going to call" would have been able to get into the house? She had locked the doors and, supposedly per Gene's instructions, taken all the keys with her to Newnan. The doctor — like the police when they arrived — would have been locked out. Nor did Daisy make any mention of, or offer any explanation for, the mysterious "alibi letters."

The only query raised about Daisy's monologue was whether perhaps that she seemed *too* composed. The *New York Tribune* thought it had been "well-rehearsed."[7] The *New York Times* reported that the statement had been "pruned, amended and polished" over a two-month period. It did not go unnoticed that the *Journal's* afternoon edition was on the streets with the full text of her statement while she was still giving it. The boldface text covered most of the front and back pages of the paper. The *Georgian* thought the statement had been the winning throw and congratulated the unknown author: "No playwright ever worked more painstakingly" to please an audience. The *Georgian* imagined Daisy, while staying out at Kimballville farm, spending her time rehearsing her star turn while "speaking only to the birds and rabbits."

Meanwhile, Gene Grace, sensing the outcome, did not want to be around for the last act to unfold. He gathered his belongings from the sanitarium, and the Elks again took him back to Newnan that night. In the now familiar A&WP baggage car, Grace admitted to "bitter disappointment" that he had not been given the chance to tell his story. "What I could have told the jury if I had been allowed to testify, I am going to tell the public at the conclusion of the trial." On the train, everyone was reading about Daisy's statement in the afternoon news accounts of the trial—"even in the negro coach." Gene seemed in good spirits, even pointing out Judge Roan's house as the train chuntered through Fairburn. Grace joked with a sympathetic conductor, "There are only three real towns in the United States, and they're all on the same line—New York, New Orleans and Newnan." Sam Hill's wagon was there once again, waiting at the depot. With Gene's cot laid carefully in the back, the wagon "creaked up the hill slowly but steadily, the horses jerking their heads gaily in the cool night air."

CHAPTER 22

Inhuman Creature or Persecuted Woman

It had been a stressful week for all. The heat was exhausting. Still, this was Atlanta in August, which was known to hold the "choicest heat." Ninety-eight degrees was the city's official record set on an August day in 1900. No records were broken during the trial. Of course, the Weather Bureau's thermometer was on the pinnacle of the Empire Building, and the temperature on the streets below was always a few degrees warmer. Daisy that Friday morning appeared drawn and tired. The *Washington Times* described her as "wan and haggard with dark circles under the eyes." The conditions in the courtroom were one thing; her fear of the prison farm if convicted may have been more responsible for the strain plainly written on her face. She seemed to have aged ten years since Monday. She leaned heavily on the arm of the ever-present nurse Wilson. Daisy told a supporter, "I am very, very tired and so uncomfortably warm." For the occasion she had selected a blue satin suit with a white waist of Irish linen and a billowy tie secured at the throat by a horseshoe diamond brooch. She wore blue satin pumps with blue silk stockings. She was wearing the large Panama hat that she had worn every day, having used it deftly to shield the emotions on her face from the intruding eyes of the press and spectators.

Long before the judge had entered the room, the public seats had all been taken. The early birds had been roosting since six. Some interlopers even had to be removed from the press table. It promised to be a spectacle. The lawyers were among the giants of the Atlanta bar, and forensic fireworks were certain. The General Assembly was then in session a few blocks away at the state capitol; so many legislators had been sneaking off to attend the trial, they had been told that further absences would not be tolerated. But again this day the public chairs were filled overwhelmingly by women.

146

Because the defense had chosen to call witnesses, they had, as mentioned, lost the privilege of speaking last to the jury. Judge Roan had decided to allow each side two-and-a-half hours for their closing statements. Mr. Dorsey opted to use one hour of the State's time to speak before the defense, holding in reserve the last 90 minutes to make his case before the jury. For reasons of narrative clarity, the arguments will be summarized in order: the defense, followed by the State.

Given the courtroom conditions and the emotions at play, the defense team decided to share the workload. John Moore would take the first ninety minutes, and the more vehement Rosser would be left to handle the last hour. Moore began by savaging Dorsey's "so-called" chain of circumstantial evidence. "It is pure rot and nothing but rot and they know it." Patent medicines cannot be used to drug anyone. The claim that she had tampered with the phone was based on no more than a crumpled nightcap found on the floor near the phone. The police thought so little of this piece of evidence that they had lost said nightcap. Moore asserted that everything was normal that morning at 29 West Eleventh Street. The mysterious note left for the Ruffins was no mystery at all; Daisy left notes for her servants every day. Martha Ruffin had come upstairs twice at Daisy's request and had been in and out of the room. Would any reasonable woman have called a servant into the room not once but twice, with her wounded husband in his bed?

At ten o'clock, several hours after he was supposedly shot, Mr. Grace answered the phone when Meckel called. While that call had established that Gene Grace was awake and able to hold a conversation, Moore declared that it was not Meckel's phone call that changed things that morning. It was the call from Mr. Lawrence. At last, some money was starting to come in to the Grace-Lawrence partnership, and perhaps it would not be necessary to sell Daisy's Spruce Street home after all. A home she had wished to pass on to her little blind son. Retrieving from the defense table the tattered power of attorney, Moore declared it to be the most powerful evidence supporting Mrs. Grace's testimony of the events that led to this unfortunate accidental shooting. "In a Christian country," Moore continued, the State had shamefully tried to keep the document from the jury. He held it out for them now. Did it not look like the crumpled piece of paper had been something that had been fought over? Had the jurors not been told of the bruises to Mrs. Grace's wrists, arms and throat? In her own words, Daisy had told the jury exactly what happened. They fought over this power of attorney; it was a terrifying struggle in which her husband brandished a gun. Mrs. Grace's testimony had been all true, from start to finish, in her own words and bravely delivered:

Here, in our fair Southland ... this poor persecuted woman, in a land of strangers, was made the object of a theatrical attempt to force a breakdown while she was making her simple statement. [Looking at Dorsey] You thought when you brought Eugene Grace in here that you would make her break down; but your theatrical plot failed miserably.

Moore thanked the jurors for their attention and said he knew they were eager to go home to their families. So, too, he said, is Mrs. Grace. Standing beside Mother Ulrich, Moore finished with: "Will you let this old and broken mother lead her blind grandson over the red hills of Georgia in search of the prison home of their daughter and mother?" Several jurors had tears in their eyes. For the first time, Daisy Grace cried. The *Journal* called Moore's speech "oratorically effective and impressive."

If Moore's job was to bring tears, Rosser rose to entertain. His portion of the closing argument for the defense would rely less on oratory and more on personality. He mimicked solicitor Dorsey, strutting about like a rooster. He mocked Dorsey's way of pronouncing Day-sey with an "S" rather than Day-zey with a "Z" that everyone else seemed to prefer. The entire case, Rosser sneered, was based on "Mr. Dorsey's suspicions," and they were no more than that. He scoffed at the idea that Gene Grace had been drugged with paregoric. That stuff was for "tummy aches." The police had never suggested any drugs were involved, and, in Rosser's words, "a policeman's mind is as full of suspicion as a n****r's head is full of lice."

Rosser had also been left the task of dealing with the "alibi letters." He insisted that Daisy could not type, and the prosecution had never produced a single piece of paper to prove otherwise. He had embarrassed Dorsey's supposed typewriter expert as a failure. As for the penciled note, Rosser said he was sure that the jurymen would see for themselves that it was in Grace's handwriting. The motive for writing these letters was obvious. Gene Grace was a scheming womanizer who had hoped to clear the way for yet another clandestine meeting. Rosser asked that the jury read the letters closely: "I can smell the male sex in every line. There is not a feminine touch in their four pages."

In the end, this case was about money, Rosser concluded. Mrs. Grace was supposedly the mercenary party. Really? Rosser ticked off the ways she had managed to expend something like $20,000 on her husband and his family. She even bought her own engagement ring in Savannah. She had loaned money to Mr. Hill. She had paid for Gene's stepsister to attend Shorter College; when Daisy stopped paying, Nannie Sue had to withdraw. Daisy had laid out almost her last $6,000 to set Gene up in his business. But it was never enough for him. Now he wanted to join clubs and buy motorcars. To do that he wanted to sell what was really Daisy's last asset, the home on Spruce Street in Philadelphia. It was that home that Daisy hoped to save for her blind son. Yet she agreed to sign a power of attorney. Why? Rosser asked the jury to understand that Daisy was fascinated by Gene Grace, who possessed the "charm of a serpent." Even the life insurance, the supposed motive for this crime, was actually Gene Grace's idea — he felt that the bigger the policy, the more important the man. Rosser concluded:

> This is the trouble with Grace. How pitiful is vanity? He has the society germ, the most dangerous germ on earth. Why I'd rather have the cholera germ, the diphtheria germ, or the typhoid germ. They would rob me only of my health. While the society germ takes your manhood away. With women it is different. God put a butterfly in a woman and she can't get out of it. They can't help wanting to rule their little world and usually they do. But, gentlemen, the man who has the society germ must be watched. No woman since the days of Adam has ever killed a man who fascinated her.

At his conclusion, Rosser pleaded exhaustion and begged Judge Roan to permit him to leave the courtroom to seek some clean air. He apologized to Mr. Dorsey that, regrettably, he would not have the pleasure of remaining to hear his closing remarks.

Before considering the State's case, one has to wonder why Dorsey had not been more insistent on having Gene Grace remain in Atlanta to be present in the courtroom for the final arguments. The man was clearly suffering from the ordeal, but every effort could have been made to have him remain for one more day. The supine figure of the victim, lying there pathetically on a cot in a corner, his legs occasionally twitching, would have been a most sympathetic figure for the prosecution. His presence would certainly have clashed visually with all the defense talk of "male sex" and serpents. But Gene Grace was that day resting in his country bedroom on Greenville Street.

The prosecution's side was opened by Lamar Hill. Holding the Smith and Wesson .32 in his hand, Lamar Hill stepped to the front of the jury box. He acknowledged that much had been said to besmirch the name and character of Eugene Grace. That was none of their business. Mr. Grace's conduct was not on trial. Further, "the only attack on his character has come from the lips of a woman who crept up on him like a serpent and there, in her bed, placed this revolver to his side and sent a bullet of death into him." There was only one question that the jury had to answer: "Was it the finger of *that* woman that pressed the trigger on *this* gun and did she intend to kill Gene Grace?"

Hers was a mercenary plan, diabolically carried out, Hill stated. She was so well prepared that she had placed an oilcloth (and here Hill held that famous article aloft) on the bed so that her husband's spilling blood would not cost her the price of a new mattress! How could she place the gun to where she thought she was firing a bullet into his heart? She had outright asked him, "Where is a man's heart?" How did she get him to lie in just the right place on the bed? She had drugged him. Hill, looking squarely at the defendant, continued: "The figure of Lucretia Borgia, the most fiendish murderess of all time, comes marching down from history, but in this twentieth century there has come one to take her place, and it is the woman in this case." But Hill recalled that even the infamous Borgia made sure her victims were dead. "The crime is bad enough, but God save us from a woman who will bar the doors of the house and leave that man shot helpless and dying and go deliberately to the woman who bore that man into the world and keep her lips sealed of the horrible truth. Inhuman creature!" Here, to be sure, the physical presence of Gene Grace in the room would have been of some assistance to the entire presentation.

Nevertheless, Hill's attacks scored, at least at the defense table. While the prosecutor was linking her name with Borgia, "the great steel-gray eyes of Mrs. Daisy Grace flashed fire, her bosom lifted and fell with emotion, and her hands twitched nervously," according to the *Constitution*. When Hill sat down, Daisy turned to nurse Wilson and confidentially dismissed it all as "such rot."

It would be a test for Dorsey to continue this assault, as he had come in to court that Friday morning feeling quite poorly. During the defense speeches he had sat sullenly, with head in hand. When he rose to speak at last, his voice was raspy at best. He blamed the wretched conditions that he and everyone associated with the case had suffered through, now for a fifth day. He would have to speak softly.

Carrying a copy of the *Georgia Code*, Dorsey urged the jurymen to understand that circumstantial evidence is a powerful force. Reading from a bookmarked page, Dorsey translated the legal verbiage for the panel: "In the absence of direct evidence, jurors must look seriously at the circumstantial."[1] He hoped that they would not let "trivial objections" interfere with their decision making. Do not fall victim to this fascinating woman, he pleaded. "Do not be swayed by any Jennie worship. Do not sacrifice your oaths on the altar of emotionalism but go down in history as twelve men who measured up to the responsibility placed on them by the great state of Georgia." He then slammed the law book down with a loud crack, which startled the room.

The solicitor said he resented the almost personal nature of the attacks on his conduct of the case by the defense. "It is not my intention to persecute anyone," he growled. To the jury, he conceded, "I have no sympathy for Mr. Grace and the life he has lived." There had been "something rotten" about the relationship between Gene Grace and Daisy Opie, but the two of them had eventually married. He brought her home to his family in Georgia. This was the too-often-familiar story of a man who fell into the clutches of an evil woman. Curiously, Dorsey sought to illustrate his argument by quoting, for the first but not the last time, from the poetry of Rudyard Kipling. He read to the jury *The Vampire*:

> A fool there was and he made his prayer
> Even as you and I!
> To a rag and a bone and a hank of hair
> We called her the woman who did not care,
> But the fool he called her his lady fair
> Even as you and I![2]

How that elucidated matters for the jury is unknown.

Dorsey reminded the jury that the defendant's story, though very well delivered, was not given under oath. The things she said and events she recalled could not be verified or challenged. Frankly, much of it, Dorsey stated, was unbelievable. She tried to make "a lover's act to lift her onto the rail of a ship" into an act of attempted murder. Who really knows how she got those scars? She claims she spent thousands of dollars on her husband — but where are the checks? She claims there were other women, but where was the evidence? The defense was not able to introduce a single name or any evidence that Grace had ever spent one night or one dollar on another woman. "Gentlemen, I want better proof than the words of this woman."

Dorsey also made an interesting pitch for support from an all-white Southern jury. Throughout this entire case it is plain that very little sympathy had been shown to or expressed about any of the numerous "colored people" who had become involved. The N-word had been jarringly used numerous times in a court of law, and it appeared un-asterisked in the public prints.[3] But Dorsey asked that the jurymen spare a moment of concern for the figure of J.C. Ruffin who had appeared before them:

> Would any Southern woman, any woman with a righteous feeling, no matter what she has promised her husband, have failed to speak out when she knew that Ruffin, an innocent Negro, was likely to be accused of the crime? It was she who had accused him. She planned to send a poor Negro to the gallows for a murder she committed. If Grace had died, she would have sent him to the gallows.... Then she would have returned to revel in her forbidden pleasures in Philadelphia.

But, Dorsey went on, Mrs. Grace had not relied solely on casting this ugly accusation at a poor Negro. She had also created these two mysterious alibi letters. Dorsey assured the jurymen that Eugene Grace had absolutely no motivation to write the letters. If the jury cared to believe that the pencil note had been written by Gene, then they should understand that she "seduced this trusting boy to sign his own death warrant." He again referred to the missing typewriter and placed the blame for its disappearance on the defense.

Dorsey read the two notes again. He declared the pencil note to be free of any grammatical errors. The typed letter, however, contained several errors. Dorsey read from that letter: "After saying good-by to you at the station to-day, *I run into a fellow.*" Dorsey reminded the jurors that Gene Grace was a college man and knew his grammar. "It is no sin to be ungrammatical, but in this case it fastens upon Mrs. Grace this black crime." [Begging Mr. Dorsey's pardon, if anyone reads Gene's early letters to Daisy, he didn't quite have the grammar thing locked down. Of course, those letters were not in evidence.] The alibi letters, Dorsey continued, were intended by Mrs. Grace to plant the suspicion on a phantom "Carolina bum." Dorsey paused to read the letter silently to himself. Looking back up at the jury, he asked the jury to think about the innocent closing instructions contained in that letter. He reminded them that Daisy was planning to return to Atlanta that Friday. The writer of the letter had concluded, "Bring mother back with you." Dorsey could not imagine anything more despicable. It was Daisy Grace's wish that "the mother of this handsome beautiful son return with her and fall prostrate over the maggots and flies on his cankering body." Mr. Rosser may have told the jury the letters had no female sachet about them, but Dorsey told the jurymen, "What they do have is the stink of a wildcat."

Dorsey ended with another baffling Kiplingian foray. Let it be understood that he was within his rights to quote poetry. The Georgia courts will permit an attorney, from either side, "to read brief extracts of literary or historical matter to illustrate and make effective a discussion of the fact."[4] The efficacy of such readings in this case seems a stretch. In the solicitor's defense, however, the English poet was then at the height of his fame. It was not uncommon, even in Atlanta, for a hostess to plan a "Kipling evening" where guests would recite from memory "The Road to Mandalay" or "Danny Deever" out of the poet's book of barrack ballads.[5] Dorsey was a fan to be sure. He knew that a jury of Southern gentlemen might not be able to comprehend how any woman could be so evil. But he could remind them that "when women are bad, men know nothing comparable." And to back up this gender-based conclusion, Dorsey opened his well-thumbed book to Kipling's, "The Female of the Species":

> And Man knows it! Knows, moreover, that the Woman that God gave him
> Must command but may not govern — shall enthrall but not enslave him.
> And She knows, because She warns him, and Her instincts never fail,
> That the Female of Her Species is more deadly than the Male.[6]

The solicitor had spoken for ninety minutes. His voice at times broke under the strain. Amid oppressive heat, the only sound in the room other than the solicitor was the beating of a hundred fans. The *Journal* called it "a brilliant summation." Through it all, Daisy Grace sat with a look the *Georgian* described as "dull tired care."

The case for the defense of Daisy Grace had come down to self-defense. She had acted in reasonable fear for her life. Self-defense is not an unlimited right; the defense must be proportionate to the threat. You don't shoot someone who shakes a fist in your face. In her statement, Daisy had detailed numerous previous incidents of violence. She said Gene had brandished a gun before. She claimed that on the morning of March 5 it was again Gene who reached for the gun. She reasonably feared he would use it, and they struggled. The State then attacked that argument with the evidence of prior intent, the events pre-dating the shooting, down to the morning of March 5. The "diabolical plot" would show that this was no *crime passionelle*; Mrs. Grace had carefully crafted her murderous plan.

It was up to the jury—did they accept the circumstantial evidence to prove that Daisy Grace had the deliberate intent to kill her husband? After four-and-a-half wearying days, Judge Roan's instructions were brief and free from poetry. He reiterated the point that Mrs. Grace had every legal right to give her statement in her own words. She could not be sworn. The jury can only take it for what it is worth. They might well ask why, if she could speak, Mr. Grace was not allowed to have his say as well. But Roan declared that the laws of the state of Georgia were clear on the subject. And so it must be. Mr. Grace could not testify against his wife. The judge concluded with the customary caution that the jurors must be certain *beyond all reasonable doubt* before casting a guilty verdict. "If you believe there was an altercation and the pistol went off accidentally—then I charge you to give this defendant a verdict of acquittal." If they determined that she was guilty of intending to murder Mr. Grace but they nonetheless wished to make some recommendation for mercy, he would be willing to hear that appeal, but the exact term of the sentence would be entirely his decision in the end. It was now 2:30, the final arguments had continued through the usual lunch recess. The judge would allow the jurors a lunch break before they would begin their deliberations.

Getting an all-white male jury to send a white woman into the Georgia prison system was always going to be a tall task. In 1903 a white woman named Mamie De Cris, the "Diamond Queen" from Savannah, was sent to Milledgeville for stealing jewelry. While at the prison she was horse-whipped by guards for "putting on airs."[7] When word leaked out, the story prompted outrage across the country.[8] "Georgia will stand disgraced," declared the *Amer-*

icus Times Recorder, "until that inhuman beating of a defenseless white woman is blotted out."[9] The De Cris whipping and the 1908 exposure of the "barbarous" abuses of the convict-lease system forced reform.[10] The state had created a new prison farm near Milledgeville. It was meant to be self-sustaining, indeed profitable. Crops were planted to feed the inmates; cotton was grown to clothe them. If found guilty, Daisy would be sent to the farm and there assigned "such labor as is best suited to her sex and strength." There were separate white and Negro barracks in Milledgeville, and the races were to be kept apart "as much as is practicable." The male breakdown was something near 60–40 black to white; fewer than ten percent of the women were white. The female prisoners were housed separately. Of the incarcerated females, 78 percent had the "mental level of a 12-year-old or less." Juries of white men were simply reluctant to send a middle or upper class white woman "to the farm." The *Georgian*, in an editorial written December 18, 1911, after another acquittal, declared, "It is a common saying that a woman, if she is young and pretty, cannot be punished for any crime."

The jurymen were left alone at 3:30. The presumption was that the jury might need a night to sleep on it, but at 4:40 Judge Roan was informed that a verdict had been reached.

CHAPTER 23

"We, the jury"

When the jury had first left to begin its deliberations, it was thought that the process might be a lengthy one. The various trial principals scattered to seek a respite. Solicitor Dorsey had gone back home in a state of near collapse. His assistant, Thomas Goodwin, would be deputized to represent the office at the finale of the "great shooting trial." Daisy Grace had gone to ground back at the Peters Building in the offices of attorneys Moore and Branch. But those spectators who held a prized seat in the steaming courtroom had no choice but to remain. With the end now in sight, they could not risk surrendering their position.

Upon hearing the news that a verdict had been reached, Daisy all but "raced" back to the Thrower Building. When she re-entered the courtroom she looked "white as a sheet," described the *Journal* reporter. At the defense table she sat down in a heap, and her Panama hat seemed to have been arrayed even lower to shield any show of emotion. Nervously, "her fingers beat the table like little strokes from a trip-hammer." Nurse Wilson, presumably with one of those ready hypodermics, was at her side. Meantime, what the *Constitution* called "the morbid sweltering crowd" kibitzed among themselves while waiting for the jury's return.

Judge Roan entered the room first. From his bench he immediately warned all those present that when the verdict was read no outbursts would be tolerated, and anyone indulging in such would face arrest. He asked the deputies to summon the jury. The twelve men entered from the door nearest Judge Roan and, in a single file, passed before the defense table, but Daisy seemed not to look for any inkling of her fate. The jury foreman was William Laird, the sales manager at the Swift Fertilizer Works in northwest Atlanta. He was a son of the late police commissioner.

All were seated and the courtroom hushed. Roan spoke next, "Mr. Laird, has the jury reached a verdict?" The foreman stood and replied that they had. He was asked to read it. "We, the jury, find the defendant not guilty."

An over-excited bailiff began rapping for order before any sound had been made. Then it began — what the *Constitution* called a "peculiar sound like the muffled steam valve on an engine." The *Journal* heard "one hysterical scream in which the falsetto voices of the women congregated there predominated." The *Georgian* simply reported the room erupted in applause and cheers. Even the barking commands of Sheriff Mangum shouting "Keep order!" were unavailing.

All eyes were on the acquitted woman. The *Constitution* wrote that a "startled cry fell from her quivering lips." The *Georgian* saw that "color returned to her face, her breasts heaved and she gave a small cry." Lips, breasts ... Daisy's powers of fascination had not waned. After hearing the two words that set her free, she seemed to be bordering on collapse, trembling from head to foot. Mother Ulrich was sobbing. It took several minutes to restore something approaching order. Judge Roan thanked the jurymen for their service and their patience. He praised the lawyers for both sides for the quality of their arguments. Attorney Moore requested that Daisy be allowed to say something to the jury. In a soft voice, with great emotion, she told them, "I feel like kissing and hugging you all. I trusted you all the time. I knew you would not believe what they said about me."

A woman in the crowd screamed, "She's free!" Judge Roan slipped out of the room. It was over. Women "struggled frantically" to reach Daisy, but the bailiffs kept them away. The *Constitution* thought the celebration was a bit overwrought: "It was the triumph of the female, and class distinctions swept down and away in the flood of raw human nature which was unloosed." For the last time Daisy Grace would walk down those concrete stairs and out of the benighted Thrower Building and into the street. A crowd of 300 people, evincing "intense excitement," followed her back across the Whitehall viaduct to her lawyers' offices. The *Journal's* final edition was already out; in three-inch bold face type, all caps, the headline blared: MRS. GRACE FREED.

The jurymen would finally get to go home. One juror took with him a unique souvenir: St. Elmo Massengale, a prominent advertizing man (he helped do the early boards for Coca-Cola), was allowed to keep the Smith and Wesson revolver. Laird, the foreman, turned aside all the press requests for a comment. Some juryman talked because the *Georgian* later reported that it had taken three ballots to reach the verdict. The first was nine for acquittal, one for guilty and two undecided. The undecideds went over to acquittal on the second ballot and the lone holdout gave in on the third.

Judge Roan, before heading off to the Terminal and the evening train to Fairburn, was brief but frank: "I'm glad it's over. Fresh air is what we all need now." From his home, solicitor Dorsey issued a statement, "I did my duty, and if I had to try the case over again, I would have proceeded exactly as I did. It was a matter for the jury to decide. Personally, I believe in the guilt of the defendant." Luther Rosser had been in his office and received the news of the verdict by telephone. "I knew it," he cheered. He left the Empire Building to go to the offices of Moore and Branch for the impromptu victory reception. Moore told the newsmen, "The verdict was just and right and the men on that jury will go down in history as men who did their duty as they saw it."

Daisy's emotions were shattered; she was either laughing or crying. She was exhausted. With her mother, she went out to Nurse Wilson's home at Ashby Street. Hundreds of congratulatory telegrams were soon arriving from across the country, again almost exclusively from women. So many telephone calls were received that Mrs. Wilson had to disconnect the phone. History does not record whether she asked Daisy for instructions.

In Newnan, reporters had gathered at 112 Greenville Street in anticipation of the verdict. On the summer evening Grace was resting on the front porch of the farmhouse. When the word came that his wife had been acquitted, Grace at least feigned some shock. "That's rotten, absolutely rotten. They might just as well put dynamite under the court houses now," he said with his eyes flashing. "I don't care what the jury said. She's as guilty as hell and she knows it." There was gloom everywhere in the house. Mother Hill was in tears, her son, crippled for life, now had had his reputation blasted.

He never struck a woman in his life, Grace insisted. "Respect for women has been instilled in me throughout my life." The scar on Daisy's face came from being kicked by a horse when a child. Keeping his promise to reveal the truth he could not tell to the jury, Grace said Daisy's tale of a quarrel was all a fraud. After returning from the theater on Monday night, he was unwell. She gave him some medicine; he kissed her good night. It was about one A.M. "Sometime in the night, she shot me. I think I was shot about 6 am." He was too drowsy to even know it at the time. When he realized what had happened, it was too late. He couldn't move, and he begged her to call in Dr. Cromer. She said she would but then she went away. No doctor ever came. He should never have trusted her, claiming that there was something fishy about the death certificate following the passing of her first husband. The injuries to Opie's arm "would not have killed a child." Grace said there was nothing for him now but to hope for surgery to restore the use of his legs. "I have one consolation. She has gone out of my life forever." In November he would be able to get his divorce. No one would blame him.

The *Newnan Herald and Advertiser*, although believing Daisy to be "surely guilty," was not surprised by the verdict. "The sinuosities and inconsistencies of the law are many and varied. It is to be hoped that she will return to the purlieus of her beloved Philadelphia, and that Georgia will see her no more forever."

Daisy was, indeed, making plans for a rapid journey north. The morning after the trial she went to the Peters Building to meet one more time with her lawyers. It was still thought to be of some interest to the public to describe her clothes. She wore a dress of pale blue Irish linen with a black silk overwaist, black suede slippers with sterling silver buckles, black silk stockings, and a white Milan hat trimmed with corn flowers and black velvet. She smiled broadly, telling the press, "This is my first day on earth in months; I am a free person again." Perhaps she had come to discuss her bill. The *Georgian* estimated the cost of her defense at $10,000 and speculated that she will likely have to seek work, although "she has no professional training or any particular accomplishment which might be turned into an income." The paper claimed that she had already received offers from theatrical managers about going on the stage.

Daisy declined numerous requests for interviews. Instead, she gave the newspapers a handwritten statement, which later appeared, in her script, on the front pages:

> I have been asked to make a statement since my acquittal. I am grateful beyond expression but not surprised. I knew that God would not forsake me in my trouble. I was taught to believe that he will never forsake the innocent. I am thankful to all who have helped me. I will return to my little boy in a day or so and devote the rest of my life to him. I will live with my mother in Philadelphia and try to comfort her for the rest of her life. Daisy Grace

On Monday night, August fifth, Mrs. Daisy Opie Grace left the "city of her greatest sorrow." With her mother, they left from the Union Depot on the 9:10 Central of Georgia train to Savannah. She wore a "neat traveling suit of tan." The plan was to catch the steamer up the east coast. When she arrived in Savannah at Union Station on West Broad Street, she seemed surprised that so many reporters were waiting. She posed for pictures and flashed the big ring she had purchased when last in the city. The S.S. *Frederick* steamed north on the seventh.

Atlanta had begun to move on at last. A great Southeastern Manufacturer's Association trade show opened the Monday following the trial. Even the heat had broken; Monday was the coldest fifth of August in city history. The reports on Daisy's departure were now relegated to page five. The *Georgian* wrote: "The spotlight is spluttering into dimness, the theater is darkening, and the crowd is passing out into the fresh air discussing the plot and players. The final curtain has fallen upon the strange tragedy of West Eleventh Street and the star has gone into retirement."

After all curtains come the critics. In the end, the city had spent most of five months reveling in the minute details of a dismal squalid domestic quarrel between two unpleasant and pretty much insignificant people. Eugene and Daisy Grace were never "society figures." Gene grew up on a red clay farm in Newnan. Daisy was a small-town girl from Pennsylvania. She was never a millionairess; she had no money of her own but what she inherited from Webster Opie, and that was all but gone. Basically they were a pair of social climbers, the very people that Atlanta's social gatekeepers were always on the watch for: "vulgarians in fine feathers." Not to mention leopard skins.

> Atlanta society accepts newcomers on their own merits, it is true, but these new-comers must have merits. Any newcomer, no matter how much money she has, how well she dresses or entertains, makes herself unpopular ... if she cannot be one in spirit with the well-bred, unpretentious leaders of the smart set.[1]

Nothing about Daisy Grace said unpretentious.

Gene and Daisy Grace were simply used by the newspapers. What a great story, damn the facts. The mysterious shooting on West Eleventh Street was tailor-made for the Hearst system. The *Georgian's* reporter, Herbert Asbury, later wrote, "Hearst immediately seduced journalism in that pearl of the Southland." When Hearst bought the *Georgian* in February, the paper's daily circulation was 38,000; by year's end it neared 60,000. The momentum carried on through the drama of the Frank case the following year. This is not meant to pile on the oft-reviled Mr. Hearst. The *Constitution* and *Journal* were every bit as frenzied in their pursuit of the story, but, as Asbury noted, "their editors had never before known the terrors of competition with America's journalistic wildcat."[2] But the "whole mad bunch" was in on it, according to the *Macon Telegraph*. In all, the three daily papers had collectively spent almost $15,000 over the five months the Grace case demanded headlines.

It was an entirely newspaper driven sensation. The papers created the myth of riches and social status. The papers sold the story of the great romance between "Daisy of the Leopard Spots and the young Adonis from a country town." Some were not to be fooled by it all. The *Griffin Daily News*, for instance, professed to find no romance but rather a "slimy tale of greed":

> By their own admission the lives of these two people must have been a veritable hell on earth, and it is tremendous warning to all who are so pitifully foolish to have been attracted by the false glitter thrown around two miserable lives by a bit of ephemeral newspaper notoriety over a spotted leopard's skin, a handful of gaudy jewels, and a fictitious heap of filthy dollars.[3]

The obsession was typical of the Atlanta dailies that delighted in peddling what the *Atlantian* had labeled "mental garbage."[4] Most troubling was the fascination the entire affair had on women. Each day of the trial, far more women than men were seen in the fourth floor courtroom. "Society girls" and women from all classes were willing to suffer through the sweltering day locked in attention. Mrs. Joseph Morgan of the Atlanta Federation of Women's Clubs proclaimed that something should be done in the future to prohibit young girls from attending such trials at which "the evidence must inevitably be of a salacious nature."[5]

It was obviously time to move on. Over at the *Constitution* the word was that the staff was pretty much exhausted. The prosecution of Daisy Grace had already been anointed the "trial of the century," albeit a young century.[6] But everyone now needed a break. Yet, before too much longer, reporters, being the men they were, would all be "fretting and fuming" over when the next "sensation" could be found.

It would not be long. On April 26, 1913, the body of Mary Phagan was found in the cellar of the National Pencil Factory on Forsyth Street. Hugh Dorsey would prosecute Leo Frank for the murder of Mary Phagan. Luther Rosser defended. Judge Leonard S. Roan presided. The coverage of the Grace case would seem meek and mild when compared with what was to come.[7]

CHAPTER 24

Purely Speculation

Before considering what might really have happened in the bedroom at 29 West Eleventh Street, the reader's indulgence is requested for a brief detour.

Gene Grace had said that his wife was fascinated with crime stories and read all about them in the papers. To be sure, then, it is of some interest to point out the incredible similarities between the Grace case and a shooting that took place in Philadelphia in December of 1910.[1] The parallel facts in these two events are so numerous as to be startling. Herbert Mason Clapp, an heir to a shoe-blacking fortune, was a "well-known clubman and man about town" in Philadelphia. His first marriage had ended amid allegations of drunkenness, beatings and adultery. He had re-married; his second wife, Marie, was a former manicurist. They soon separated but had reunited.

At 3:30 in the morning of December 12, 1910, at their home on Girard Avenue, Clapp claimed that his wife stood over his bed with a pistol and shot him. The bullet went through Clapp's mouth and emerged beneath his left ear. Clapp was expected to die and made a complete "ante-mortem statement." But, as in the case of Gene Grace, despite his ghastly wound, Clapp survived.

Marie Clapp told a variety of stories but eventually admitted that she shot him in self-defense while "struggling for possession of a revolver." Marie claimed that he had thrown her to the floor and was trying to inject her with morphine. Clapp denounced his wife as a lying she-devil who wished to cover up her simple wish to kill him. In the end, no charges were ever filed.

This Philadelphia scandal occurred while both Daisy and Gene were residing in that city. At the time she was still unhappily married to Webster Opie, and Gene was the newly arrived well-dressed bond salesman. They almost certainly knew or knew of the Clapps, who also figured in Philly's pre-war "gilded café life." Incredibly, Mrs. Clapp had come to be known as "the tiger lady" for a tiger-striped coat that she claimed her husband forced her to wear. "I hated that coat," she whined. The sentiment among Philadelphians at the time was that Marie Clapp probably shot her husband while he slept, but he pretty much deserved it.

The facts of the Clapp case so closely match the Grace case that it is no leap to believe it had some effect on Daisy's thinking 15 months later. Things were not turning out as she had envisioned them. She did not much care for Atlanta, let alone playing dominoes with the bucolic ladies of Newnan. Her "aristocratic" young husband was no more than the son of a farmer's wife. She had grown tired of being tapped for the expense of their lavish travel and lifestyle. About all she had left was the Philadelphia property intended for her blind son. Now Grace wanted that as well. If you believe Daisy's version of their marriage, Gene was also abusive to her and, with less certainty, unfaithful. Perhaps Daisy dreamed that she could rid herself of him with a pistol shot and follow Mrs. Clapp's lead and plead self-defense.

Clearly, however, Daisy could not have hoped to reenact Marie Clapp's actions down to the near miss bullet and agonizing wound, but it happened. Getting the police, the public and a jury to believe it was self-defense was the greater challenge. Gene Grace did not have the public reputation of a brute that H.M. Clapp held in Philadelphia. Daisy had but her one chance to make that case in her hour-long appearance in court. She succeeded.

So what might really have happened that morning?

Daisy's defense team mocked the idea that the collected patent medicines could have been used to drug anyone. The facts are less exculpatory. Radway's Ready Relief is basically "flavored alcohol"—the alcohol content was said to be 27 percent. Dr. King's New Discovery was a concoction of morphine and chloroform in a sugar syrup and pine tar solution. The amount of morphine was listed at one-fifth of a grain per one ounce. The bottle found in the Grace home held three ounces. Morphine was generally prescribed by doctors in amounts from an eighth to a half grain. If Grace had drunk the entire bottle, the three-fifths of a grain of morphine would have had a "decidedly injurious effect,"[2] but it would certainly not have been fatal. But add in the alcohol from the Radway's and the combined effect would likely put someone into a good sleep. The police should have looked for any evidence that there was drink in the house—wine or spirits. Did they? Alcohol would have greatly increased the drowsiness caused by this cocktail of meds. Daisy, the "modern day Borgia," could have put Gene into a compliant stupor. If it was her diabolical plot to have him lie down directly over the oilcloth, he was probably in no condition to object.

It should be remembered that Gene had originally told the police when they arrived, "I might have been drugged." Here again we encounter yet another way in which Gene Grace's will to live cost him legally. If he had died that day there would have been a post-mortem and the stomach contents analyzed. The use of such evidence was not unknown in 1912, even in Georgia; the state chemist had testified in many poison cases.[3] But Gene Grace was in no condition to have his stomach pumped. The procedure was done either by aspiration (pump) or expression — by pressing down on the stomach, "imitating the act of straining in defecation"— if the patient could bear it.[4] Given Gene's grave condition, it was not likely that the doctors would have risked either.

Accepting the possibility that Gene had been rendered "loopy" in some way, there are a few possible scenarios for the events of that morning.

1. She incapacitated him and shot him before the servants arrived (Dorsey's theory).
2. She incapacitated him and shot him after the servants left.
3. Gene had not been drugged but was simply unwell. There was a physical argument with a gun involved, and the gun went off. Either one of them could have been holding the gun (Daisy's version).

The state went with version 1. Dorsey set the time of the shooting as some time before the Ruffins came into the house at 7:30. Neither J.C. nor Martha ever talked of hearing a shot. Therefore the shooting had occurred before the servants came into the house that morning. Clearly, if Daisy intended to shoot her husband, then she intended to kill him. If that was her plan — to shoot him while he slept in the night — it follows that when the morning came she would have a dead man in her bed. What would she have done then? If Gene was lying there dead, could she really have risked allowing the servants access to the room? But if the servants were barred from the room, that would eventually have raised questions with the police once, come Friday, Gene's body was "discovered."

But, of course, she had not killed him. The morning did come, and — so the prosecution claimed — Gene was lying in bed, bleeding and in pain. The same question arises: would any reasonable woman have then brought a servant into the room? How could Daisy be certain that Gene would not have suddenly summoned the strength to simply say, "Help me, I've been shot"? Yet Martha was called upstairs and into that bedroom twice, first to light the fire and later to fasten up Daisy's dress. Martha reported seeing nothing amiss, save that Gene had not eaten anything off his breakfast tray. Either important evidence was missed or she just had not seen anything. Was Gene under the covers? Where was Gene on the bed? Maybe a female servant was trained not to look at the master's bed. The fireplace was against the east wall of the house, opposite the foot of the bed. Martha scuttled into the room with her head down and tended to the fire, then left. But lighting a fire is not a quick task. Yet all Martha could recall from her visit of at least a few minutes was that she heard Mr. Gene "groaning." All of this leads to the conclusion that Daisy allowed Martha into the room because nothing had yet happened. Gene Grace may have been sickened by a cocktail of "drugs" or he may have been simply suffering from a very bad winter cold. But he had not yet been shot.

That brings matters to about ten o'clock and the Meckel phone call. The Peachtree grocer stuck to his story under Dorsey's fierce assault; he insisted that he spoke to a man on the phone at ten. There was only one phone in the house. It also seems clear that Meckel's call came after the Ruffins had left to go to the "negro moving pictures." As the Ruffins had heard no shots, it seems clear they never heard a phone ring. If the defense knew that the Ruffins had been in the house when Meckel's call came in, Messrs. Rosser et al. would have put very simple questions to them on the stand. Did you hear the telephone ring that morning? The question was not asked. The Ruffins must have already gone out. From his end of the phone line, Meckel did not sense anything was amiss as of ten o'clock.

Ellis Lawrence called Ivy 469 after Meckel had rung off, but Ellis did not speak to Grace. Daisy asked the jury to believe that the shooting had occurred as a result of an argument that began *after* Lawrence's telephone call. Gene's partner had some good news: a large payment had come in and the check needed to be banked. The firm's prospects were improving. Daisy expressed her hope that this news might defer any plan to sell the Philadelphia house, which she had bitterly opposed. The discussion became heated; she went to take the power of attorney out of Gene's jacket pocket, and one thing led to another. The gun was produced, they struggled, and the gun went off.

Also about this time, Sylvester Kenny, servant at a neighbor's house, came to the door on some unstated errand and interrupted Daisy at the piano downstairs. It is surprising that the prosecution did not make the suggestion to the jury that Daisy was so wicked that she banged away on the piano below to cover the sound of her wounded husband's anguished suffering and calls for help while she awaited his death. Now *that* is diabolical.

Let's look at the whole issue of the oilcloth. The prosecution's theory was that Daisy took this fairly large caliber gun and, while Gene dozed, put the muzzle as close to his body as she dared and pulled the trigger. The prosecution suggested that Daisy had somehow cajoled Gene to lie on top of a four-by-five foot oilcloth. Gene was a large man. As best we know, Daisy was not a marksman, nor was she a blood spatter expert. Shootings are never neat. Did anyone believe that she was willing to go so far as to shoot her husband in the heart on the bed but only if she could get her breakage deposit back?

There are myriad domestic reasons why there may have been an oilcloth on the bed. It seems rather a reach for the prosecution to have put so much emphasis upon it.

It bears repeating: if she intentionally shot him, she meant to kill him. If the first bullet did not do the job, why did she not fire a second shot? The State's case was that Daisy apparently realized that Gene would eventually bleed to death, which served her purpose just as well. So she locked the doors and went off to Newnan as she had planned. But she did not count on Gene being able to somehow get to the telephone. As Chief Ball suggested in the early days of the investigation, not disabling the phone was an important slip-up on Daisy's part.

Additionally, why did she take all the keys with her but leave the gun? A crafty shooter would certainly have left Gene's keys in the room but, like the phone, placed them well out of reach. What possible reason would she have had to leave the gun behind the drapes on the first floor? From the time she left the house and the time her train left for Newnan, she had a minimum of two hours. This was ample time for a "diabolical" murderess to have disposed of the gun. Leaving the gun behind and poorly hidden in the house would seem to be an act of panic or confusion more likely to have occurred after an accidental shooting. Thomas Felder, one of the few Atlanta lawyers not employed by either side in the Grace case, made the point at the time: "The strength of the prosecution's case is, as I see it, its weakness." Dorsey had painstakingly welded together his chain of evidence to prove that this diabolical murderess had laid out a deadly plan to eliminate her husband. Yet she also committed several inexplicable errors in carrying it out: the gun, the keys, why say anything to the servants about a doctor? Felder concluded that "no person of the intelligence and worldly knowledge of Mrs. Grace could have committed such a string of blunders if she had planned the assassination."[5]

Daisy's unsworn statement of what took place was, at the very least, entirely plausible. Was it entirely true from start to finish? Unlikely. Was Gene Grace as much of a brute, a leech and philanderer as she made him out to be? Probably more so than not. Did it all happen the way she described? We will never know, but certainly her statement was artfully crafted to give the jury reasons to believe it did. Gene had hit her before, he had pulled a gun on her before, she had overpowered him before (remember she was 5'7, he was 6'3), she had disarmed him before, and she hid a gun behind some drapes before. It was all very well done. But some sticking points remain.

The weapon: Published reports state that the gun was a "Smith and Wesson Safety Hammerless Revolver." Such a gun was touted as "A Perfect and

Safe Arm for the House and Pocket."[6] It featured an "automatic safety bolt" which was designed to prevent firing "until the pistol is firmly gripped for use." *Farrow's American Small Arms Encyclopedia*, referring to the Smith and Wesson hammerless revolver, declares: "To discharge this arm in any but the proper manner is an impossibility."[7] Why did the prosecution not call a weapons expert? Was it even possible for the gun in question to be fired accidentally? Moreover, the author of the 1910 book *Hints on Revolver Shooting* thought the weapon was unsuitable for a woman: "I should not recommend a lady to use these or any other short, light self-defense revolvers unless it be actually necessary, as the recoil is heavy and apt to hurt a lady's hand."[8] Did police examine her hands on the day of the shooting? If so, the results were either inconclusive or unreported.

The wound: In her statement, Daisy claimed that Gene was holding the gun in his left hand. This was a very important detail and skillfully slipped into her story. One can picture her on the witness stand providing all the appropriate hand gestures to demonstrate the point. It would have been helpful to know if Gene Grace was right or left handed. The path of the bullet that entered the body of Gene Grace would more likely have been produced if Gene were holding the gun in his left hand. The bullet entered below the heart, through the lower left lobe of the lung and into the central backbone. For a right-handed man, or if Gene was holding the gun in his right hand, the muzzle would have to have been quite severely twisted for the bullet to have followed that path. Still, to be fair, it was not impossible. The questions of the path of the bullet and/or the angle of entry were non-issues at the trial.

On the other hand, the police and prosecution made much of the "dried blood." Whether Gene Grace had been shot at six A.M. or eleven A.M., by the time the police chopped their way into the bedroom at 2:30 that afternoon, more than enough time would have passed, under the then accepted three-hour rule, for Gene's blood to have dried on his nightshirt and the bed clothing. The science of time-dating bloodstains in 1912 was not yet capable of determining when the wound was first opened.[9] A more interesting issue, not raised at the trial, was whether Gene Grace could have lived at all if he had been bleeding from this untreated wound since six A.M.? Would he have bled to death before being able to make the phone call?

The weakest part of Daisy Grace's remarkable speech was that portion dealing with what occurred after the gun went off. She and Gene hastily arranged this mysterious pact of silence, and sealed it on a Bible, no less. In the days after the shooting, Daisy repeatedly professed her love for Gene, and she went on about how someday she would wheel him about and care for him, etc. A woman who truly felt that way would have called him a doctor immediately. The idea that the shooting was "too embarrassing" is ludicrous. Some story could just as hastily have been concocted to make everyone think it was an accident. "I dropped the gun," or some such fabrication comes easily to mind. The world did not have to think that there had been a "n****r row" in that bedroom. And going beyond that, did either of them really think that they could somehow explain this accidental shooting and *still* get a membership in the Piedmont Driving Club? There was a phone in that room; the natural human response for a wife who cared for her husband was to call a doctor, whatever he said. Other than the "fascination" that she had for Gene, Daisy never explained why she went along with his supposed plan. We are asked to believe that she left her husband in bed bleeding from a gunshot wound on his word that the wound was nothing serious. Like the Black Knight from *Monty Python and the Holy Grail*, he said "'tis but a scratch." So Daisy left the house but locked him in and took his keys. She did not think to call and check on him until three hours had passed. Nor did she ever explain how, if she had decided to summon one, a doctor would have gotten in. She had all the keys with her! Gene lay abed expecting her back with a doctor. By 2:00 he knew he had been betrayed. He realized she had left him to die. Using his elbows, he dragged himself to the phone and called the police.

And what of Gene's singular conduct? At what time in the roughly three hours he was left there did he figure out that no doctor was coming? Perhaps he had passed out from the pain and blood loss. But the fact that Grace waited for so long to make the call seems to demonstrate that he had been expecting help to arrive and finally gave up. Here it seems that attention has to be called to the police report on the day of the shooting. The call officers asked Grace flatly who shot him. He gave a most curious reply: "Someone I thought was my friend. I will tell you about it later." Was it your wife, they asked. "It could have been but, please God, don't make any arrests." This isn't Daisy's version; this is what an admittedly wounded and delirious Gene Grace told the cops. Gene's cryptic words do, it has to be said, lend some credence to Daisy's story.

The best guess at an answer to the mystery is to accept Daisy Grace's explanation. These two ill-matched people by that stage thoroughly despised one another. The bedroom fracas seems totally believable. The jurymen were eager to go home. They were tired of it all and not willing to apportion blame between two unlikable people. There was no certainty as to what happened in that bedroom. There was reasonable doubt aplenty, and to send this woman off to a south Georgia prison farm for any length of time was too formidable a punishment for what might just have been an accident.

If that was all to the story, then it seems a fair cop. But just when the mind settles comfortably on some way or another to exonerate Daisy from intentionally trying to murder her husband, we get back to the baffling "alibi letters." Hugh Dorsey spoke nothing but the truth when he told Judge Roan that without them they had no case. It is possible that Gene had prepared them both. He had access to the typewriter, and he could type. We have the advantage of having seen and read some of Gene's other "Philadelphia" letters; the jury did not. In comparing the early letters with the "alibi" letters, there are enough similarities in style and salutation to reasonably believe Gene Grace had typed/penciled both of the alibi letters as well. If one wants to believe that Gene wrote those letters so as to clear the deck for a hookup with a lady friend that Tuesday night, then why would he have sent both letters to Newnan? It seems clear that only Daisy might have had reason to send both letters to Newnan, presuming that she had not yet decided which one to employ when the time came.

The typewritten letter undoubtedly was done well in advance of the shooting. The letter has no date, not even a day of the week. The Graces left North Boulevard (and the Smith Premier number 2) on January fifteenth, 50 days before the shooting. Rosser said Daisy could not type. Of course, anyone can type if given the time to peck it out one letter at a time. Daisy may well have typed up this undated alibi letter to have around when the conditions might be arranged to employ it. Perhaps, however, she became uncertain about the typed letter and thought one in Gene's handwriting would be more useful. So on March 3, the Sunday before the shooting, she somehow cajoled her husband into writing a similar note in pencil. We have Gene Grace's baffling public admission that he had done just that. He claimed that he had only done it to please his playful wife. Her powers of seduction must have been formidable indeed to be able to dictate this devious note and have her husband faithfully take it all down and then sign it. For what possible purpose? As Dorsey said, the gullible man had prepared and signed his own death warrant. Gene Grace did not deserve his fate, but he was never the sharpest pitchfork in Newnan, to be sure.

Subscribers to the "diabolical plot" theory may conclude that on March 4, her two letters now ready, Daisy set the plot in motion for Tuesday. Before bed on Monday night she tried to weaken him with a cocktail of patent medicines. In his woozy state she got him to lie down on the bed where she had discreetly placed the oilcloth. At some time, having hurried the servants away (I believe after 10:30 Tuesday morning), she surprised her dozing husband with the gun. She aimed at the heart but missed the target. Still, he was bleeding. He was immobile. She presumed he would eventually bleed to death. She left and locked the door, not to return for 72 hours. What an awful scene would have greeted Daisy and Gene's aged mother on Friday. Daisy, through her tears, would then sobbingly recall that letter she'd received while in Newnan. It would all be clear that poor Gene's good-hearted act of bringing an old friend home for a meal had cost him his life. Everyone would be greatly saddened at his passing. The police would set off to pursue their inquiries in Charleston. Daisy probably would have gotten away with all this if only Gene had just gone ahead and died.

"It is a common saying that a woman, if she is young and pretty, cannot be punished for any crime." In the end, it seems that Dorsey's fears were justified. A jury of men could not believe a woman could be so calculatingly villainous. Dorsey had failed to convince them that Daisy had *intended* to kill Gene. Maybe a jury of twelve Kiplings might have convicted her, but twelve Atlanta men decided to let her walk. Nor was Daisy Grace alone; in the first two decades of the twentieth century, several "society" women were accused of shooting, stabbing, poisoning or otherwise doing-in their husbands or lovers but were acquitted after sensational trials. A few weeks after the Grace verdict came down, John Wayman, the prosecuting attorney for Cook County and the city of Chicago, bemoaned the fact that "all a woman needs to do is to retreat behind the protecting wall of her sex, and an avalanche of tears, and make no other defense." Wayman thought it was clear that the time had come for the traditional bar against having women on juries had to be lifted. The "avalanche of tears" will not fool another woman. Until that happened, Wayman boldly predicted, "There will be an epidemic of husband slaying in this country."[10] In fact, however, Daisy Grace agreed with Wayman; she told a reporter that women should be on juries: "Women understand women. They know the real human side of life as a man never sees it. They can look at one of their sex and see if she is shamming and they can tell whether she is guilty of a crime. No deceit or false tears for them, for they can read a woman's heart through every time."[11] At least in Georgia, the time for women jurors was not at hand. Not until 1953 did the State of Georgia give women the right to serve on a jury.[12]

CHAPTER 25

The Final Chapter

It was always a curious fact that no one heard a shot on March fifth. Not the Ruffins who slept in the rear yard; not any of the neighbors. The experts in such things contend that a handgun fired at night can be heard as far as two miles away. In the daytime, with other competing noises, the sound of the gunshot will travel one mile.[1] But those estimates are based on a gun fired outdoors. Gene Grace was shot inside a well-built house; the windows were closed on a March day and the heavy drapes drawn. Still, West Eleventh Street was a quiet residential street, and the homes were no great distance from each other. Someone must have heard a shot.

There was understandable excitement, then, when a man did come forward a few days after the trial had concluded to claim that he had heard a gunshot at about 5:30 that March morning. Incredibly, the ear-witness was none other than the solicitor-general, Hugh Dorsey.[2] The *Georgian* reported this most amazing scoop:

> On the morning of March 5, Mr. and Mrs. Dorsey were in bed in their rooms on the 2d floor of the Goldsmith Apartments [12 West Eleventh Street] across the street from Grace's home. "I tossed restlessly all night and I was still lying awake just as the sky began to lighten and the first gray streaks of daylight came through the half opened window of our apartment. My wife was sleeping soundly. Suddenly I heard the crack of a pistol shot, and from where I lay I could tell it came from the direction of the Grace house across the street." He heard nothing more; it was instantly quiet once again. Dorsey recalled that he thought someone was shooting a cat. He dozed, heard the milk man, and that helped him to put the time at somewhere between half past 5 and 6 that morning. He thought no more of it for several days until he got involved in the Grace case. "The prosecution of Mrs. Grace devolved on me through my office, and I knew my evidence regarding the firing of the shot would destroy her defense. But the very fact of being Prosecutor placed me in a remarkable position, and when eminent Judges and lawyers advised me for ethical reasons not to go on the stand, I followed their advice."

170

To be accurate, Dorsey's apartment was not "across the street" from the scene of the shooting. It was on the opposite side of West Eleventh Street, but the apartments were several lots to the east, across Crescent Street, whereas "the Kiser home" was west of Crescent. Still, it is possible that Dorsey could have heard the shot. The only caveat Dorsey offered to explain his decision not to come forward with this startling intelligence was that he was unwilling to swear that he had heard the shot on the morning of March fifth, although he was certain in his own mind that he had. In the September 1912 edition of *Law Notes*, a contemporary legal monthly, the editor thought that Dorsey's decision was commendable but not necessary. The relevant passage in the A.B.A. code of ethics of the day read: "Except when essential to the ends of justice, a lawyer should avoid testifying in court in behalf of his client." Certainly that proviso fit the facts in the Grace case. Dorsey, the article concluded, could have given his evidence with "perfect propriety."[3] When Daisy was told of Dorsey's claim, she seemed more annoyed than anything. It was "very unfair" of him to make such a statement after the fact.

Despite losing the Grace case, Dorsey easily won election to a full term as Fulton County Solicitor.[4] But the Grace verdict was the first in a series of much publicized courtroom setbacks for the ambitious prosecutor. In the months following the Grace trial, Dorsey lost two big murder cases — Kell Potts and Mrs. Appelbaum.[5] The latter was interesting. A traveling salesman from Chicago was shot and killed in his room at the Dakota Hotel on North Pryor Street. The "Mrs. Appelbaum" in his room was not his wife. She was defended by the firm of Moore and Branch, and acquitted. Down in Newnan, Gene Grace had followed the trial and saw something of Daisy in the attractive shooter in the Appelbaum case. "Speaking from a standpoint of the experience I have had with the vampire type of woman, there is nothing conceived by God or nature more dangerous than such a character. She has been the downfall of mankind. The bachelor is the happiest and sanest person, after all, and, in many cases, the livest."[6]

The losses Dorsey suffered in this series of prominent cases had an effect. Students of the Leo Frank mystery believe it explains the solicitor general's all-consuming pursuit of a conviction for the murder of Mary Phagan.[7] The Frank jury was treated to Byronic references from Dorsey in lieu of Kipling.[8] That verdict was won, and Dorsey's popularity was restored, at least among his contemporaries. In 1917, Hugh Manson Dorsey was elected governor of Georgia, and he built a record as a fairly progressive figure over his two terms.

In late August of 1913 the body of Martha Ruffin was found in a pea patch off Ponce de Leon; she had been stabbed.[9] Amid the tension of the final days of the Frank trial, the murder of a poor colored woman received scant notice in any of the city's three papers. Martha and J.C. Ruffin had separated soon after losing their jobs with the Graces. The killing was done in what the *Constitution* called "the regular 'Jack the Ripper' style." This was a reference not to the infamous London ripper but to a killer who preyed on black women in Atlanta. Martha was said to be his eighteenth victim. The Atlanta police had no leads.

Those who would wish to seek out the scene of the "great Atlanta shooting" will search in vain. The Kiser home stood on the north side of Eleventh Street. It was torn down some years ago, and the lot is now in the shadows of the hulking Atlanta Federal Reserve Building at Peachtree and Tenth. It is worthy of note that the Kisers continued to own the home following the shooting, but they obtained the city's permission to renumber the house. The former 29 was to become 35 West Eleventh Street in 1913. Perhaps the Kisers were hoping to confuse the "morbidly curious" sightseers of the day. Or is it possible that, as with Daisy Grace and her concern over being given room 613 at the Kimball House, the Kisers also shared some sense of "hoodoo" numbers.

Incredibly, the Thrower Building, the original shell of it anyway, is still standing at the corner of Mitchell and Pryor. In 1913 the preliminaries in the Leo Frank case were held in Judge Roan's fourth floor courtroom. Frank's trial was to begin almost a year to the day after that of Daisy Grace; the opening session was July 28. With the memories of the previous oppressive conditions still fresh, Solicitor Dorsey, with the support of the defense counsel, including Luther Rosser, decided to uproot the Frank trial to the "old City Hall" on East Hunter Street. A new "ozonator" system had been installed there. The Thrower Building went through a few owners but continued to house Kutz's Millinery Warehouse. Most recently the building was gutted and renovated, to be marketed as "Capital Center," with an atrium lobby and six-story indoor water feature. Alas, the real estate market cratered, and the building now stands vacant.[10]

The *Georgian* enjoyed a circulation surge created by Daisy Grace, the Frank trial, etc., and soon claimed at varying times to be the best-selling paper in the city. But for a variety of reasons the *Georgian* was in retreat by the 1930s. In 1937, Hearst sent his youngest son, Randolph, to Atlanta to be the assistant news editor at the age of 21. In 1938, Randolph married Catherine Campbell of Atlanta; of their five daughters, one was the celebrated Patty Hearst. William Randolph Hearst sold the *Georgian* to the owners of the *Constitution* in 1939. "His efforts to win a foothold in Atlanta alone were calculated by him to have cost 21 million dollars before he gave up."[11]

Readers will perhaps appreciate, in closing, a few brief notes explaining "whatever happened to" the two leading figures in this captivating drama.

Gene Grace underwent a second operation a week and a half after the trial. On August 14, 1912, the doctors were again unable to remove the bullet. They told reporters that Grace was "no better no worse" after the surgery, which he once again bore with "wonderful nerve." It was now almost certain that he would "lie on his back helpless from the waist down for the rest of his life ... under such conditions the vitality of the man cannot last much longer."[12]

The same day as Grace's operation, Daisy and her mother steamed up the Delaware River aboard the S.S. *Frederick*, arriving at the Lombard Street dock in Philadelphia. Daisy's brother-in-law, Henry Kreider, led the welcoming committee, but there were so many people assembled at the dock that Daisy became frightened and remained on board. After going aboard to talk with her, Kreider returned to urge the crowd to leave; he told them that Daisy was in such a "highly nervous state" that she would not get off and might even return to Savannah. After some little further delay, Daisy and Mother Ulrich came down the gangway. The reporters had stayed, of course, and when a passing remark was heard that was critical of Gene, Daisy barked, "You will kindly stop talking in that manner. Please remember he is my husband and he is a cripple at present, but I hope to see him well before a great while." Daisy pleaded to be left alone henceforward: "I wish people would stop talking about [the shooting]. The incident is closed." She and her mother then left in a taxicab for 4246 Spruce Street and their reunion with little Webbie.

Regardless of her dockside comments, Daisy Opie Grace moved speedily to shed her aforementioned husband. In September she filed for a divorce in the Common Pleas Court of Philadelphia. The suit cited "such indignities to the person of the libellant as to render her condition intolerable and life burdensome, thereby, compelling her to withdraw from his home and family and that the respondent by cruel and barbarous treatment, endangered her life." Gene Grace did not answer the petition and instead filed his own divorce action that November in the Coweta County court in Newnan. Neither suit was ever prosecuted to conclusion.

The two Graces remained out of the news for all of 1913, with the exception of a bizarre story from Downingtown, Pennsylvania. A "Mr. and Mrs. Oldham" were evicted from the Swan Hotel in that Dutch country town where they had been living as man and wife. According to several news reports, "Mrs. Oldham" was, in fact, Daisy Grace.[13] From Newnan, Gene Grace had a brief comment: "God pity the man!"

Gene Grace remained paralyzed and at home in Newnan. He told the *Constitution* that, for a diversion, he was thinking of writing up a screenplay for "the movies" about his case. There were periodic brief statements from his doctors, typically glum about his long-range prognosis. At last, in January 1914, the *Constitution* reported, "Eugene H. Grace is dying at his home in Newnan. One of the pluckiest battles for life ever made by a human being is ending in failure." On January 11, the *New York Times* quoted Gene as saying:

> I am sure that Daisy is guilty. If I finally lose my long fight for life, I will appeal from the earthly courts to the Higher Tribunal. She will not come clear then. Maybe I shouldn't talk that way, but I am thinking of it all the time and it has eaten into my soul. She did it! She did it! She shot me and left me locked in the room. I can't forgive and, although a jury acquitted her, God won't. I am dying because of her act and she ought to be punished.[14]

At 1:45 on the morning of Monday, January 12, Gene Grace died in his room at 112 Greenville Street. The *Newnan Herald and Advertiser* reported that he had been failing since before Christmas. He had become increasingly nervous, and persistent nausea had robbed him of his strength. "The end came peacefully at last and the dauntless spirit that had battled so long and so bravely in the unequal struggle found rest in an eternal sleep that must come to us all sooner or later." His mother and his Hill stepfamily were with him at the end. The *Constitution* called it the "final chapter in one of the greatest tragedies that has ever stirred the people of Atlanta. His long brave fight centered the attention of the medical world and excited unusual interest all over the country." The doctors reported that his death was due to uremic poisoning which had inevitably set in about the bullet that remained in his spine. Gene Grace was 30.

The funeral was held at the farmhouse the same day. The mourners were limited just to family, "out of respect for their wishes for a quiet service." A great number of beautiful floral offerings were displayed. Most of the flowers had come from Newnan, but others had arrived from Atlanta and beyond, from the "wide circle of friends who had stood with him through all the changing fortunes of his life." The Reverend H.L. Edmondson of Newnan's First Methodist Church spoke but "made little if any reference to the tragedy."[15]

Ironically, the *Washington Times*, noting the death, still paraded out the old references to Gene Grace as "the wealthy clubman."[16] While in Newnan, Grace's plain wooden coffin was placed aboard the family wagon for the short journey up Jefferson Street to the Oak Hill Cemetery. A contemporary guide book declared, "There is not a burial ground of the dead in Georgia more beautifully kept than Oak Hill ... it is one of the beauty spots of the State."[17] On a cold but clear day, Gene Grace's funeral wagon was followed by family,

The grave of Eugene H. Grace, Oak Hill Cemetery, Newnan, Georgia (author's photograph, September 2011).

friends and "the usual throng of the idle curious." The procession passed the phalanx of white crosses marking the graves of more than 200 sons of Newnan who died for the Confederacy. Not far beyond, on the left in Section 34L, Row 4, Grave 6, is the marker for Eugene H. Grace, 1883–1914.[18] To the right are the graves of his mother and stepfather, both of whom lived into the 1920s.

In some of the papers it was reported that before he died Grace vowed that his spirit would live on, and he had hoped to "haunt" his wife until her dying day. "I wouldn't want to be in that woman's shoes for all the riches of the earth," said one unidentified "Atlanta friend" who claimed to have visited Grace just before his death.[19] "Not even the grave can keep down the publishing of Grace stories," the *Athens Banner* fussed. But Daisy was unconcerned; she told Philadelphia pressmen, "The man is dead. Let him lie. I am not worrying about his coming back and haunting me or anything of the kind. That is silly. I have no fear of ghosts."

Some overheated stories also appeared speculating that she might now be re-tried for murder. Daisy had no fear of that ever happening either. In fact, she claimed to have received a letter from Gene (which she never submitted for verification) in which he exonerated her of all guilt. Her mind was at peace. "I did not shoot my husband. He was satisfied of that when he died, in spite of all reports to the contrary. I am not in fear of any prosecution. I was acquitted of the shooting of my husband once. That is enough. I will say nothing about my plans for the future or whether I intend to marry again."

Daisy Grace did, in fact, marry again. When her mother died in 1916, the Lebanon paper listed among the mourners Mrs. Ulrich's daughter — Mrs. D. Elizabeth Bender — and her husband William. The more flamboyant appellation "Daisy" had been discreetly retired. The story of Daisy's third marriage never made the newspapers. She died on March 25, 1934, at the Delaware County Hospital in Upper Darby, near Philadelphia. She was 57 and had been ill for several months. The brief death notice in the *Philadelphia Bulletin* made no mention of the events of 1912. Apparently the once infamous "Daisy of the Leopard Spots" was now simply D. Elizabeth Bender, wife of William H. Bender of 640 Old Forest Road, Carroll Park, in West Philadelphia. She was buried at the Westminster Cemetery in Bala Cynwyd.[20]

Daisy never had another child. Her only son, little Webbie Opie, lived a long life. He died in 1995.

Whichever the reader chooses to conclude — that Daisy Grace shot Gene in cold blood, or the gun went off during their last argument — there is no disputing the fact that the woman walked out of that house and locked the door. She never called Dr. Cromer; she never spoke again with Gene. She surely believed that she was leaving him there to die. She took a cab to the Terminal Station and boarded an A&WP train to go on her pre-planned visit to the dying man's family. Trox Bankston watched her on that journey and thought this well-dressed woman had not a care in the world. On that train ride of about an hour, Daisy must have consoled herself with the thought that she was finally rid of this man. She was likely steeling herself to play the role of the grieving wife for a few days or weeks as necessary, but then she could leave Georgia forever. At Newnan she was incredulous at the news that he still lived. "How could a man live who was shot through the lung?" she spluttered.

Solicitor Dorsey had tried to prove that all this was a planned and diabolical crime, but, hampered by a lack of any direct evidence and opposed by a skilled defense team, he failed. Her actions may not have been diabolical, but she displayed a calculated, pitiless cruelty. Yet the charge against her was assault *with intent* to murder. The jury accepted the claim that the shooting was accidental. She indisputably left him to die, but she had not been charged with the crime of manslaughter. The jury could not be certain beyond a reasonable doubt that Daisy Grace on the morning of March 5, 1912, set out intending to kill her husband Gene. So she walked.

In Gene's letter to Daisy, written after Opie's death in February of the previous year, he had begged for a special kind of friendship: "I just want to be the kind of a friend that you can know, down in the depths of your heart, if you have one true friend in the world, it is I. Not the kind that sticks only as long as good fellowship lasts but the kind that grasps you by the hand and says, 'No matter what your trouble is or what is wrong, I am with you to the finish.'" That day Daisy showed that she was no such friend at all. She did not take his hand—rather, she turned her back on him and walked away.

As he lay paralyzed in Newnan, awaiting a certain death, Gene Grace must have often reflected on what he had also written in that letter, when he admitted, "My only curse has been women."

Chapter Notes

Preface

1. Walter Hines Page and Arthur Wilson Page, *The World's Work* (New York: Doubleday, Page, 1901), Vol. 1, 113.
2. Edward Hungerford, "The Personality of Atlanta," *Travel* 26–27 (1916): 23.
3. Arthur C. Inman, *The Inman Diary: A Public and Private Confession*, ed. Daniel A. Aaron (Cambridge, MA: Harvard University Press, 1985), Vol. 1, 33–35.
4. Rev. Anthony Harley, *Southward Ho! Notes of a Tour to and Through the State of Georgia* (London, 1886), 117.
5. Walter G. Cooper, "Atlanta, the Gate City of the South," *Southern Merchant* 19 (January 7, 1907): 3.
6. Robert Alexander Kraig, *Woodrow Wilson and the Lost World of the Oratorical Statesman* (College Station: Texas A&M University Press, 2004), 50.
7. "Hearst Buys Atlanta Paper," *New York Times*, February 6, 1912.

Chapter 1

1. "Grace, Dying, Sues Wife He Accuses: Legal Fight Begins for Policies on Life of Rich Georgian Strangely Shot," *New York Times*, March 9, 1912, 24.
2. The author has relied almost exclusively on the reports of the shooting, the ensuing investigation and the eventual trial as they were published in Atlanta's three daily newspapers: the morning *Constitution*, and the afternoon papers, the *Journal* and the *Georgian*. The reports in the *Constitution* would generally refer to events of the previous day, while the afternoon papers would report what had happened earlier that day. To spare the reader a surfeit of notes, the account that follows is an amalgam of the Atlanta press coverage and will be sourced only when felt necessary.
3. "Grace Wouldn't Permit Wife to Go on Stage," The Atlanta *Journal* (*Journal*), March 10, 1912, 5. Mrs. Ruffin (the "negress") was interviewed while being held as a material witness. Among other subjects, Martha revealed that Mrs. Grace had talked of going on the stage but "Mr. Gene" would not hear of it.
4. *New York Times*, March 6, 1912.
5. *The Atlanta Georgian and News* (*Georgian*), December 1, 1910, 8.
6. http://www.atlantapd.org/apdhistory.aspx.
7. William J. Matthias and Stuart Anderson, *Horse to Helicopter: First Century of the Atlanta Police Department* (Atlanta: Georgia State University, School of Urban Life, 1973).
8. Ray Stannard Baker, "The Atlanta Riot," *American Magazine*, April 1907.
9. S. Mays Ball, "Prohibition in Georgia, Its Failure to Prevent Drinking in Atlanta and Other Cities," *Putnam Magazine* 5 (1909): 694–701.
10. *The Atlanta Constitution* (*Constitution*), July 8, 1911, 4.
11. "Shortage in Men Not Inefficiency Hampers Police," *Constitution*, March 3, 1912, 1.

Chapter 2

1. The term "goober train" was not unique to the A&WP but was used to refer to most any rail line that served the rural South. Goobers were, originally, peanut farmers. *Goober* came from

Africa where the Bantu word for peanut is *nguba*. David K. Barnhart and Allan A. Metcalf, *America in So Many Words: Words That Have Shaped America* (Boston: Houghton Mifflin, 1997), 134.

2. "Mrs. Grace Happy on Journey to Newnan," *Journal*, March 10, 1912, 5.

3. Wilbur W. Caldwell, *The Courthouse and the Depot: The Architecture of Hope in an Age of Despair: A Narrative Guide to Railroad Expansion and Its Impact on Public Architecture in Georgia, 1833–1910* (Macon, GA: Mercer University Press, 2001), 148.

4. Obediah B. Stevens, *Georgia, Historical and Industrial* (Atlanta: Georgia Department of Agriculture, 1901), Vol. 3, 615–618.

5. Edwin T. Arnold, *"What virtue there is in fire": Cultural Memory and the Lynching of Sam Hose* (Athens, GA: University of Georgia Press, 2009).

6. "Bill Arp's Letter," *The Sunny South* [Atlanta], May 6, 1899, 6.

7. "I'm Innocent Mrs. Grace Declares," *Journal*, March 6, 1912, 1 & 5.

8. See "Husband Accuses Wife of Trying to Kill Him," *The New York Tribune*, March 7, 1912, 1; "Mrs. Grace Insists Her Husband Was Shot by a Burglar," *The Washington Times*, March 7, 1912, 1.

Chapter 3

1. "Descendants of William Grace," http://familytreemaker.genealogy.com/users/c/o/o/Linda-Cooper-Gatesville/GENE1-0014.html (April 27, 2011).

2. "Georgia News," *Daily Enquirer-Sun* (Columbus, GA) October 27, 1882, 3.

3. Newnan-Coweta Historical Society, *History of Coweta County* (Roswell, GA: Wolfe Associates — Historical Publications Division, 1988).

4. Ibid.

5. *Register of Students of the Georgia School of Technology* (UA351, UA352).

6. "Georgia School of Technology," *Scientific American* 52 (August 24, 1901).

7. John Irving Dillon, "Old-Time Drinking Places in Philadelphia," http://www.ushistory.org/philadelphia/drinkingplaces.htm (May 7, 2011).

Chapter 4

1. 1880 Census. Stanley & Martha Ulrich were residing in Lebanon, PA with three sons and daughter, Daisy, who was registered as being born in 1877.

2. *Obituary Record of Graduates of Yale University* (New Haven: Yale University, 1910), 1373.

3. The author is grateful for the assistance provided by Ms. Susie Hainie, Administrative Coordinator, Lebanon County Historical Society, February 25, 2011.

4. Rebecca Trumbull, "Spruce Hill Historic District: Statement of Significance," prepared for the University City Historical Society, http://www.uchs.net/sprucehill.

5. Robert Morris Skaler, *West Philadelphia: University City to 52nd Street* (Charleston, SC: Arcadia, 2002), 51.

6. "Approve the Turkey Trot; Philadelphia Society Leaders Are Taking Lessons in Latest Dance," *New York Times*, December 22, 1911, 13.

7. For more on the subject of the "turkey trot," etc., see Mark Knowles, *The Wicked Waltz and Other Scandalous Dances: Outrage at Couple Dancing in the 19th and Early 20th Centuries* (Jefferson, NC: McFarland, 2009).

8. "Chauffeur's Fracture," *Therapeutic Gazette* 26 (1910): 588. Reprinted from *The Medical Record*, March 12, 1910.

9. A reference to Bishop Warren A. Candler, Bishop of the Methodist Episcopal Church, South, in *The Christian Advocate* 92 (1917): 2.

10. "Grace's Own Letters to His Wife Refute His Sensational Charges," *Georgian*, March 6, 1912, 1. The so-called Philadelphia letters were printed in all of the Atlanta papers with the usual varying transcriptions. I have relied on the version that appeared in *The Georgian*, March 26, 1912. This letter from Gene to Daisy was written on February 7, 1911.

11. Http://www.usinflationcalculator.com (October 27, 2011).

12. Letter from Gene to Daisy, February 23, 1911, *Georgian*, March 26, 1912.

Chapter 5

1. Christopher Gray, "The Little Church Around the Corner," *New York Times*, April 5, 1998; "Hasty Marriages Barred," *New York Times*, February 26, 1919.

2. Mitchell Mannering, "The Grunewald, Monument to Louisiana Progress," *National Magazine* 35 (1912): 669–672.

3. "Southern Society: Newnan," *Georgian*, November 28, 1907, 3.
4. Paul O'Neill, *The Oldest City: The Story of St. John's, Newfoundland* (St. Philips, Newfoundland & Labrador, Canada: Boulder, 2003), 752–754. The *Florizel* was wrecked off Newfoundland in February 1918 with a great loss of life.
5. The "Philadelphia letters" were published in the *Journal* and *Georgian* on the afternoon of Tuesday, March 26, 1912. The transcriptions varied slightly and the author has chosen the letters as they appeared in the *Georgian*. Letter from Gene to Daisy dated August 26, 1911.
6. Letter from Gene to Daisy dated November 2, 1911.
7. Letter from Gene to Daisy dated November 4, 1911.
8. Ibid.
9. Ibid.
10. "Business in Empire Building Backed by a Billion Capitol and Much Splendid Brains," *Constitution*, September 17, 1911, 12.

Chapter 6

1. Franklin M. Garrett, *Atlanta and Environs: A Chronicle of Its People and Events, 1880s–1930s* (Athens: University of Georgia Press, 1969), Vol. 2, 440.
2. Dewey Grantham, *Hoke Smith and the Politics of the New South*, paperback ed. (Baton Rouge: Louisiana University Press, 1958), 142.
3. "The Gal in the Fountain Receives Fair Visitors," *Georgian*, January 9, 1908, 9.
4. Garrett, *Atlanta*, Vol. 1, 746. William Bailey Williford, *Peachtree Street, Atlanta*, paperback ed. (Athens: University of Georgia Press, 2010), 29–30.
5. John Temple Graves, "Atlanta Will Never Know a Residential Section to Surpass Ansley Park," *Georgian*, September 17, 1906, 2.
6. *Georgian*, October 12, 1910, 2.
7. C. Olen Teate, "Insurance Swap Planned by E.H. Grace and Wife," *Constitution*, March 31, 1912, 4.
8. For the Forsyth Theatre, see Arthur Frank Wertheim, ed., *The Papers of Will Rogers: From Vaudeville to Broadway* (Norman: University of Oklahoma Press, 2001), Vol. 3, 236, note 14.

Chapter 7

1. Inman, *Diary*, 34.
2. Wallace Putnam Reed, ed., *History of Atlanta, Georgia* (Syracuse: Mason & Co., 1889), 99–100.
3. "Kiser-Read," *Georgian*, June 28, 1906, 8.
4. "The Avenger of Blood Abroad in the Land," *The New York Age*, March 21, 1912, 4.
5. *Macon Telegraph*, March 7, 1912, 1.
6. Prof. Dr. Schwarzacher, "Bloodstains," *The American Journal of Police Science* 1 (1930): 374.
7. *Constitution*, December 8, 1911, 6.
8. "15 Are Arrested for Burglaries," *Constitution*, February 19, 1912, 1.
9. *New York Times*, March 7, 1912.
10. *New York Tribune*, March 7, 1912.
11. Ibid.

Chapter 8

1. "A Million Dollar Fire—Burning of the Kimball House in Atlanta," *New York Times*, August 13, 1883.
2. "The End of a Great Work," *Constitution*, May 1, 1885, 4.
3. *The San Francisco Call*, November 27, 1912, 6.
4. Thomas Gibson, "The Anti-Negro Riots in Atlanta," *Harper's Weekly* 50 (1906): 1457–1459.
5. Franklin M. Garrett, *Atlanta and Environs: A Chronicle of its People and Events, 1880s–1930s* (Athens: University of Georgia Press, 1969), 363.
6. Herbert Aptheker, ed., *A Documentary History of the Negro People in the United States* (New York: Carol, 1990), Vol. 3, 319.
7. "Woman in the Tower Takes Her Own Life," *Georgian*, January 13, 1911, 1.
8. For Adam Stanley Ulrich, see *Universities and Their Sons* (Boston: R. Herndon, 1900), Vol. 4, 103. For Walter Grace, see George H. Watkins, *Coweta Co GA, 12th Battalion Georgia Light Artillery—Co A*, http://files.usgwarchives.net/ga/coweta/military/civilwar/rosters/coal2batt.txt.

Chapter 9

1. *The Code of the State of Georgia*, adopted August 15, 1910, Volume 1, Chapter 17, Article 1, 1261.
2. Candler and Evans, *Georgia* (1906):80–81.
3. "Dougherty Dead by a Bullet Fired in Accidental Fall," *Georgian*, September 16, 1911, 1.
4. "Rube Arnold's Burglar Captured in Tennessee," *Georgian*, September 20, 1911, 7.
5. See Eugene J. Watts, "Atlanta Police 1890–1905," *The Journal of Southern History* 39 (1973): 165–182.
6. Rebecca Burns, *Rage in the Gate City: The Story of the 1906 Atlanta Race Riot*, rev. ed. (Athens: University of Georgia Press, 2009), 86–87.

Chapter 10

1. Dana F. White and Victor A. Kramer, eds., *Olmsted South: Old South Critic, New South Planner* (Westport, CT: Greenwood Press, 1979), 233.
2. "Vast Improvement Is Well Under Way at Piedmont Park," *Georgian*, May 20, 1909, 16.
3. John R. Hornady, *Atlanta, Yesterday, Today and Tomorrow* (N.p.: American Cities Book Company, 1922), 206.
4. "Styles Come from Hell, Says Len. G. Broughton," *Georgian*, June 12, 1911, 2.
5. "Cigarette Plea Gets Wolmesley [sic] Short Term," *Georgian*, October 28, 1911, 5.
6. "St. Joseph's Infirmary," *Atlanta Journal-Record of Medicine* 8 (1906): 198–99.
7. American Surgical Association, *Annals of Surgery* 56 (1912): 66.
8. Ibid., 64.
9. William Williams Keen, *Surgery, Its Principles and Practice* (Philadelphia: W.B. Saunders, 1906), 896–898.
10. *Daily Times Enterprise*, Thomasville, GA, March 12, 1912, 1.
11. "Mrs. Grace's Plight as Seen by a Woman," *Georgian*, March 11, 1912, 4.

Chapter 11

1. *The Code of the State of Georgia*, adopted August 15, 1910, Volume 2, § 1037, par. 4. (Atlanta, 1911), 215.
2. §1026 Dying Declarations, *Park's Annotated Code of the State of Georgia*, Volume 6, 1914, 654.
3. Harry Clay Underhill, *A Treatise on the Law of Criminal Evidence* (Indianapolis: Bobbs-Merrill, 1912), 187ff.
4. *Shepard v. US*, 290 US 96, 100, 54 S.Ct. 22, 24 (1933).
5. "Grace's Dying Statement," *New York Times*, March 15, 1912.
6. "Insurance," *The New International Encyclopedia* (New York: Dodd, Mead, 1905), Vol. 10, 682.
7. "Wife Supported Grace: Disclosures Change Atlanta Sentiment toward Accused Wife," *New York Times*, March 12, 1912.
8. E.g., "Grace's Story Now Doubted, Sentiment in Atlanta Veers to His Wife," *Richland* [Ohio] *Shield and Banner*, March 14, 1912, 1.
9. Eric Partridge, *A Dictionary of the Underworld: British & American* (London: Routledge & Paul, 1968).
10. "Graces Exchange Rings, Dying Man Gives Rings Back to Wife Accused of Shooting Him," *New York Times*, March 16, 1912, 24.
11. Steve Oney, *"And the dead shall rise": The Murder of Mary Phagan and the Lynching of Leo Frank* (New York: Pantheon Books, 2003), 49.
12. *Valdosta Times*, March 26, 1912, 1.

Chapter 12

1. "A True Story of Love, Hatred and Hypnotism Puzzles the Police of the South," *The Day Book*, Chicago, March 13, 1912, 3.
2. "Grace Case Gets Too Much Space," *Constitution*, March 18, 1912, 5.
3. "Ellenwood Points Moral in the Grace Case," *Georgian*, March 20, 1912, 5.
4. Myrtle Reed, *A Weaver of Dreams* (New York: G.P. Putnam's Sons, 1911).
5. "Did Myrtle Reed Foreshadow Her Tragic End in Her Last Book?" *New York Times*, September 10, 1911.

6. *Railway World* 54 (1910): 802.

7. "Southern Train Held Up," *Georgian*, February 18, 1911, 1. Five "yeggmen" removed the safe and blew it up, making off with all of $700.

8. "Mrs. Grace Here; Denies She Shot Young Husband," *The Washington Herald*, Washington, DC, March 21, 1912, 1.

9. *Philadelphia Evening Bulletin*, March 21, 1912.

10. "Mrs. Grace Raising Funds," *New York Times*, March 22, 1912, 9.

Chapter 13

1. *Official Railway Guide* (Atlanta & West Point Railroad).

2. *Newnan Herald & Advertiser*, March 29, 1912.

3. "Grace's Boyhood Neighbors and Friends Honor His Character," *Journal*, March 25, 1912, 4.

4. David Stewart Rudstein, *Double Jeopardy: A Reference Guide to the United States Constitution* (Westport, CT: Praeger, 2004), 95.

5. "Strange Grace Case Still Puzzling to All Atlanta," *Milledgeville News*, March 15, 1912, 1.

6. "Saw Two Fleeing From Grace Home," *New York Herald*, March 29, 1912, 4; "Woman Resembling Mrs. Grace Seen," *Washington Herald*, March 30, 1912, 8.

7. The official record can be found in the Orleans Parish Grooms' Marriage Index (vol. 33, p. 261). Grace, Eugene Hamilton, 27 (Male), married "Webster Hughes," 31, on 05/10/1911.

8. *Hill v State* (1871) 41 Ga. 484. The fact set in this case is the reverse; the woman/mistress was allowed to testify against the man with whom she lived. "The exclusion of the wife of a party is based upon principles of public justice, arising out of the sacredness of the domestic tie, which cannot be considered applicable to one whose condition did not involve this relationship."

9. *The Athens Banner*, April 12, 1912, 4.

Chapter 14

1. *Atlanta: A City of the Modern South*, compiled by Workers of the Writers' Program of the Work Projects Administration in the State of Georgia (Atlanta Board of Education, 1942), 94ff.

2. Ben Procter, *William Randolph Hearst: The Later Years 1911–1951* (New York: Oxford University Press, 2007), 21.

3. John Dittmer, *Black Georgia in the Progressive Era, 1900–1920* (Urbana: University of Illinois Press, 1977), 130.

4. "The Reign of Terror Must End," *Georgian*, August 24, 1906, 6.

5. "Why Mr. Barber Left Atlanta," *Voice of the Negro* (November 1906), 470–72.

6. "Hearst Buys Atlanta Paper," *New York Times*, February 6, 1912.

7. Herbert Asbury, "Hearst Comes to Georgia," *American Mercury Magazine* (January 1926), 87–95.

8. Ibid.

9. Willard G. Bleyer, *Main Currents in the History of Journalism* (Boston: Houghton Mifflin, 1927), 387.

10. *Atlanta Constitution*, March 26, 1912, 4.

11. Ibid.

12. *Daily Times Enterprise*, Thomasville, GA, March 19, 1912, 2.

13. "On Trial (Special to the Banner)," *Athens Banner*, March 13, 1912, 5.

14. *Macon Telegraph*, March 15, 1912.

15. Charles Whibley, *American Sketches* (London: Blackwood & Sons, 1908), 125–6.

16. *Atlanta Georgian*, March 14, 1912.

17. *Atlanta Journal*, April 16, 1912.

18. *Atlanta Constitution*, April 17, 1912, 1.

19. *Atlanta Constitution*, May 7, 1912, 1.

Chapter 15

1. "Mrs. Grace Is Indicted: 'Glad of it,' Says Accused Woman Who Expects to Be a Mother," *New York Times*, May 7, 1912, 1.

2. "Aaron Morris Is Killed by Negro," *Constitution*, March 22, 1912, 1; "Nearly $2000 Subscribed for Morris Family," *Constitution*, March 30, 1912, 1.

3. "'Cocaine Ben' Ready to Meet His Fate," *Constitution*, May 7, 1912, 5.

4. "Mrs. Grace Faints at Gallows," *The Sun* (New York, NY), May 10, 1912, 1.

5. "Evils in Society Scored by Jones," *Constitution*, June 5, 1912, 9.
6. *Constitution*, July 9.
7. *Ector v. State*, 10 Ga. App. 777, 74 S. E. 295 (1912).
8. "Kimballville Farm — Will V. Zimmer, Prop.," *Georgian*, July 1, 1911, Poultry, Pet and Live Stock Section, 2 [insert C].

Chapter 16

1. "Courts, Courts, Everywhere; Here's Where You Find Them," *Constitution*, July 11, 1911, 4.
2. "Southside Boom Has Now Started," *Constitution*, January 19, 1911, 9.
3. Ward Greene, "Notes for a History of the Klan," *American Mercury Magazine May to August 1925* (Whitefish, MT: Kessinger, 2003), 140.
4. Wayne W. Daniel, *Pickin' on Peachtree: A History of Country Music in Atlanta, Georgia* (Urbana: University of Illinois Press, Champaign, IL, 1990), 19.
5. "Memorial of Leonard Strickland Roan," *Report of the Annual Session (1915) of the Georgia Bar Association*, Vol. 32, 255–257.
6. Oney, "And the dead shall rise," 95–96.

Chapter 17

1. §5729. *The Code of the State of Georgia*: Adopted August 15, 1910, Vol. 1, 1328.
2. The three Atlanta newspapers devoted several pages each day, during each of the five days of the trial of Mrs. Grace. The narrative of the trial that follows here is a compilation of that reporting. Endnotes will only be used where felt essential for sourcing or clarity.
3. "Detective Wood Is Fired from Force After a Fair Trial," *Georgian*, December 8, 1910, 1.
4. Oney, "And the dead shall rise," 49.
5. Please note, however, that when Martha Ruffin spoke with a reporter from the *Journal* on March 10, she was quoted as declaring, "[Mr. Grace] was covered up to the shoulders." Again, this book relies on the ability of newspaper reporters to scribble down as much of the Q&A as possible; perhaps they missed Dorsey's question. The original court records have not been preserved.
6. "Mrs. Opie Grace Collapses When Husband Appears," *The Washington Herald*, July 30, 1912, 1.
7. "Mrs. Grace Trembles as Husband Appears," *New-York Tribune*, July 30, 1912, 3.
8. *Constitution*, April 15, 1912. Dr. Bailey denied reports that Grace had been seen in a "rolling chair."
9. See www-personal.umich.edu/~abw/charles_thomas_swift_story.html.

Chapter 18

1. E.g., "Sensational Case up in Atlanta, Couple Prominent Socially," *The Telegraph Herald*, Dubuque, IA, July 28, 1912, 1. In their defense, however, it should be noted that the *Journal* was still describing Gene Grace as a "clubman and dashing society figure" as late as July 28, 1912.
2. *Philadelphia Inquirer*, July 30, 1912, 1.
3. "Women See a Marriage Lesson in Grace Trial," *Georgian*, July 30, 1912, 3.
4. Arthur Joseph Cramp, *Nostrums and Quackery* (Chicago: American Medical Association, 1921), Vol. 2, 738.
5. Samuel Hopkins Adams, "Preying on the Incurables," *Collier's Weekly*, January 13, 1906. Quoted in *The Journal of the American Medical Association* 46 (1906): 205.
6. The Harrison Narcotics Act (December 17, 1914); see Ruth Clifford Engs, *The Progressive Era's Health Reform Movement: A Historical Dictionary* (Westport, CT: Praeger, 2003) 155.
7. §1024, *Park's Annotated Code of the State of Georgia*, 1914, 648.
8. Paul S. Milich, *Georgia Rules of Evidence* (St. Paul: Thomson West 2002).
9. Ashe sold them for $50. *Georgian*, July 1, 1907, 18.
10. "Ashe Makes Study of Typed Letters," *Georgian*, July 31, 1912, 2.
11. "Court Drama: Wife and Paralysed Husband," *Poverty Bay Herald*, Gisborne, NZ, September 28, 1912, 3. Available online at paperspast.natlib.govt.nz.

Chapter 19

1. "Admit Alibi Letters Against Mrs. Grace," *New York Times*, August 1, 1912, 20.
2. *Milwaukee Sentinel*, July 31, 1912, 2.

3. *Diaz v. United States*, 223 U.S. 442 (1912).
4. Conversation with the author, March 3, 2011.
5. "Grace Death Notes Read," *Georgian*, July 31, 1912, 1.
6. "Enthusiastic Meeting in Interest of H.M. Dorsey," *Constitution*, August 2, 1912, 11.

Chapter 20

1. Anne Taylor, "Bouffant Lines Prevail," *The Woman's Magazine*, February 1914, 13.
2. §1029, *Penal Code of Georgia* (1895).
3. "Mrs. Grace Gets Short Freedom: Grace-Lawrence Building Company Affairs Go Into Court," *Constitution*, May 22, 1912, 8.
4. Joel Chandler Harris, *The Bishop and the Boogerman* (New York: Doubleday, Page, 1909).
5. However, at about this time, *booger* also had the usage as a "playful term of endearment" usually with a child, as in "Come here, you little booger." See "Dialect Notes, A Word List from East Alabama," *Bulletin of the University of Texas* 73 (1909): 292.

Chapter 21

1. §1036, Prisoner's Statement, *The Code of the State of Georgia* 2 (1910): 215.
2. *Ferguson v. Georgia*, 365 US 570 (1961).
3. "Here Is Mrs. Grace's Own Story of Shooting, as Told to Jury," *Journal*, August 1, 1912, 1.
4. Baedeker, *The Dominion of Canada* (1907): 31.
5. Built by developer Joel Hurt at Edgewood Ave and Exchange Street near Five Points.
6. The husband of Rebecca Sams.
7. "Grace Shot Himself, His Wife Tells Jury," *New York Tribune*, August 2, 1912, 16.

Chapter 22

1. §5743 Jury Right to infer, *The Code of the State of Georgia* 1 (1910): 1330.
2. Rudyard Kipling, "*The Vampire*," from *Departmental Ditties, Ballads, Barrack-Room Ballads and Other Verses* (New York: The Lovell Company, 1899), 251.
3. E.g., for Rosser's "lice" remark, see "Grace Case Has Gone to the Jury," *Journal*, August 2, 1912, 5.
4. T.T. Molnar, *Georgia Criminal Law* (Atlanta: The Harrison Company, 1935), 157.
5. "Dr. Memminger Delights Audience with Kipling," *Georgian*, May 13, 1910, 12.
6. Kipling, *The Female of the Species: A Study in Natural History* (New York: Doubleday, Page, 1912).
7. "Miss De Cris Was Whipped: Brutal Treatment of a Woman Prisoner on Georgia Convict Farm," *New York Evening Telegram*, August 12, 1903, 1.
8. "Brutal Lashing May Bring Death," *San Francisco Call*, August 10, 1903, 7.
9. "A Brutal and Inhuman Act," *Americus Weekly Times-Recorder*, August 14, 1903, 4.
10. Alex Lichtenstein, *Twice the Work of Free Labor: The Political Economy of Convict Labor in the New South* (New York: Verso, 1996).

Chapter 23

1. Annulet Andrews, "Southern Society and Its Leaders," *Everybody's Magazine* 12 (1905): 54–63.
2. Circulation numbers, etc., from Asbury, *American Mercury Magazine* (1926).
3. *Griffin Daily News*, August 3, 1912.
4. "What Atlanta Needs," *The Atlantian*, March 1912, 5.
5. "Protecting Young Girls," *Constitution*, August 3, 1912, 4.
6. "Grace Case Georgia's Most Famous Trial," *Georgian*, August 3, 1912, 2. The Grace trial, it was asserted, had usurped the title from the 1894 trial of Will Myers for the murder of Forrest Crowley. The victim, a local businessman, was found slain in a thicket near Atlanta's Westview Cemetery. He'd been robbed of $700. Myers was sentenced to the gallows for an "almost unaccountable crime." Following an appeal, he was tried again with the same result. Awaiting a new appeal, he escaped from the old city jail and was never re-captured. For more see Garrett, *Atlanta and Environs*, 301–304.
7. Leonard Dinnerstein, *The Leo Frank Case* (Notable Trials Library, Indiana University, 1987), 29.

Chapter 24

1. "Charge Wealthy Woman with Shooting Husband," *Washington Times*, December 12, 1910, 1; "Philadelphia Clubman Shot by His Wife," *Gettysburg Times*, December 13, 1910, 3; "Says She Shot in Self-Defense," *Detroit Free Press*, December 14, 1910, 1.

2. *The Pharmaceutical Journal and Transactions* 24 (1894): 653.

3. E.g., "Sentence of Death for Dr. M'Naughton," *Georgian*, October 20, 1910, 4.

4. John Herr Musser, *A Practical Treatise on Medical Diagnosis for Students and Physicians* (Philadelphia: Lea & Febiger, 1913), 382.

5. "Thos. B. Felder Dissects State's Case in West 11th Street Shooting Mystery," *Georgian*, March 11, 1912, 4.

6. Advertisement, *The Century* 38 (1889): 985.

7. Edward Samuel Farrow, *American Small Arms* (New York: Bradford Company, 1904), 287.

8. Walter Winans, *Hints on Revolver Shooting* (New York: G.P. Putnam's Sons, 1910), 120.

9. See Chapter 7.

10. "Prosecutor Says Justice Needs Women on Juries to Try Women Who Take Life," *Toledo News-Bee*, August 24, 1912, 12.

11. "Women Juries & Crime," *New York Post*, December 20, 1912.

12. Rebecca Davis, "Overcoming the 'Defect of Sex': Georgia Women's Fight for Access to Jury Service," *The Georgia Historical Quarterly*, Vol XCI, No. 1, Spring 2007.

Chapter 25

1. For more on the subject, see Harry Francis Hollien, *The Acoustics of Crime: the New Science of Forensic Phonetics* (New York: Plenum Press, 1990).

2. "Dorsey at Daybreak Heard Grace Shot," *Georgian*, August 8, 1912, 1.

3. "Professional Ethics in Practice," *Law Notes* 16 (1912): 101.

4. "Atlanta's Solicitor General," *Constitution*, August 22, 1912, 3. (Dorsey won the vote handily over Madison Bell, 6230–2738.)

5. "Jury Frees Potts Twenty Minutes After Case Ends," *Constitution*, February 21, 1913, 1; "Not Guilty Verdict Ends Appelbaum Case," *Journal*, April 26, 1913, 3.

6. "Eugene H. Grace Gives Views of Appelbaum Case Drawn From Own Famous Shooting," *Constitution*, February 28, 1913, 1.

7. Oney, "And the dead shall rise," 94.

8. *American State Trials*, ed. John Davidson Lawson (St. Louis: Thomas Law Books, 1918), Vol. 10, 302. In his closing statement, Dorsey mentioned Frank's defense counsel, attorneys Luther Rosser and Reuben Arnold: "They have had Rosser, the rider of the winds and the stirrer of the storm, and Arnold (and I can say it because I love him), as mild a man as ever cut a throat or scuttled a ship."

9. "Mrs. Grace's Maid Is Murdered; Eighteenth Victim of 'Ripper,'" *Constitution*, August 25, 1913, 1.

10. Details on the recent history of the Thrower Building courtesy of Kyle Kessler, Atlanta Preservation Center.

11. Edwin H. Ford, *Highlights in the History of the American Press: A Book of Readings* (Minneapolis: University of Minnesota Press, 1954), 322.

12. "Grace Has Small Chance to Recover from Wound," *Constitution*, August 14, 1912, 2.

13. "Hotel Evicts Mrs. Grace; Learned She Was Not the Wife of C.H. Oldham," *New York Times*, June 4, 1913, 1

14. "E.H. Grace Near Death," *New York Times*, January 11, 1914, S4.

15. "Grace Lies at Rest in Newnan Cemetery," *Constitution*, January 13, 1914, 3.

16. "Dies Two Years After Shooting," *Washington Times*, January 12, 1914, 10.

17. Lucian Lamar Knight, *Georgia's Landmarks, Memorials, and Legends* (1914), 435.

18. *Coweta County, Georgia, Cemeteries*, compiled by the Coweta County Genealogical Society (1986), 394.

19. *Daily Times Enterprise*, January 13, 1914, 4.

20. *Philadelphia Bulletin*, March 27, 1934.

Bibliography

Newspapers

Atlanta Constitution
Atlanta Georgian
Atlanta Journal
Macon Telegraph
New York Times
Newnan Times Herald
Chronicling America, a joint project of the National Endowment for the Humanities and the Library of Congress.
The Digital Library of Georgia including newspapers from Atlanta, Athens, Columbus, Macon, Milledgeville, Valdosta and more.

Books (* denotes those works most essential for the period)

Aptheker, Herbert, ed. *A Documentary History of the Negro People in the United States.* New York: Carol, 1990.

Arnold, Edwin T. *"What virtue there is in fire": Cultural Memory and the Lynching of Sam Hose.* Athens: University of Georgia Press, 2009.

Barnhart, David K., and Allan A. Metcalf. *America in So Many Words: Words That Have Shaped America.* Boston: Houghton Mifflin, 1997.

Bleyer, Willard G. *Main Currents in the History of Journalism.* Boston: Houghton Mifflin, 1927.

Burns, Rebecca. *Rage in the Gate City: The Story of the 1906 Atlanta Race Riot.* Athens: University of Georgia Press, 2009.

Caldwell, Wilbur W. *The Courthouse and the Depot: The Architecture of Hope in an Age of Despair: A Narrative Guide to Railroad Expansion and Its Impact on Public Architecture in Georgia, 1833–1910.* Macon, GA: Mercer University Press, 2001.

*Code of the State of Georgia, Adopted August 15, 1910. Atlanta: Foote & Davies Printers, 1911.

Cramp, Arthur Joseph. *Nostrums and Quackery.* Chicago: American Medical Association, 1921.

Daniel, Wayne W. *Pickin' on Peachtree: A History of Country Music in Atlanta, Georgia.* Urbana: University of Illinois Press, 1990.

Dinnerstein, Leonard. *The Leo Frank Case.* Notable Trials Library; Indiana University, 1987.

Dittmer, John. *Black Georgia in the Progressive Era, 1900–1920.* Urbana: University of Illinois Press, 1977.

Engs, Ruth Clifford. *The Progressive Era's Health Reform Movement: A Historical Dictionary.* Westport, CT: Praeger, 2003.

Farrow, Edward Samuel. *American Small Arms.* New York: Bradford, 1904.

Ford, Edwin H. Ford. *Highlights in the History of the American Press: A Book of Readings.* Minneapolis: University of Minnesota Press, 1954.

*Garrett, Franklin M. *Atlanta and Environs: A Chronicle of Its People and Events, 1880s–1930s.* Athens: University of Georgia Press, 1969.

Grantham, Dewey. *Hoke Smith and the Politics of the New South.* Baton Rouge: Louisiana University Press, 1958.

Harley, Rev. Anthony. *Southward Ho! Notes of a Tour to and Through the State of Georgia.* London, 1886.

Harris, Joel Chandler. *The Bishop and the Boogerman.* New York: Doubleday, Page, 1909.

Hollien, Harry Francis. *The Acoustics of Crime: The New Science of Forensic Phonetics.* New York: Plenum Press, 1990.

*Hornady, John R. *Atlanta, Yesterday, Today and Tomorrow.* N.p.: American Cities Book Company, 1922.

Inman, Arthur C. *The Inman Diary: A Public and Private Confession,* ed. Daniel A. Aaron. Cambridge, MA: Harvard University Press, 1985.

Keen, William Williams. *Surgery, Its Principles and Practice.* Philadelphia: W.B. Saunders, 1906.

Kipling, Rudyard. *Departmental Ditties, Ballads, Barrack-Room Ballads and Other Verses.* New York: The Lovell Company, 1899.

_____. *The Female of the Species: A Study in Natural History.* New York: Doubleday, Page, 1912.

Knowles, Mark. *The Wicked Waltz and Other Scandalous Dances: Outrage at Couple Dancing in the 19th and Early 20th Centuries.* Jefferson, NC: McFarland, 2009.

Kraig, Robert Alexander. *Woodrow Wilson and the Lost World of the Oratorical Statesman.* College Station: Texas A&M University Press, 2004.

Lichtenstein, Alex. *Twice the Work of Free Labor: The Political Economy of Convict Labor in the New South.* New York: Verso, 1996.

*Matthias, William J., and Stuart Anderson. *Horse to Helicopter: First Century of the Atlanta Police Department.* Atlanta: Georgia State University, School of Urban Life, 1973.

Milich, Paul S. *Georgia Rules of Evidence.* St. Louis: Thomson West, 2002.

Molnar, T.T. *Georgia Criminal Law.* Atlanta: Harrison, 1935.

Musser, John Herr. *A Practical Treatise on Medical Diagnosis for Students and Physicians.* Philadelphia: Lea & Febiger, 1913.

Newnan-Coweta Historical Society. *History of Coweta County.* Roswell, GA: Wolfe Associates — Historical Publications Division, 1988.

Obituary Record of Graduates of Yale University. New Haven, CT: Yale University Press, 1910.

O'Neill, Paul. *The Oldest City: The Story of St. John's, Newfoundland.* St. Philips, Newfoundland & Labrador: Boulder, 2003.

*Oney, Steve. *"And the dead shall rise": The Murder of Mary Phagan and the Lynching of Leo Frank.* Pantheon Books, 2003.

Page, Walter Hines and Arthur Wilson Page. *The World's Work, Volume 1.* New York: Doubleday, Page, 1901

Park's Annotated Code of the State of Georgia, 1914: Embracing the Code of 1910 and Amendments and Additions Thereto Made by the General Assembly. Atlanta: Georgia General Assembly, 1914.

Partridge, Eric. *A Dictionary of the Underworld: British & American.* London: Routledge & Paul, 1968.

Procter, Ben. *William Randolph Hearst: The Later Years 1911–1951.* New York: Oxford University Press, 2007.

Reed, Myrtle. *A Weaver of Dreams*. New York: G.P. Putnam's, 1911.

Reed, Wallace Putnam, ed. *History of Atlanta, Georgia*. Syracuse: Mason, 1889.

Rudstein, David Stewart. *Double Jeopardy: A Reference Guide to the United States Constitution*. Westport, CT: Praeger, 2004.

Skaler, Robert Morris. *West Philadelphia: University City to 52nd Street*. Charleston, SC: Arcadia, 2002.

Stevens, Obediah B. *Georgia, Historical and Industrial*. Atlanta: Georgia Department of Agriculture, 1901.

Underhill, Harry Clay. *A Treatise on the Law of Criminal Evidence*. Indianapolis: Bobbs-Merrill, 1912.

Whibley, Charles. *American Sketches*. London: Blackwood, 1908.

White, Dana F., and Victor A. Kramer, eds. *Olmsted South: Old South Critic, New South Planner*. Westport, CT: Greenwood Press, 1979.

*Williford, William Bailey. *Peachtree Street, Atlanta*. Athens: University of Georgia Press, 2010.

Winans, Walter. *Hints on Revolver Shooting*. New York: G.P. Putnam's, 1910.

Writers' Program of the Work Projects Administration in the State of Georgia. *Atlanta: A City of the Modern South*. Atlanta: Board of Education, 1942.

Journals & Periodicals

Adams, Samuel Hopkins. "Preying on the Incurables." *Collier's Weekly*, January 13, 1906.

Andrews, Annulet. "Southern Society and Its Leaders." *Everybody's Magazine*, 1905.

*Ashbury, Herbert, "Hearst Comes to Georgia." *American Mercury Magazine*, January 1926.

*Baker, Ray Stannard, "The Atlanta Riot." *American Magazine*, April 1907.

Ball, S. Mays, "Prohibition in Georgia, Its Failure to Prevent Drinking in Atlanta and Other Cities." *Putnam Magazine*, 1909.

"Chauffeur's Fracture." *Therapeutic Gazette*, 1910.

*Cooper, Walter G. "Atlanta, the Gate City of the South." *Southern Merchant*, January 7, 1907.

Davis, Rebecca Davis. "Overcoming the 'Defect of Sex': Georgia Women's Fight for Access to Jury Service." *The Georgia Historical Quarterly*, Spring 2007.

"Dialect Notes, A Word List from East Alabama." *Bulletin of the University of Texas*, 1909.

"Georgia School of Technology." *Scientific American*, August 24, 1901.

Gibson, Thomas. "The Anti-Negro Riots in Atlanta." *Harper's Weekly*, 1906.

*Hungerford, Edward. "The Personality of Atlanta." *Travel*, 1916.

Mannering, Mitchell, "The Grunewald, Monument to Louisiana Progress." *National Magazine*, 1912.

*"Memorial of Leonard Strickland Roan." *Report of the Annual Session (1915) of the Georgia Bar Association*.

"Professional Ethics in Practice." *Law Notes*, 1912.

"St. Joseph's Infirmary." *Atlanta Journal — Record of Medicine*, 1906.

Schwarzacher, Professor. "Bloodstains." *The American Journal of Police Science*, 1930.

Trumbull, Rebecca. "Spruce Hill Historic District: Statement of Significance," *University City Historical Society* (http://www.uchs.net/sprucehill).

*Watts, Eugene J. "Atlanta Police 1890–1905." *The Journal of Southern History*, 1973.

Index